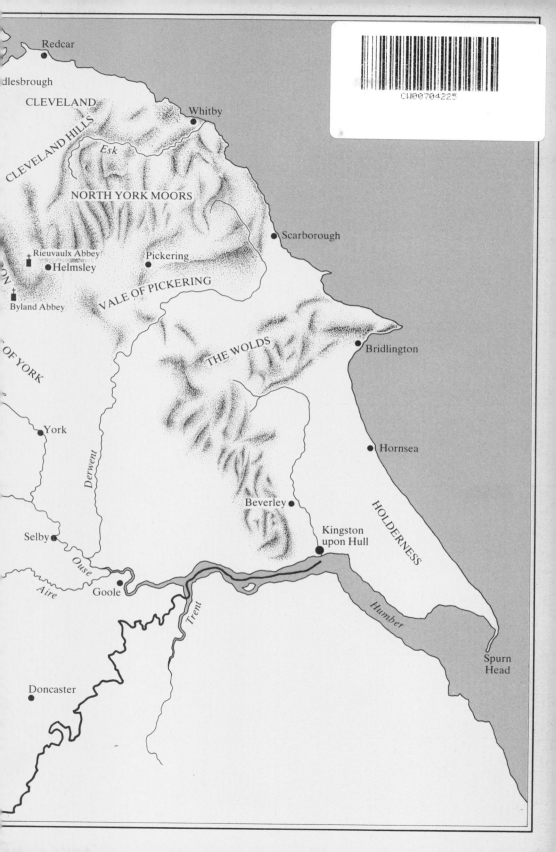

Redcar

dlesbrough

CLEVELAND

Whitby

CLEVELAND HILLS

Esk

NORTH YORK MOORS

Rieuvaulx Abbey

Helmsley

Pickering

Scarborough

Byland Abbey

VALE OF PICKERING

OF YORK

THE WOLDS

Bridlington

York

Derwent

Hornsea

Beverley

HOLDERNESS

Selby

Kingston
upon Hull

Ouse

Goole

Aire

Trent

Humber

Doncaster

Spurn
Head

Fred Trueman's Yorkshire

Fred Trueman's Yorkshire

Fred Trueman and Don Mosey

Stanley Paul

London Melbourne Sydney Auckland Johannesburg

Stanley Paul & Co. Ltd

An imprint of the Hutchinson Publishing Group

17–21 Conway Street, London W1P 6JD

Hutchinson Publishing Group (Australia) Pty Ltd
PO Box 496, 16–22 Church Street, Hawthorne, Melbourne, Victoria 3122
PO Box 151, Broadway, New South Wales 2007

Hutchinson Group (NZ) Ltd
32–34 View Road, PO Box 40-086, Glenfield, Auckland 10

Hutchinson Group (SA) Pty Ltd
PO Box 337, Bergvlei 2012, South Africa

First published 1984
© Fred Trueman 1984

Set in Sabon by Butler & Tanner Ltd

Printed and bound in Great Britain by
Butler & Tanner Ltd, Frome and London

ISBN 0 09 158420 5

Contents

History

Food and Drink

Foreword by the Earl of Scarbrough

There are many great cricketers of the past who are still household names, but it is often difficult for many of us to remember which counties they played for. However, I think that even a large number of those who are not followers of the game know that Fred Trueman played for Yorkshire.

This book is not about cricket – except in two chapters. It is an adventure of Fred through his native countryside, accompanied by a most able navigator and Sancho Panza in the form of Don Mosey. They meet and visit a remarkable cross-section of Yorkshire people and places far removed from the pavilions of Headingley and Scarborough.

This is a book to delve into. It is two Yorkshiremen discovering Yorkshire, but it should not upset a Lancastrian or alarm anyone from south of Watford.

I commend this book. All it lacks – and this only because of the laws of libel – are some of the very personal and colourful reminiscences produced around almost every corner during a drive in the company of Fred Trueman!

Acknowledgements

Apart from acknowledgements and other credits mentioned in the text of this book, the authors would like to offer special thanks to Bill Mitchell and the staff of the Dalesman Publishing Company who provided many shortcuts in our research, David Howes at Rugby League headquarters in Leeds, Mrs Florence Dodsworth for her invaluable help with the early history of free education in Bradford, and Gabrielle Allen for imaginative and extensive picture research.

Photographic acknowledgements

The author and publishers wish to thank the following for permission to reproduce photographs:

All-Sport, pages 121, 125, 127, 129 below and 221, photo Adrian Murrell; BBC Hulton Picture Library, pages 123, 136, 153 above and below, 194, 196/197 and 209; Bradford City Economic Development Unit, page 22; City of Bradford Metropolitan Council, Local Studies Library, pages 180/181 and 189; British Tourist Authority, page 23 above, 34 and 35 below; Barney Colehan, BBC Leeds, page 211; Dairy Crest Creameries, pages 247 and 252; Dalesman Publishing Company, photo P. Fox, page 202; Patrick Eagar, pages 134, 135 and 137; John Foster and Son plc, Black Dyke Mills Band, pages 88 and 89; Barbara Heller Photo Library, photos Fay Godwin, pages 23 below, 44/45 and 62, photo Charles Walker page 35 above; Huddersfield Choral Society, page 72; Keystone Press Agency, pages 114/115, 129 above, 132 and 147; Leeds City Council, page 233; *Radio Times*, page 208; Harry Ramsden's, page 227; Scottish Opera, photo Eric Thorburn, page 99; Sport and General, pages 171, 219 and 220; T. & R. Theakston Ltd, pages 238 and 239; Varley Picture Agency, pages 150 and 151.

Colour section:

Ace Photo Library, photo Rolf Richardson, page 4 below, photo Crysse Morrison, page 5, photo Chris Arthur, page 8 below; All-Sport, photo Adrian Murrell, page 7 below left; Bradford City Economic Development Unit, page 8 above; British Tourist Authority, pages 1, 3 above and below and 4 above; Barney Colehan, page 7 below right; Gerry Cranham, page 6 below; Patrick Eagar, page 7 above; Barbara Heller Photo Library, photo Fay Godwin, page 2; Huddersfield Choral Society, page 6 above.

Dales sketches by Gillian Riley.

Introduction

Any book on Yorkshire, no matter how extensive the research or how wide the experience of its authors, must necessarily only scratch the surface, so vast is the range of subject matter to be reviewed. Yet, according to the Department of the Environment, no such place as Yorkshire exists. There is – as a modern atlas will show – a collection of autonomous local authorities known as North, South and West Yorkshire, Cleveland and Humberside, but there is nowhere that is simply called 'Yorkshire'. Well, that may satisfy the bureaucrats and the cartographers but it cuts no ice whatsoever with around three and a half million men and women who regard themselves as 'Yorkshiremen' and 'Yorkshire women', and that figure includes the authors.

They met through cricket – Fred Trueman as one of the great fast bowlers of all time, Don Mosey as a man who has written and broadcast about the game for more than twenty-five years. As professional relationship developed into personal friendship, the two found a common bond not merely in cricket but in a shared love of the county's countryside, its wildlife and its characters. This book, then, is the result of a thousand conversations and as many expeditions amongst the hills and dales of their native county. Mosey was born in Airedale and explored every road and village of the Dales on his bicycle whilst still a schoolboy; Trueman discovered the Dales when he was already an adult, and an England fast bowler, and made up for lost time via a less energetic form of transport but with no less zeal and enthusiasm. Together, they have watched birds and yarned in pubs, played cricket and searched out characters, listened to music and eaten fish and chips, examined the county's history and its culture, looked at its personality and its humour. This is a pooling of their experiences, discoveries, hobbies, interests, emotions, reactions. It is not a book about cricket, although when two Yorkshiremen write about Yorkshire, cricket has got to enter into it. Most of it is an expression of their love of, and pride in, their native county.

The Countryside

The Dales

The Norsemen left their placenames all over Yorkshire and so we have 'dales' in the east – Ryedale, Farndale, Rosedale – and in the north of the county, where streams cut deep into the Cleveland Hills, but it is in the extreme west, in the High Pennines, that the real Yorkshire Dales, as most of us know and accept them as a geographical area, begin. There are five of them and, from north to south they read Swaledale, Wensleydale, Nidderdale, Wharfedale and Airedale. The only one which does not take its name from its river is Wensleydale. Instead, the valley forsakes its natural artery, the River Ure, and takes its name from the attractive village of Wensley which was an important market town until a large percentage of its population was wiped out by the plague in the sixteenth century.

All the Dales have remarkably distinctive attractions and histories; all provide different kinds of scenery; all have their individual character, accent and dialect words and phrases. Two of them have individual breeds of sheep named after them. Only one thing do they seem to have in common – their waters all end up mingled together in the River Ouse. First the Swale and Ure join together north of York, in the plain between the North York Moors and the Pennines which admitted the Great North Road to connect the opposite ends of the country as the coaching roads were developed. Next, the Nidd twists and dodges its way past Harrogate and Knaresborough to join the Ouse, which is then the confluence of three rivers as it flows serenely through York. And here it has been landscaped superbly to form yet one more attraction in a jewel of a city which was a metropolis for the Romans, then the Vikings, and a commercial and military centre in the Middle Ages. There was a beautiful Georgian York and in the nineteenth century it became an important centre for the railway system, as well as for chocolate confectionery manufacture. To emerge from the station at York in springtime, leaving behind the high-speed trains and electronic signal boxes of the 1980s, and see the daffodils in bloom underneath the medieval city walls takes the breath away. And beyond the walls are the three towers of the sublime Minster – yes, York has a special place in the hearts of all Yorkshiremen.

As the Ouse flows on towards the North Sea it is joined next by my favourite of the five Dales rivers, the Wharfe, which has first threaded its way through forty miles or so of England's loveliest scenery, levelling out into fertile farmland beyond Otley and meeting the Ouse near Cawood, just south of York. That leaves only the Aire, with its own story – starting mysteriously in Malham Tarn and finding its way through the limestone honeycomb of the great Cove, then past Skipton, bidding farewell to its rural innocence as it heads for the once great textile empire which began at Keighley. From this point, the Aire is tainted with industrialism, skirting Bradford but unable to avoid Leeds. It winds shamefacedly through the coalfields until, with a final shudder of relief, it collapses into the Ouse at Goole, and barely has time to recover its self-respect as a river before the Ouse becomes the Humber estuary, its story now of seagoing ships.

The five dales all have their own tale to tell and we shall look at each of them in turn. If favouritism filters through my travels in Wharfedale it is because it is there that my love affair with the Yorkshire Dales first began. My knowledge of Yorkshire, as a young man, was largely confined to that part of the extreme south of the county where I was born, and the towns or cities where first-class cricket was played. The Dales were simply a mysterious area far away to the northwest which I had vaguely heard of, but never seen. Then I was called to a beginning-of-the-season practice match in Settle, far away on the main road through the Aire Gap which takes Yorkshire families to summer holidays in Morecambe or the Lake District. From the east coast, where my journey began, I took the most direct route according to the map (no motorways then) and found myself climbing over craggy hills and dropping down into one valley after another until at length I topped just one more summit. And I stopped, my breath caught by the beauty of the panoramic view. I had climbed past the workings of the old lead mines on Greenhow Hill out of Nidderdale, and now I was looking down on Wharfedale for the first time. There and then I promised myself that somehow I would have a home there, one day. It took twenty years for that day to arrive, but I finally achieved it and, since 1970, once in my home, I have been able to let the world pass me by.

Here, between still-rural Airedale and the limestone splendour of

Wharfedale, is parkland which was at its noblest when the fine houses were the homes of families who had been there for centuries (the Currers, Wilsons, Hammertons, Carrs). Other residences were built in Victorian times with the new wealth accumulated in the mills of Airedale. The houses are now mostly private schools or homes for the elderly. Some have disappeared altogether, although their fine dressed sandstone or gritstone is incorporated into a hundred smaller but newer buildings. Only the trees remain, solitary and magnificent, like sentries who know relief will never come – oak and elm, beech and sycamore. Simply to stand and look at one of these proud giants in the grounds of Flasby Hall or Eshton Hall gives me an indefinable pleasure. I can do it by walking William and Tara (my old English sheepdog family) for two minutes down my country lane. Such immense pleasure from so simple an act ... in my home I am a very happy man.

Swaledale

The upper reaches of the Swale are so remote that the area seems to have undergone little change in something like two thousand years. There were three periods of major industrial activity and they all involved the mining of lead from those wild and lonely fellsides. First, the Romans valued lead so highly that they laid their roads and marched their legions over these hills, and then had to defend themselves against the warlike tribe, the Brigantes, whose land this was. Incursions by Romans, Normans, Scots, Norsemen and Celts obviously mixed up the bloodstock considerably, but I often think – indeed I *like* to think – that there is something of the Brigantes' character remaining in most Yorkshiremen. The rest of the country seems to consider us awkward, stubborn, independent blighters and certainly that is how the Romans must have found our ancestors.

The Normans were the next to mine the lead in great quantities and it was carted out of the valley to cover the roofs of castles and abbeys throughout the north and much farther afield as well. And then came the next 'boom' in the eighteenth and nineteenth centuries, which went on right up to 1880 when it became cheaper to import lead into England than to dig it out ourselves, much as our great wool and cotton textile industries came to be priced out of world markets after the Second World War, I suppose.

The head of Swaledale is just beyond the village of Keld and, ironically, this has been opened up to the outside world as much by the establishment of the Pennine Way as by any form of mechanized transport. It is a land of bare moorlands and spectacular waterfalls with, here and there, more sheltered patches of farmland. Thwaite, the next village, with a purely Norse name (meaning clearing or paddock), is hemmed in by the High Pennines and, in particular, three individual peaks called Great Shunnor, Kisdon and Lovely Seat; and the next Swaledale village of Muker also bears a Norse name meaning a cultivated enclosure. The memories of those wild invaders who savaged their way inland, then settled peaceably to graze their stock in clearings they must have created themselves, are everywhere around us. In their day, the fells would have been covered with thick scrub and forest, and finding 'paddocks' and turning them into 'cultivated enclosures' must have been damned hard work.

At Gunnerside, the water of the Swale gathers reinforcement from a beck which has carved out a course down the slopes of Rogan's Seat which towers 2200 feet above the valley. This was 'Gunner's pasture' to the Norsemen and a very extensive lead-mining area to the Normans. Today, it is as quiet and peaceful as it must have been a thousand years ago, though the forests have been cleared and the hillsides are scarred with the burrowings of the miners. It's a glorious area in summer sunlight, yet I can still enjoy it when the clouds sit low on the tops of the fells and the day is grey and forbidding. Somehow this seems to give Swaledale a character very much its own. There is an eerie quality about this part of the dale; it seems haunted by ghostly memories.

At Reeth, tucked away in the shelter of Fremington Edge, we begin to move into tourist country with a charming village green surrounded by shops and hotels, and Arkengarthdale springs suddenly upon us from the northwest. This superb little valley leads out to Tan Hill where the highest inn in England stands hospitably firm against the bleak winters. For miles in all directions the moorlands stretch to the horizon, dotted with those flat-faced, curly-horned sheep which bear the name Swaledale.

Back in the main valley we run into folklore at Swale Hall where, it is said, the great British institution of a pot of tea first arrived upon the social scene. James Raine and his wife were supposed to have been given a brass kettle, together with a supply of tea and (apparently) rather imprecise instructions, as a wedding present. They put the tea and water in the kettle, then mixed in cream and sugar before boiling up the whole concoction and serving it to their guests in bowls, with spoons to eat the mess. Well, that's the way the story goes and I can't help wondering how many guests survived that wedding feast! The greatest pot-of-tea man I've ever known was my friend Brian Close. On the odd English summer's day when it was warm enough to justify drinks on the cricket field, he always used to moan that he would much rather have tea than orange squash, which is the usual offering. On his last day in county cricket, at Weston-super-Mare, they finally quietened him by taking out a teapot and all the trimmings.

Marske-in-Swaledale (to avoid confusion with Marske-by-Sea on the Yorkshire coast, which, incidentally, has a cricket club with a notable history) has a fair claim to rival Burnsall, in Wharfedale, for its setting of exquisite natural beauty. It has so much natural charm, with its surround of thick woods and lush valley bottom, that the high moors do not dominate it as they do so many of the villages farther upstream. The Huttons of Marske Hall were a remarkable family, producing two Archbishops of York, one of whom went on to Canterbury in the eighteenth century.

As the dale begins to open out onto the northern part of the Vale of York, the Swale finally reaches Richmond, one of the most interesting towns in the whole county and the Gateway to the Dales in the north, as Skipton is in the south. Everything is dominated by the magnificent red sandstone castle on its cliff above the river. It is from a cavern under the castle that, according to legend, King Arthur and his Round Table knights will emerge in England's hour of need. Also for the romantics, what about that 'Sweet lass of Richmond Hill'? Don't let anyone try to kid you that she was anything to do with Richmond (Surrey). Absolutely not. She was Frances I'anson, born on 17 October 1766, at Leyburn in Wensleydale, and as a young girl she lived in Richmond (Yorks.). It was here that she was courted by Leonard McNally, a dashing Irishman, who was bound to win her after writing:

On Richmond Hill there lived a lass
More bright than Mayday morn,
Whose charms all other maids surpass,
A rose without a thorn.

They were married in 1787 and McNally's tribute to his love became top of the pops in Dr Johnson's London.

A less well-authenticated story – and one without a happy ending – is that of a drummerboy who was sent down a secret passage in Richmond Castle which was reputed to lead to Easby Abbey, a mile away. He was supposed to drum his way along the tunnel so that its route could be charted by people up above. It seems a remarkably hamfisted way of going about things to me, and so it turned out for the little lad with the drum: he was never seen again. But they do say that by putting your ear to the ground between Richmond Castle and Easby Abbey you can still hear the drumbeat!

That's Richmond ... full of folklore and romance and tragedy. No wonder it has been designated by the British Archaeological Society one of the thirty-five 'most precious' English towns.

The Swale now leaves the high moorlands behind, but what is left of its course is just as fascinating as its upper reaches, if only for the fact that it takes in Catterick which is known (possibly without any great affection) to thousands of ex-servicemen. It was Lord Baden-Powell (better known and probably much more warmly regarded as the founder of the Boy Scout Movement) who, as an Army Commander in the north before the First World War, was asked to find a suitable site for a military training centre and his report was an important factor in the decision to build the camp at Catterick. It is really an Army *town* now, spread over a vast area, and from being a dreary place, remote from any major centre of population and with few amenities beyond the NAAFI, Catterick Camp has been developed to a remarkable extent since the war. Its Rugby Union team, in the days of National Service, won everything in sight, largely because it included many of the professional stars of Rugby League. Those palmy days have gone, but recreational facilities include a theatre and cater for thirty major sports, including a golf course. Aye, it's a bit different from *my* National Service days.

Long before, the Romans had appreciated the strategic importance of the route between the Pennines in the west and the Hambledon and Cleveland Hills to the east. Caracteronium was a Roman city and it still rated the title of 'town' in the Middle Ages. In the Second World War the area took on a new military significance as the whole Vale of York was dotted with airfields. From Catterick and Leeming Bar and Topcliffe and Dishforth first the Wellingtons, Whitleys and Hampdens started out on their bombing raids in Europe, and later came the Stirlings, Halifaxes and Lancasters. It is between these airfields that the Swale now winds the last few miles of its course towards Boroughbridge and its meeting with the Ure. Swaledale meets Wensleydale and the River Ouse is born.

Wensleydale

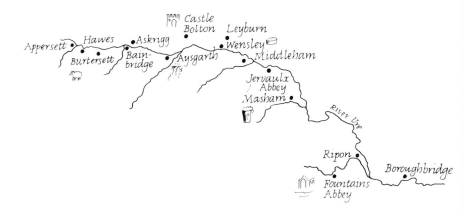

Through one of its many original tributaries, the River Ure starts its eastward journey to the North Sea within a mile or so of the source of the Eden, which flows northwestwards before slipping neatly around the side of Carlisle to empty itself into the Solway Firth. The altitude is something over 2000 feet where the infant Ure begins to wind its way down the high fells, or rather its several ways, because there are half a dozen or more tributary streams, descending in a series of waterfalls, to the floor of the valley proper. The Norsemen left their mark here, as in Swaledale, with their name for summer grazing pastures – *saetrs* – which became simplified into 'sett' or even 'seat', so that around Hawes, which really marks the start of the dale proper, we find Appersett and Countersett and Burtersett.

Hawes itself is a delightful market town (unless you are trying to motor through it on a Tuesday, when market day has been held since King William III gave it a charter nearly three hundred years ago). Then, the narrow road to the east becomes heavily congested with farmers' cars, usually towing boxes of sheep, plying to and from the auction mart just off the road to Leyburn. Wensleydale cheese – milky-white, crumbly and delicious – is world famous, even though it is now almost all factory produced in Hawes. There's nothing like apple pie eaten with a bit of Wensleydale. It is still possible to find an isolated farm where the wife might sell you a pound or two of the real farmhouse Wensleydale, usually made to a recipe which has been in the family for generations. To the north of the town is the 100-foot waterfall of Hardraw Scaur which is set in a natural amphitheatre and forms a spectacular backdrop for brass-band concerts which are staged there in the summer – a nice day out for the family, as the sounding brass booms back from the rock face.

From Hawes, the Ure winds along the valley bottom (though still around 700 to 800 feet above sea level) to Bainbridge, the historian's dream village. Here, the Bain, having splashed its way down from Lake Semerwater, joins the Ure to earn itself the title of the shortest river in England. Its course runs just three miles, yet, unlike the dozens of 'becks' which have by this time swelled the waters of the Ure, the Bain alone gets the title of a fully fledged river. Why, I've always wondered. Bainbridge is a sheer delight, with the Rose and Crown overlooking a picturesque village green, and the whole scene domi-nated by a huge grassy mound which once housed a Roman fort.

The inn itself, which can trace its ancestry to the reign of Henry VI, is a place of immense character. The horn once used to summon foresters from their labours is kept there and is still blown during the evenings between Michaelmas and Shrovetide. In the days when Tom Woodmass was the landlord I've seen orphaned foxcubs, which he's taken in and reared as family pets, running around a pen at the back of the pub with his own dogs. I've drunk at the bar in the company of a donkey, and of a duck with a liking for brown ale. And, of course, I've enjoyed a glass or two with customers of a more orthodox charac-ter, too.

A few more miles to the east and we move into the history of England in the Middle Ages. On the northern side of the valley stands Bolton Castle, built by the powerful Scropes in the fourteenth century and in those rough and ready days it must have been a very desirable mod. res., designed as it was to give the maximum amount of comfort as well as military protection. This was the first English 'home' of Mary, Queen of Scots, in flight from her rebellious Scottish lords; it held out staunchly for King Charles in the Civil War. It is now partly a restaurant, partly a museum with many relics of Dales life, but viewed from the valley bottom, on the southern side of the Ure, its square shell with corner towers is imposing.

If this was simply a historical survey of Yorkshire, the Scropes would rate two or three chapters to themselves for they must rank as one of the county's greatest families. They appear in Shakespeare, they

The great
limestone crag
of Kilnsey

LEFT
A steep climb
to the Brontës'
Parsonage

Robin Hood's Bay on Yorkshire's North Sea coast

were Kings of Man, they produced two earls, a Lord Chancellor, a Lord Chief Justice or two, innumerable barons and baronets. They fought in the Crusades and were at Crécy and Agincourt. They inter-married with the Nevilles and the Percys, produced an Archbishop of York who was beheaded by Henry IV, and were granted the right to a private family chapel by a papal bull. And, yes, the name is pro-nounced Scroop.

Aysgarth is perhaps the most popular tourist centre, especially for those with cameras, because here the Ure dashes over limestone plat-forms, providing three series of spectacular falls, all backed by curtains of trees; and if catering for the modern tourist's requirements has taken something away from the village's charm, mercifully all this has been kept well clear of the natural beauty of the falls themselves.

Leyburn, which can claim to be Wensleydale's capital – certainly since the tragedy of Wensley itself – figures in the Domesday Book. It has town fairs in May and October, is the home of the Wensleydale Agricultural Society Show and the Wagnerian-titled Wensleydale Tour-nament of Song, as well as a colourful horse show. From here the valley begins to flatten out into the Vale of York and the traveller has the choice of straight ahead, towards the Great North Road and an early meeting with the River Swale, or a gentle diversion to the south-east and back into medieval history.

Middleham, to the modern racegoer, is the centre of stables which have a proud name on the Turf going back as far as Charles Kingsley, author of *The Water Babies* (although we associate him more with Airedale). Kingsley described Middleham in 1845 as 'quite a racing town ... jockeys and grooms crowd the streets and I hear they are a most respectable set and many of them regular communicants'.

But the most famous resident of Middleham was undoubtedly that grossly maligned monarch, Richard III. It was a nephew of the Con-queror who built the first castle at Middleham and FitzRandolph's Norman keep still stands. Then came that most powerful of medieval families, the Nevilles, to add great walls and new turrets. It was the chief home of the Kingmaker, Richard of Warwick, the dominant figure of the Wars of the Roses until he changed sides and was killed supporting the Lancastrian cause at Barnet. And it was under the protection of Warwick, at the time when he was the greatest of the Yorkist magnates, that Richard III spent a happy childhood at Middle-ham Castle. Here he learned the knightly virtues and martial arts, and read of the chivalry of King Arthur and his Round Table; here he enjoyed hunting in the Dales with the Earl and his retinue, who would eat six whole oxen in a single day. Here young Richard grew up with

Francis Lovell and Robert Percy, who were to remain his friends for the rest of his short and tragic life. Here, too, he first met the young Anne Neville, who, for another brief period of happiness in his life, became his queen.

The great days of Middleham Castle ended with Richard's death in 1485; the buildings were severely dismantled during the Civil War but the ruin is still impressive. A walk of only a minute or so, after parking in the market place, brings you up against the massive curtain walls; but if you are prepared to take a slightly longer walk to the south of the castle, the view from there is much more rewarding, looking down a gentle slope at the buildings as a whole. Here, it is much easier to picture its life in the fifteenth century, the young Duke of Gloucester growing up with his friends, and then returning to Middleham as King of England. Here, in the south tower, his son was born and died as a small boy, but not before he had been proclaimed Prince of Wales at York – possibly the only trip he ever made out of Wensleydale.

So Middleham had its great days of pageantry and its grim days of royal sorrow. It's a little corner of Wensleydale which merits several pages in England's story.

And so, I suppose, does Jervaulx Abbey although, compared with some of the other Yorkshire abbeys, the ruins are not so interesting. Here settled the industrious Cistercians rather than the more academically inclined Benedictines and, apart from being credited with the original recipe for Wensleydale cheese, they were great horse breeders. The abbey's dissolution came in 1537, which seems rather hard luck on the last abbot, Adam de Sedbergh, for only one year earlier he had been hanged for taking part in the most gently named of all northern uprisings, the Pilgrimage of Grace.

On now, to Ripon, steeped in its own traditions, some of which go back to Alfred the Great, who granted a charter of incorporation in 886, so the 1100th anniversary will come round fairly soon. The traffic can be a bit tricky in that splendid old market square but it's worth the struggle. Until 1604, Ripon was ruled by a 'Wakeman' who was responsible for dealing with all crimes committed in the night, i.e., between the hours of curfew and sunrise. The last Wakeman, who became the first mayor, was Hugh Ripley, and the office is remembered by the blowing of the Wakeman's horn each evening at the corners of the market place. It is one of great tourist attraction and Americans in particular love to tape-record the ceremony. I have a personal interest in that square too – some of the best pork pie in Yorkshire can be bought there, if you can manage to find somewhere to park the car!

25

Between Ripon and Pateley Bridge, with estates in both Wensleydale and Nidderdale, stands one of the loveliest abbey ruins in the country and certainly one of my favourite beauty-spots: Fountains Abbey, the greatest Cistercian abbey in England. I sometimes wonder if the Christmas story of Good King Wenceslas was not drawn, in part, from the tale of those thirteen monks from St Mary's in York, who were, in fact, Benedictines when they first decided to found an abbey in that wild and inhospitable stretch of country (as it was in the first half of the twelfth century). The story goes that during their first two years at Fountains, living in terrible poverty, beset by winter weather and predatory beasts, they were asked for food by a blind beggar. The monks and lay brothers were near to starvation themselves, with only two loaves of bread to share amongst the lot of them, but from the first they had established a principle that no man might ask for help and be refused. The abbot, accordingly, ordered one loaf to be given to the beggar and the other shared by his flock. And scarcely had this been done than the starving monks saw a wagon, laden with food, coming down the hill from a landowner in Knaresborough. And from that moment the monks in that 'wild and rocky place, thick set with thorns and a fitting lair only for wild beasts', began to prosper. What faith those men must have had, clearing the land, chasing off predators, and building day after day. After thirteen years their work was almost complete when it was destroyed by fire and they had to start all over again. The nave, aisle and transepts which you can see today date from the resumption of their labours in 1147 and it is still possible to see much of the beauty of the original masonry.

Meanwhile, the River Ure has moved quietly on through Ripon, with its modern marina and bridge-building soldiery, across the Vale of York to join the Swale.

Nidderdale

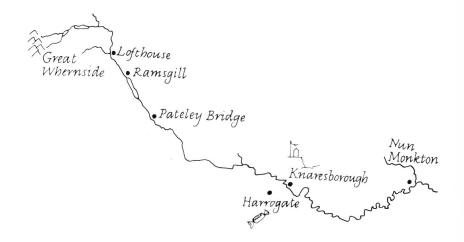

Nidderdale differs from the other four dales in that it is, to the motorist, a cul-de-sac. All the others have a western outlet, whether it is a major road like the A65 through the Aire Gap or the B6270 which climbs spectacularly over the tops out of Swaledale. For those who explore Nidderdale by car, it peters out at Scar House and Angram reservoirs and even these reaches of the High Pennines are attainable only by use of a waterworks road. But they are well worth a visit for the magnificent scenery on all sides, for a series of picnic areas and the fascinating labyrinth of caves leading from Goyden Pot – though, as ever, warning to the inexperienced is necessary about keeping well away from any pothole system when the waterlevel is high, or when sudden rain may bring about a dramatic rise in level.

The Nidd rises on the northeastern slopes of Great Whernside, although this 2310-feet peak is really one of the Wharfedale hills, towering as it does above Kettlewell. This is very much potholers' country and it has seen many a nailbiting rescue of the unwary and the foolhardy. One of these, in 1958, went on for two or three days and brought, in the wake of the cave-rescue organizations, a great gathering of newspapermen who were far less at home in this territory even than the unfortunate, if ingenuous, band of explorers trapped below. One *Daily Express* reporter, panting and wild-eyed, arrived back at his base headquarters (comfortably established in the Bluebell Hotel in Kettlewell) to report that he had been pursued down the fellside by a wolf! It was, of course, a wolf in sheep's clothing and I cannot see its 'pursuit' being of a particularly energetic nature, but there is something rather endearing about a born-and-bred Londoner, in the middle of the twentieth century, being utterly convinced that wild beasts still roamed the Yorkshire Dales.

From Great Whernside, the infant Nidd (like the Aire) quickly plunges underground and can be seen rushing through its subterranean courses by those who go to explore the cave system of Goyden Pot; then, towards Lofthouse and Ramsgill, it resumes a more orthodox march to the sea. This is the land of the walker and the caver, the angler and the birdwatcher.

There are superb circular walks around the fells, and a ten-mile tramp over into Wharfedale from Stean provides panoramic views of two dales and a visit to the old lead-mine workings of Yarnbury, on the moors above Grassington.

Gouthwaite Reservoir is a private nature reserve of endless fascination for those privileged to be granted access to it. The reservoir itself was built around the turn of the century and as its wildlife has been rigorously guarded for more than eighty years some very rare specimens indeed have been observed here – golden eagle, pied-billed grebe, red and black kites, Temminck's stint and red-necked phalarope, for instance. Ramsgill, at the head of Gouthwaite Reservoir, is, without much argument, the prettiest of the villages in the dale, though Wath, at the foot, would certainly put forward claims as a haven for those who love peace and tranquillity.

Another mile and we reach the metropolis of Upper Nidderdale – the attractive market town of Pateley Bridge, surrounded by high moors which are reached by steeply sloping roads and footpaths. In fact the area was called Little Switzerland when the railways opened it up to the townsfolk of the industrial West Riding in the mid-nineteenth century and its popularity as a 'day-out' venue grew, and continued, over the next fifty years, to such an extent that, when the reservoirs were built at the head of the valley, a single-line light railway was constructed giving access to the more remote areas above Wath. It was, in fact, the first municipally owned passenger railway in Britain when it was opened in 1907, taking 'trippers' as far as Lofthouse, until the valley was made more accessible by the arrival of motorbus transport.

For some reason which is not quite clear, the locomotives and coaches for the six-and-a-half-mile line from Pateley Bridge to Lofthouse were brought from London – from the Metropolitan Railway. If railway engines have souls, as steam enthusiasts insist they have, then those Cockney locos must have felt pretty lonely in rural Nidderdale. One of them was called 'Holdsworth', very much a North Country name, which suggests it was either christened, or rechristened, on its arrival in Nidderdale, via the great railway centre of York, and there is a famous photograph of it outside the engine sheds there in 1907.

Sadly, its life as a passenger line came to an end in 1930, and after the opening of Scar House Reservoir in 1936 there was deemed to be no further use for it as a freight line either, and plant and equipment were sold at Pateley Bridge in September 1937.

The annual show of the Nidderdale Agricultural Society is held at Pateley Bridge in late September and if it is now shorn of some of its former glory (like a visit from the Yorkshire County Cricket Club, travelling by horsedrawn wagonette), it is still a popular and important date in the diary of the farming community and, indeed, of the whole dale.

By the time it reaches the singularly attractive village of Ripley, the river has begun to leave behind the high fells and uplands. It now skirts Harrogate on the northern side. Harrogate grew up around its mineral springs and now, with a population of more than 60,000, is by far the major centre of population in this particular dale. I am very fond of Harrogate. There are few more pleasant towns in the whole country to visit during those weeks when the icy grip of winter is being prised loose at last and first the snowdrops, then the crocuses and finally the daffodils lay down their carpets over the wide green spaces of the town centre. On a very personal note, I have taken part in a number of epic matches on the pleasant St George's Road cricket ground and I have drunk champagne more than once there when Yorkshire have rounded off another season as champions. Harrogate, too, was the home of that much loved cricketer, Maurice Leyland, and for that alone it will always have a special place in the heart of every Yorkshireman. And yet, in spite of all this, I can't help thinking of Harrogate in the feminine gender. It's a woman's town, in essence – perhaps because it has a grace, elegance and charm which is so different from the more rugged qualities of most other Yorkshire towns, perhaps because it is renowned as a shopping centre with a particular appeal for the ladies. All the same, a gentle walk around the middle of Harrogate in March is calculated to warm the heart of anyone.

Once clear of Harrogate, the Nidd plunges straight into a narrow limestone gorge where tiny cottages with red-tiled roofs cling precariously to the steep slopes and where a defensive fortification has existed for more than a thousand years. This is Knaresborough, which had a recorded existence in King Alfred's time, was an important centre when the Domesday survey was carried out, and was a royal burgh of Edward III. Beside the twelfth-century castle ruins is the cave of Mother Shipton, the soothsayer of Henry VII's reign, who foretold:

> Iron in the water shall float
> As easy as a wooden boat.
> Learning shall so ebb and flow
> The poor shall most wisdom know
> Carriages without horses shall go
> And accidents fill the world with woe.
> Under water men shall walk
> In the air men shall be seen
> In white, in black and in green.

Not bad, that, for a view of the twentieth century from around 1500, was it?

The Nidd has but a short journey to join the Swale and Ure, now flowing together as the Ouse, and, as if reluctant to relinquish its identity, it starts to twist and loop and turn back on itself before finally giving up the struggle at Nun Monckton, six miles from York. But first it has passed the boyhood home of a most infamous Yorkshireman, Guy Fawkes. He is supposed to have been a bellringer at Cowthorpe, just south of the river, and it's pretty certain that, as his triple bob majors rang out over the watermeadows of the Nidd, he had no idea that, for the next three hundred years, his name would live on, as bonfires blazed over the whole country on the night of 5 November.

He was, of course, pretty daft to imagine that, along with his fellow-plotters – Catesby, Percy and the rest – he could ever get away with such a farfetched and ill-conceived conspiracy, but I like to think he showed a bit of Yorkshire character when it was discovered. One of his judges recorded: 'This handsome young red-headed Yorkshire captain lies tonight in the deepest dungeon of the Tower. Tomorrow for him is nothing but torture, ruin and death yet he sleeps the sleep of a child whilst we, his judges, toss uneasily beneath the canopies of Hampton Court.'

Wharfedale

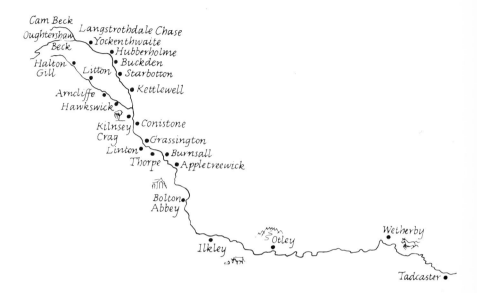

Wharfedale has long been my favourite of all the Yorkshire Dales for a number of reasons. It was my first glimpse of the middle section of this valley which started my love affair with the Dales. It has a characteristic loveliness all of its own, compounded of steep valley slopes, criss-crossed by miles of dry-stone walls (walls without mortar between the stones) so painstakingly built; of peat-brown water rushing over polished limestone platforms; of grey old villages huddled round their greens where summer sports take place in much the same way as they have since the first Queen Elizabeth; of woodlands carpeted by springtime violets and primroses; of good pubs with good ale and marvellous characters in their taprooms.

Wharfedale is not historic in the sense that Wensleydale has a clearly recorded history. Wharfedale goes back into the misty realms of Celtic folklore and Viking saga. It is not a valley of ghostly legend like Swaledale, but its ghosts are there just the same. It claims none of Airedale's industrial archaeology and yet it has its old mills by its old streams. Above all, Wharfedale delights the eye and sets the pulses racing. The ponderous face of Kilnsey Crag makes you doubt your eyes, whether viewed from two miles away or in close-up as you stand under that awesome overhang, especially if you happen to catch a couple of climbers suspended beneath it by the highly technical hardware of modern mountaineering.

The Wharfe starts its life very close to the birthplace of the Ribble, which chooses to plunge southwest and head for the Lancashire coast. The Wharfe, however, chooses an easterly route out of the wilderness of Langstrothdale Chase and over its first six or seven miles splashes merrily beside the road linking Wharfedale with Wensleydale as it climbs dramatically over Fleet Moss. But down in the valley the farms and hamlets seem snug and secure, even if you do tremble a little at the thought of their isolation in the winter snow – Cam Houses, Oughtershaw and Yockenthwaite. But in summer there is no thought of snow as families choose from a score of ideal picnic spots at the riverside.

At length the river reaches Hubberholme which, although merely a collection of farms grouped around a pub and St Michael's church, may reasonably be described as the first community of any size. Here a Viking chief named Hubba ruled the roost a thousand years ago and he might well have been the man who instituted the village 'Parliament' which sits once a year, on New Year's Day, very sensibly in the bar of the George. There is only one item of business – the letting of Poor's Pasture, a piece of grazing land owned by the church – and it doesn't take very long, not with the more pressing business of drinking the first New Year pint at hand. Next comes Buckden, where a road goes left over Kidstones Pass and into Wensleydale. Do-it-yourself entertainment is provided by self-taught musicians on a variety of instruments in the Buck at Buckden and the White Lion at Cray.

Next comes Starbotton, and here the Wharfe is trickling for the first time into recorded history, for the existence of Starbotton was recorded by the Domesday survey. And then, as it reaches Kettlewell, the valley of the Wharfe begins to broaden which has the effect of enhancing the beauty of the dale. Kettlewell is one of my favourite villages and the Racehorses is one of my favourite pubs. It was here that the Saints Cricket Club (which includes quite a number of former Yorkshire players and committee-men in its membership) held its annual dinner in December 1982. Festivities were fairly well advanced when the phone rang and on the line, from the sunshine of Australia, F.S. Trueman offered his good wishes to his clubmates as they watched the snowflakes flutter down outside. It didn't really matter because, if you are going to get snowed up in the heart of the Dales, the Racehorses is a better place than most to experience that sort of thing.

The B6160 crosses the Wharfe at Kettlewell, although a narrower road will obligingly take you down the northern bank of the river if you prefer, under the shadow of Great Whernside, giving you an earlier view of Kilnsey Crag. The main road, however, leads direct to the shadow of the great crag.

First, though, it joins the little road winding out of Littondale and the Wharfe is joined by its main tributary, the Skirfare. Between the two valleys stands the massive rampart of Old Cote Moor, all outcrops and scree and grazing for thousands of hardy sheep. There are walks over this moor for the ambitious and energetic, involving a precipitous ascent and an equally dramatic drop on the other side, but these were paths of necessity for, first, the shepherd monks and later the lead miners. Littondale, taking its name from one of the valley's five villages (Arncliffe, Halton Gill, Foxup and Hawkswick are the others), is largely unspoiled because its visitors are mainly walkers, anglers or birdwatchers, all of whom, mercifully, have strong feelings for the countryside. Arncliffe is the largest of the villages. The church has a roll of honour for those who fought not, as one might expect, in either of the two world wars, but at Flodden Field in 1513 when the flower of Scottish chivalry was decimated and James IV killed. Charles Kingsley loved Arncliffe, and if *The Water Babies* was conceived and part written high above on the Malham plateau, much was also written here, in a house called Bridge End.

But back in the main valley, the Wharfe has now reached the twin villages of Kilnsey and Conistone. The huge crag forms a remarkable backdrop to the annual show and sports day of the Upper Wharfedale Agricultural Society, held immediately after the summer Bank Holiday. Here you can see the few remaining exponents of dry-stone walling at work; they start at the beginning of the day and their work is judged at the end of it. For those who demand more energetic forms of entertainment, there is the race to the top of the crag (via the steep grassy surrounds – not up the face itself) and back to the showground. Kilnsey Show is one of Wharfedale's most colourful annual events. Across the river, Conistone church is perhaps the oldest in the dale and both villages have a road which leads directly to Grassington, the capital of Upper Wharfedale.

For a spot with a population of no more than 1200, Grassington is remarkable. On the lower slopes of the moors (where there was once extensive and profitable lead mining), it is possible to trace the outlines of a large Celtic settlement. Edmund Kean and Harriet Mellon performed classical tragedies in a theatre which is now a couple of cottages. John Wesley preached in what is now a barn. Down the main street stood the smithy of Tom Lee, who was hanged for murder in York and his body brought back to hang on a gibbet near Grass Woods (just a step northwest of the village). There are those who will

Richmond's castle and bridge over the Swale

Malham Cove at the
head of Airedale

Rievaulx Abbey on the
edge of the North York
Moors

not walk past that spot at night, even today. Iron Age, Bronze Age, Celtic settlements – all have left their mark in or near Grassington, which sprawls across the northern slopes of the valley and so has a splendid aspect, with its back to the cold winds of winter and its face looking happily into the summer sunshine. The river itself is serenely beautiful in the valley bottom as it winds towards the picture-postcard village of Burnsall. First, though, it passes just to the north of the 'secret' village of Thorpe-in-the-Hollow.

Apart from a couple of signposts, which are easy to miss, there is nothing to indicate Thorpe's existence. There would have been nothing *at all* to suggest it before roads were built and certainly not in the days when the Scottish reivers came swarming over the hills in search of cattle and any other loot they could lay their hands on. Those who could get there quickly enough headed for Thorpe as soon as warning came of the approach of the Scots and those who couldn't sent their valuables – and their daughters!

And so to Burnsall, which must stand very high on any list of England's prettiest villages. Its setting is one of perfection, on a loop of the river which is crossed by a bridge so attractive that I would be happy just to sit and look at it all day long. The village green borders the river itself and here the summer sports have been staged for at least four hundred years. Looking down on the village is Burnsall Fell, the course for England's oldest fell race, and to the east the craggy summit of Simon's Seat, with its many legends, presides benignly over this section of Wharfedale.

As the valley narrows, the woods hurry down to escort it through a series of grottoes and glades, past the picturesquely named village of Appletreewick. Here, towards the end of the sixteenth century, lived a youngster named William Craven. At the age of thirteen, he was sent off to London to be apprenticed to a mercer. He learned his trade well, was made an alderman of the City of London, became Sheriff, then Lord Mayor in 1610, and finally was knighted. Now, have I heard that story somewhere before, dressed up a bit and set to music? That's it – a Christmas pantomime called *Dick Whittington*. However, there's no mention of a cat in the story of young William Craven. Let's see what the local boy-who-made-good did for his part of Wharfedale: he founded and endowed Burnsall Grammar School, restored and embellished the church, and built that bridge I was telling you about. And his son became the first Earl of Craven. Not bad for a lad from Appletreewick!

The valley is now narrowing every step of the way and the suspicion grows by the minute that just around the next corner something dramatic is going to happen. Before that, however, we reach Barden Tower and here, for a moment, our story overlaps that of Airedale, for the tower was built by Henry Clifford, the Shepherd Lord of Skipton Castle, just over the hill. Henry was leading the men of Craven to battle at Flodden when his call-up papers came from Henry VIII, and those lads whose names hang in the church further up the valley, at Arncliffe, would have been alongside him.

From Barden, a road winds over a stretch of moorland called Black Park and down into Skipton, and the views from the top of the hill are so breathtaking that it's worthwhile making a little detour from the valley of the Wharfe.

The Wharfe now narrows to a marked degree with beech and birch and alder crowding down through the rocks to the water's edge. But as the volume of water is compressed into an ever-narrowing defile, the lovely Wharfe becomes a death-trap at the Strid. This is probably the most famous, or notorious, stretch of water in the north of England, largely because of its toll of victims over the years. As the river plunges amongst the rocks, it reaches a width that seems to invite the adventurous spirit to jump across it. But beware. The leap itself is something of an optical illusion – it's just a little further than it looks – and the landing is uncertain on tilted, and sometimes moss-covered, rocks. The Strid's list of victims is formidable because, once in the water, it is difficult to get out. Violent undertows drag you down deep beneath the rocks and there have been few survivors. In such a sylvan setting, the Strid seems to me to be rather like an exotic jungle plant which attracts unwary insects with its beauty and then traps and devours them.

Once through this narrow glen, the river then broadens and has a bland innocence as it flows through the watermeadows of Bolton Priory where generations of mill workers from the industrial West Riding have taken their picnics. The local parish church is actually the nave of the old priory and to be married in it represents a considerable social occasion. Surrounded by the ruins of the remainder of the priory, the buildings show a variety of architectural styles – Norman, Early English, Decorated and Perpendicular, and as you drive down the road from Burnsall, the route actually takes you under an ornate stone arch which was built by the monks to bring water from a moorland stream to operate their flour mill.

From the past, we move very quickly into the present as far as I am concerned because the sixth, fifth and fourth holes of Ilkley Golf Course soon appear on the left bank. I've spent a lot of time there trying to ignore the existence of the Wharfe. The first three holes are even more hazardous, because while it is a very simple matter to drag one's opening tee shot into the water, the second and third (both par-3 holes) are built on islands in the river itself. We have many cricketers' golf days there and there has been a lot of unsympathetic laughter at the expense of those playing the course for the first time.

Ilkley itself was Olicana to the Romans, who had a small garrison here to protect one of their roads, but to the Victorians it was an inland watering place noted for its mineral springs and the bracing quality of the air on its world-famous moor. 'Ilkla Moor Baht 'at' is Yorkshire's personal anthem, sung whenever ex-patriots gather together in farflung outposts. It is, in all truth, a long and rather boring song and not a particularly good advertisement for those moorland breezes as it tells of the sad consequences of wooing a young lady named Mary Jane while bereft of headgear. It goes on for about eight verses and describes, as I remember it, the whole span of life and death. Grim stuff, but the tune fits just as well to 'While Shepherds Watched Their Flocks by Night'. But Ilkley is always worth a visit. Apart from its hospitable golf club, the walks over the moors (on both sides of the valley) are exhilarating; there is an abundance of good hotels and communications are excellent. For the ambitious walker it is first class because it marks the start of the Dalesway, which, using old-established tracks, leads the whole length of Wharfedale, over into the valley of the Ribble, through Dentdale and the Howgills, to end at Bowness on Lake Windermere – a fine hike.

Many smaller towns felt deep resentment at being gobbled up by the newly created metropolitan districts in the seventies and I don't blame any of them. It was supposed to streamline local government and effect all kinds of economies, but I'm blessed if I can think what they were. The cost of new letter-headed civic notepaper alone must have been enormous. But all this must have paled into insignificance beside the sense of civic outrage at the loss of age-old identities and I doubt if any felt this more strongly than Otley, the next town on the Wharfe.

Since the early part of the thirteenth century, Otley has had a charter to hold a market, and market day in Otley (with the pubs open all day on Friday) is rather like having Christmas once a week. The Butter Cross in the town centre marked the spot where dairy products were sold from the Middle Ages right up to the outbreak of the Second World War. Chippendale was born here and Turner painted landscapes of this part of Wharfedale for his friends, the Fawkes. The agricultural show is the oldest of its kind in England and a great social event, not only for the farming community. And after all this, the town now finds itself part of the Metropolitan District of Leeds. Otley is livid about it, and I'm not surprised.

Skirting the eastern end of the ridge called Otley Chevin and its continuation, Harewood Bank, the Wharfe now reaches Wetherby (with pleasant boating on the river, an attractive golf course and a racecourse) before at last developing a utilitarian character at Tadcaster. Here the Romans had a river crossing (Calcaria) and here, nearly two thousand years later, the town is easily identifiable by the smell of hops: Tadcaster is very much a brewery town. But by now the Wharfe is near the end of its travels. I doubt if there is a river course in the country to match it for beauty in so many guises before, at Cawood, it joins the waters of Swale, Ure and Nidd to become part of the Ouse.

Airedale

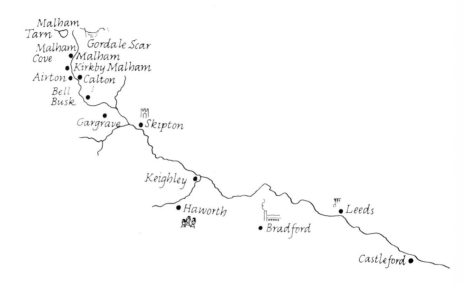

For a river which gave so much practical help to the Victorian industrialists, the Aire has a singularly romantic start to its travels – on the high limestone plateau above Malham Cove. This is great country for the geologist and naturalist alike, for the archaeologist, the botanist – and for the angler and fellwalker. As England emerged from the Dark Ages, the Malham area was an Anglian settlement taking its name from the headman, Malca; but, after the Norman Conquest, the land was divided between the Norman barons, who got the good bits, and the monks, who got the swamp and scrub and, by sheer industry, turned their wildernesses into gardens. Malham went onto the books of Fountains Abbey, miles away over what is difficult country even today, so communication with this outpost of monastic empire must have been something of a problem in the twelfth century.

The Aire begins as a clear little stream flowing out of the great natural lake of Malham Tarn which inspired Kingsley to write *The Water Babies*; indeed, much of the book was actually written at Tarn House on the northwestern shore of the lake. This, in the nineteenth century, was the home of Walter Morrison, one of the outstanding personalities of Victorian Yorkshire. More than that, he was a national and international figure, since his business interests extended to owning a railway in Argentina. But he enjoyed nothing more than to go home to Tarn House, where he entertained friends like Kingsley, Darwin and Ruskin. He loved the high fells and after travelling 250 miles by train (the last stage on the magnificent Leeds–Carlisle line), he would often dismiss the coachman, who was waiting for him at Settle with a landau, and walk the six miles or so to Tarn House. Now six miles is, I know, little more than an incompetent golfer's zigzag progress round a course, but Settle to Malham Tarn involves a climb that is almost precipitous at times. It must have been damned hard work to a middle-aged gentleman in severely formal Victorian dress, but at least it would have blown a few of the cobwebs away! Morrison did a great deal for the Craven area and it seems absolutely right that his home should now be an important centre for the Field Study Council which welcomes students from a very wide circle (both geographical and academic) to its residential courses.

No sooner has the Aire emerged from Malham Tarn than, perversely, it disappears into the limestone courses behind the face of the Cove, the massive limestone scar which encloses the village of Malham in an amphitheatre. At the foot of the Cove the Aire is reborn as it bubbles up out of the ground at a point which has been named Aire Head and which, to many, is the real source of the river. In the village, it is joined by Malham Beck, but the two together still constitute nothing grander than a stream a few feet wide which saunters amiably past the villages of Kirkby Malham, Airton, Calton and Bell Busk. Calton Hall was the home of 'Honest John' Lambert who, though born of a wealthy family, was a captain of horse in the Parliamentary forces during the Civil War. He rode with Cromwell and Fairfax in that decisive Battle of Marston Moor and was left in command of the north when Fairfax went south at the head of the Model Army. He was renowned for his rectitude, yet Lambert lived in an age when you just couldn't win. He was anti-Stuart, but he opposed plans to advance Cromwell to a status more exalted than that of Lord Protector and died an exile in Guernsey for his pains and his principles. In the church of Kirkby Malham the bells bear inscriptions commemorating the Lambert family.

At Gargrave, the Aire takes on something of the character of the Windrush, which flows so picturesquely through the Cotswolds, thanks largely to householders who have built attractive little bridges across the stream to the main road; from there it skirts Skipton to the southwest. The Springs Canal, a spur of the Leeds and Liverpool Canal, cuts right into the heart of this lovely old market town, sweeping spectacularly round the back of the splendid castle. Skipton is the model medieval town, with the High Street running straight to the door of the Norman parish church and the gate of De Romille's great castle. Here, the imperious instruction *'Desormais'* ('Henceforth') in letters of stone provides a chilly welcome for visitors. For five hundred years, from the reign of Edward II, this was the home of the Cliffords who, like the Tempests just a step down the road, were one of the great warrior families of the Middle Ages. In both cases they fought at Crécy and at Agincourt, and on most of the other battlefields of France. Here, in the heart of Yorkshire, the Cliffords were Lancastrian supporters in the Wars of the Roses and some historians 'credit' the terrible 'Black-faced' Clifford with the murder of young Edmund, Earl of Rutland and the brother of Richard III, after the Battle of Sandal. Just a year later it was Clifford's turn, in the Palm Sunday slaughter of the Lancastrians at Towton. His son was spirited away to more remote family estates in Cumberland, there, in contrast, to be brought up as the gentle Shepherd Lord, returning to Skipton when the Tudors were securely on the throne of England. He seems to have been happier in what was really a hunting lodge than amidst the pomp of life in the castle. The spiritual atonement of the Cliffords was, you might say, completed by Lady Anne, last of the line and one of the greatest personalities in Yorkshire history.

So the Aire flows on, out of a bloody era and, beyond Skipton, into the Industrial Revolution. Its waters powered the mills of the wool textile industry and even its smaller tributaries played their part. Keighley, first of the major industrial towns, takes its motto 'By Worth' from the stream which tumbles out of the Brontëland moors to join the Aire just southeast of the town, and while cartographers dignify it by the title of River Worth, to those who live beside it, it rates nothing grander than 't'beck'. The Brontë village of Haworth became part of the Borough of Keighley, which in turn was swallowed up in the 1970s by the Metropolitan District of Bradford, but to literary aficionados I suppose Haworth will always remain a community in its own right. Indeed, the pilgrims flock there from every part of the world. The Parsonage is now a museum and the present landlord of the Black Bull will gently discourage you from drinking yourself to death as Branwell did. A few steps beyond the Parsonage and you are in another world – a world of high, inhospitable moors which stretch for miles before spilling down into Lancashire's answer to Yorkshire's wool – the cotton towns of Rochdale, Oldham and Bolton. It was on these moors that Halliwell Sutcliffe set his romantic tales of feuding families with Romeo-and-Juliet overtones, and here, in the plaintive cry of the curlew, it is possible to hear the anguish of Heathcliff searching for his lost love.

At the foot of Haworth's main street is the headquarters of the Worth Valley Railway, beloved of steam enthusiasts and invaluable to film makers. Here *The Railway Children* was made and those who know the line well will have identified many a shot in television plays which call for a steam-railway sequence. It was, in fact, one of the first lines to be saved from the axe of Dr Beeching and an immense amount of hard work went into restoring and preserving the permanent way, the bridges, the tunnels, acquiring locomotives and rolling stock, and putting it all on a sensible financial basis. One of the Worth Valley line's six stations serves a hamlet called Damems which, in the 1930s, had its own claim to fame as the smallest station on the London, Midland and Scottish Railway. Then, I am told, the company built the stationmaster a house to save him a three-mile walk. It doubled the size of the station and the title was lost!

Now reinforced by the Worth, the Aire marches on through a forest of mill chimneys, skirting Bradford but unable to avoid Leeds. First, though, it casts a nostalgic eye upon Saltaire, the earliest of the 'model villages', which its power created. Titus Salt was at first a small farmer but then joined his father's business manufacturing woollens. As Bradford wrenched from Norwich its pre-eminence in wool marketing, so the manufacturers began to diversify on the outskirts of Britain's fastest growing town. Huddersfield, Halifax, Keighley all had their own areas of specialization in the type of cloth they spun. In fact, the area around Dewsbury and Batley is still known as 'the heavy woollen district' for the rough but durable qualities of its products. And on the banks of the Aire, just three or four miles from the middle of Bradford, Titus Salt built his mill. With a huge supply of alpaca wool (which for some reason no one seemed to want) lying on the dockside at Liverpool, he built up a great business. As it prospered, he passed on benefits to his workers in the form of houses, all laid out in uniform streets; and he built churches, schools, institutes, baths and a library. A whole town sprang up and, combining his family name with that of the river, he created Saltaire. And from this great industrial complex ringing Bradford was born perhaps the greatest nursery of county and Test cricketers in the world – the Bradford League. Herbert Sutcliffe, Sir Leonard Hutton, Brian Close, Ray Illingworth were just a few of its products.

The sad decline of such staple industries of the West Riding as wool and engineering has meant less industrial pollution of the Aire and, although new chemicals now sour its waters, the indefatigable anglers still sally out at weekends in search of chub and roach. How different it was in 1152 when a handful of monks trudged down the

Mill and moorland – Todmorden

Aire valley in search of a place to settle. When they founded Kirkstall Abbey they could fish happily in the clear waters of the Aire and graze their sheep in the watermeadows. But they were industrious chaps, those Cistercian monks. They pioneered the use of iron ore, started a tannery and a pottery, and introduced spinning and weaving the wool of their own sheep. And when you think that some of these sheep were grazed as far away as Holderness, in the East Riding, they'd have a bit of walking to do as well. Just to keep them out of mischief, these busy lads were simultaneously building their monastery, which was not quite complete when their first abbot, Alexander, died, thirty years after they had settled there. Now, when you think that the monks' day started at one in the morning and went through until around eight at night, it's a fair bet that trade unions hadn't started to operate!

In the twelfth century the market in the village of Leeds, a couple of miles downriver, sold the monks' wool at a better price than it fetched at the markets of Thirsk, Elmet, or farther south in Derbyshire. Seven centuries later, the city of Leeds took the cloth made in the satellite towns around Bradford and made it into clothing. But it all started with, and grew around, those monks who first set up shop down the hill from one of my favourite cricket grounds – Headingley.

Now the Aire is right out of its river valley. It joins forces with the Calder southeast of Leeds, and enters coal-mining country – and Rugby League country, too. Many of those hard-as-nails sportsmen come out of the mines around Castleford and Featherstone, and what great lads they are. I have always had a profound regard for the game and those who play it. Over the northern edge of the Yorkshire coal-field slides the Aire and out, once again, into low-lying farmland – a very different river from the sparkling stream which trickled out of Malham Tarn, sixty miles back. It winds between the great cooling towers of the power stations which take the coal hewn from the earth and turn it into energy, until, poisoned and spent, it gratefully starts a new life as part of the Ouse.

The Brontë parsonage, Haworth

Eastern Yorkshire

In spring, the little North Riding valley of Farndale is a glowing mass of gold as the wild daffodils come into bloom; five months later the moors just a little to the north are an eye-dazzling mass of purple as the heather sings its hymn of praise to high summer. And the road which winds up and down precipitous banks on its way from the picture-postcard delights of Hutton-le-Hole, north to the Cleveland villages of Castleton and Danby, is a route through a technicolour fairyland. The colours on a bright sunny day, whether it is spring or summer, are dazzling. This is all part of the immense variety of the countryside which is one of Yorkshire's greatest attractions. The moors that stretch between Pickering and Whitby, for instance, with the weather-beaten old village of Goathland as their capital, are totally different in character from those that separate Yorkshire from Lancashire, far to the west, and this is not merely because the surrealistic outline of the Fylingdales early-warning station looms out of the morning mists to the right, halfway along the journey. These, somehow, are more hospitable moors than those of the Pennines. But though one can certainly visualize the A169 being blocked by driving snowstorms, the Halliwell Sutcliffe moors which straddle the county border far to the west are more easily associated with pitiless, driving rain, and their peat hags with squelchy treachery.

At the southwest corner of the North York Moors are the gentler Hambledon Hills with the chalk outline of a horse carved above Kilburn easily visible right across the York Plain from places like Harrogate and Wetherby. And at the foot of the hills we find picturesque villages – the Coxwold of Laurence Sterne, and Kilburn, which not only has that 314 by 288-foot white horse carved in the year of the Indian Mutiny by schoolmaster John Hodgson and his pupils, but is the original home of the noted woodcarver, Robert Thompson. His personal trademark, a mouse, can be found on some of the most splendid of church woodwork. There is Ampleforth, a particular favourite of mine, with its great Roman Catholic public school, the ruined abbeys of Byland, Rievaulx and Rosedale, and Hutton-le-Hole where two small streams meet and ramble amongst the grey stone cottages and green lawns.

Helmsley is a lovely old market town with red-roofed houses entwined with flowering creepers and the ruins of a twelfth-century castle, as well as some splendid pubs with a distinctive market-day atmosphere. Eastwards runs the Vale of Pickering which, topographically as well as geologically, separates the North York Moors from the Yorkshire Wolds, and here again is a valley which provides architectural magnificence with its market towns and villages and, as a bonus, a great horse-racing, training and breeding tradition – the superb racecourse on York's Knavesmire, the stables of eminent trainers around Malton, and the Sledmere Stud of the Sykes family. Here, too, is Hovingham Hall, family home of the Duchess of Kent before her marriage and of her father, Sir William Worsley, who, as President of Yorkshire County Cricket Club from 1961 to 1973, was a man for whom I had a most profound respect and affection. Pickering, from which the vale takes its name, is just one more of those characteristic market towns which abound in the area, again with a twelfth-century castle ruin to provide an indication of its place in history as a significant centre of population.

On the south side of the valley, through which run the two main roads to the seaside towns of Scarborough, Bridlington and Filey, are the Wolds, which are really a continuation of the ridge running north–south through mid-Lincolnshire. They do not rise much above 600 feet at any point but, because they are flanked by flat, and usually fertile, plains, the view from any vantage point is always impressive. And as the roads wind through these mini-hills there is always the prospect of a superbly crafted stately home, or a village which looks as though it has been custom-built for the pages of a tourist brochure, around the next corner. This is the home of people different in character and in language from those of the industrial West Riding and, indeed, from the Dales of the far northwest as well. They take time to make up their minds; they weigh their words more carefully, I think, than the townsmen of Leeds and Bradford and Sheffield; and they take life at a more leisurely pace. But they're Yorkshire no less for that.

We have now reached the most southeasterly point of the county, the land which constitutes the northern shores of the great estuary of the Humber. This is Holderness, clearly given its name by the Norsemen, but I doubt if they would recognize much of the coastline 1100 years on. At the northern end is the 500-acre inland lake of Hornsea Mere, popular with sailors and anglers alike, but the low coastline has been subjected to a battering from the North Sea over so many centuries that it has changed shape and character quite dramatically. And yet, with that marvellous compensation which nature provides, as the coast is eaten away, much of it is swept round into the estuary, to extend and rebuild the great talon of Spurn Head which claws its way far into the mouth of the Humber. This is a land of the birdwatcher and the naturalist, lengthening by about a yard a year, yet in places no more than a few yards wide.

Looking back westwards, it is infinitely sad to see the outline of the once great port of Hull, its trawler fleet now decimated and its trade in decline. I looked the other day at a reference book, published only in 1971, and read:

Fishing fleets, cargo ships, oil-tankers and now streamlined modern car-ferries nose past Spurn Head, 21 miles southeast, and head for the forest of derricks and cranes along miles of Hull's dockland. The docks grow almost annually to cope with a surging tide of cargo: wool from Australia and New Zealand for the West Riding mills, timber from Scandinavia, dairy products from Denmark, grain and seed for the flour mills and oil-extraction plants that punctuate the Hull horizons.

It is strange and tragic to reflect that this was written less than fifteen years ago when Hull was Britain's third largest port. Alas, few would recognize it today from the description. And yet Hull always has been a city of the sea and, even now, amidst the industrial decay of the 1980s, it remains so in its pride and dignity and personality.

Bird Life

During the Third Test between India and England in New Delhi, at Christmas 1981, I had a phone call at home from the BBC in London. Even farther away in Australia, Dennis Lillee had just passed both my record of 307 Test wickets and Lance Gibbs's figure of 309. The producer of 'Test Match Special', Joanne Watson (a good Yorkshire lass), wanted a four-way conversation between Dennis in Aussie, Brian Johnston in the studio in London, Don Mosey at the Test commentary point in India, and me. Well, it was an ambitious technical exercise and it worked very well, but as they were getting near to the end of the tea interval in Delhi I asked to have a quick personal word with my old mate at the Feroze Kotla Stadium. 'You know that nuthatch in my garden that you always miss when you're here, Don? He was here this morning. I wish you could have seen him.' Quick as a flash over 6000 miles of airwaves came a classic piece of oneupmanship: 'I'm sorry about that, Fred. I hope to catch a glimpse of him one of these days because I have never seen a nuthatch anywhere. But I must tell you that I'm sitting here looking at a cricket ground with hoopoes all over the outfield.'

Hoopoes indeed! D.M. knew damn well that *I've* never seen one of *them*. But that fragment of conversation will show pretty clearly at least one – perhaps rather off-beat – interest we share. We spend hours watching the bird life of my garden, then switch to Don's home on the edge of Morecambe Bay to observe the seabirds and waders. And I don't think we shall ever tire of it, such is the endless fascination of birdwatching, whether you are an expert ornithologist or an interested amateur. Certainly it provides me with an enhanced pleasure in simply being 'at home'. What music is sweeter than the song of the blackbird after a light summer shower? Few things are more endearing than the cocky assumption of our robin that he is part of the family. On a fine morning I enjoy nothing better than breakfasting outside and watching the finches frolic on the bird table or the exquisite little goldcrest foraging for building materials when he's nesting. A walk to the bottom of the garden, where the stream dodges between alders and willows, usually reveals a flash of brilliant blue, green and orange as the kingfisher patrols up and downstream. Away over the bracken, towards the pointed summit of Sharphaw, I've seen merlins, as well as kestrels, hovering, poised for the kill.

Spring, summer, autumn, winter – the cycle goes on, the population (and its lifestyle) changes. Always there is something new to see, a new marvel of nature taking place. I suppose I ought to expect a pretty extensive cross-section of species because in a radius of, say, ten miles from my home there are deciduous trees and conifers, meadows, streams, rivers and reservoirs, bracken and hedgerow, moorland and marsh, villages and one town. But I was still absolutely staggered to find the full range of bird life when I saw the results of a census. This was the work of Peter Wright, who, apart from being on the staff of the Dales National Park Centre in Grassington, is an expert ornithologist and a member of the Craven Naturalists and Scientific Association. Peter, and some of his mates in the Craven 'Nats', carried out a survey of the area to provide an all-the-year-round view of the bird population in territory no more than 9 miles from Flasby, and this is what they came up with:

Key: R – Resident.   B – Breeding.   S – Summer visitor.   W – Winter visitor.
P – Passage migrant.   ? Known to be present but breeding not confirmed.   Species marked with an asterisk have been recorded near my home recently.   All species seen within a 9-mile radius in the last two years.

Woodlands and hedgerows

* Goshawk (*Accipiter gentilis*)	R ?	(also seen over open country)
* Sparrowhawk (*Accipiter nisus*)	R B P	(also seen over open farmland)
* Pheasant (*Phasianus colchicus*)	R B	
* Woodcock (*Scolopax rusticola*)	R B	
* Woodpigeon (*Columba palumbus*)	R B	(feeding in open country)
* Stock dove (*Columba oenas*)	R B	(feeding in open country)
* Tawny owl (*Strix aluco*)	R B	
* Green woodpecker (*Picus viridis*)	R B	
* Great spotted woodpecker (*Dryobates major*)	R B	
Tree pipit (*Anthus trivialis*)	S B	

Great grey shrike (*Lanius excubitor*)	W	(often near sewage works)
Waxwing (*Bombycilla garrulus*)	W	
* Wren (*Troglodytes troglodytes*)	R B	
* Dunnock (*Prunella modularis*)	R B	
* Garden warbler (*Sylvia borin*)	S B P	(likes undergrowth)
* Blackcap (*Sylvia atricapilla*)	S B P	(likes undergrowth and sometimes winters here)
Whitethroat (*Sylvia communis*)	S B P	(scrub areas)
* Willow warbler (*Phylloscopus trochilus*)	S B P	
Chiffchaff (*Phylloscopus collybita*)	S B occasionally P	
* Wood warbler (*Phylloscopus sibilatrix*)	S B P	(likes areas of beech)
* Goldcrest (*Regulus regulus*)	R B	(particular liking for conifers)
Pied flycatcher (*Ficedula hypoleuca*)	S B P	
* Spotted flycatcher (*Muscicapa striata*)	S B P	
* Redstart (*Phoenicurus phoenicurus*)	S B P	
* Robin (*Erithacus rubecula*)	R B	
* Fieldfare (*Turdus pilaris*)	W P	(also found in pastures)
* Blackbird (*Turdus merula*)	R B P W	
* Redwing (*Turdus iliacus*)	W P	(also found in open pasture)
* Song thrush (*Turdus philomelos*)	R P B	
* Mistle thrush (*Turdus viscivorus*)	R B	(often feeds in open)
* Long-tailed tit (*Aegithalos caudatus*)	R B	
* Marsh tit (*Parus palustris*)	R B	
* Coal tit (*Parus ater*)	R B	
* Blue tit (*Parus caeruleus*)	R B	
* Great tit (*Parus major*)	R B	
* Nuthatch (*Sitta europaea*)	R B	
* Treecreeper (*Certhia familiaris*)	R B	
* Chaffinch (*Fringilla coelebs*)	R B P W	
Brambling (*Fringilla montifringilla*)	W	
* Bullfinch (*Pyrrhula pyrrhula*)	R B	
Siskin (*Carduelis spinus*)	R ? W	(often feeding on alders)
* Greenfinch (*Chloris chloris*)	R B	
Tree sparrow (*Passer montanus*)	R B	
Jay (*Garrulus glandarius*)	R B	(likes areas with oaks)
* Magpie (*Pica pica*)	R B	

Open water and streams

Little grebe (*Tachybaptus ruficollis*)	R B P	
Great crested grebe (*Podiceps cristatus*)	R B P	
Cormorant (*Phalacrocorax carbo*)	P	(regular for some years)
* Grey heron (*Ardea cinerea*)	R B	
Canada goose (*Branta canadensis*)	R B P	(breeds on moors)
Pink-footed goose (*Anser brachyrhynchus*)	P	(makes regular crossings from the Humber to Morecambe Bay)

Mute swan (*Cygnus olor*)	R B	
Whooper swan (*Cygnus cygnus*)	W	(regularly seen on floodwater)
Bewick's swan (*Cygnus bewickii*)	W	
Shelduck (*Tadorna tadorna*)	P B	(breeding for last five years)
* Mallard (*Anas platyrhynchos*)	R B P	
Teal (*Anas crecca*)	R B P	
Gadwall (*Anas strepera*)	P	
Wigeon (*Anas penelope*)	R ? P	
Pintail (*Anas acuta*)	P	
Garganey (*Anas querquedula*)	P	
Shoveler (*Anas clypeata*)	R B	
Pochard (*Aythya ferina*)	R P B W	
Tufted duck (*Aythya fuligula*)	R B P	
Scaup (*Aythya marila*)	P	(often with tufted duck)
Common scoter (*Melanitta nigra*)	P	
Goldeneye (*Bucephala clangula*)	P W	
Red-breasted merganser (*Mergus serrator*)	P	
* Goosander (*Mergus merganser*)	R B P	(breeding on most rivers)
Water rail (*Rallus aquaticus*)	R ?	
* Moorhen (*Gallinula chloropus*)	R B	
Coot (*Fulica atra*)	R B	
Oystercatcher (*Haemotopus ostralegus*)	R B P	
Ringed plover (*Charadrius hiaticula*)	P	
Ruff (*Philomachus pugnax*)	P	
* Redshank (*Tringa totanus*)	R B P	
Greenshank (*Tringa nebularia*)	P	
Green sandpiper (*Tringa ochropus*)	P	
* Common sandpiper (*Tringa hypoleucos*)	S B	
* Black-headed gull (*Larus ridibundus*)	R B	
* Herring gull (*Larus argentatus*)	R ?	
* Great black-backed gull (*Larus marinus*)	R	
* Common gull (*Larus canus*)	W	(has bred in the area)
Black tern (*Chlidonias niger*)	P	(regular arrival in spring on the east wind)
Common/Arctic tern (*Sterna hirundo/ paradisaea*)	P	
* Kingfisher (*Alcedo atthis*)	R B	
* Sand martin (*Riparia riparia*)	S B	
* Yellow wagtail (*Motacilla flava*)	S B	(in watermeadows)
* Grey wagtail (*Motacilla cinerea*)	R B	
* Pied wagtail (*Motacilla alba*)	R B	(also found in pastures)
* Dipper (*Cinclus cinclus*)	R B	
Sedge warbler (*Acrocephalus schoenobaenus*)	S B	
* Reed bunting (*Emberiza schoeniclus*)	R B	

Limestone uplands and moorland

* Buzzard (*Buteo buteo*)	P W	
Rough-legged buzzard (*Buteo lagopus*)	W	
Hen harrier (*Circus cyaneus*)	R B	(has bred)
Peregrine falcon (*Falco peregrinus*)	R B P	
Merlin (*Falco columbarius*)	S B	
* Kestrel (*Falco tinnunculus*)	R B	
* Red grouse (*Lagopus lagopus*)	R B	
Black grouse (*Lyrurus tetrix*)	R B	(upland wooded hills)
* Golden plover (*Pluvialis apricaria*)	R B	(valleys in winter)
Dunlin (*Calidris alpina*)	S B P	(calls at reservoirs and rivers in passage)
* Curlew (*Numenius arquata*)	R B P	(valleys in winter)
* Snipe (*Gallinago gallinago*)	R B	
* Cuckoo (*Cuculus canorus*)	S B	(also in woodland)
Short-eared owl (*Asio flammeus*)	R B W	(also in areas of young conifers)
* Skylark (*Alauda arvensis*)	S B	
* Meadow pipit (*Anthus pratensis*)	R B	
* Whinchat (*Saxicola rubetra*)	S B	
Stonechat (*Saxicola torquata*)	R B	
* Wheatear (*Oenanthe oenanthe*)	S B	(likes limestone areas)
* Ring ouzel (*Turdus torquatus*)	S B	
* Yellowhammer (*Emberiza citrinella*)	R B	(marginal land with some scrub)
Snow bunting (*Plectrophenax nivalis*)	W	
Twite (*Cardnelis flavirostris*)	R B W	(valleys in winter)
* Linnet (*Cardnelis cannabina*)	R B	(marginal land, valleys in winter)
* Carrion crow (*Corvus corone*)	R B	
Raven (*Corvus eorax*)	B	(was formerly a regular breeder)

Pastures and open fields

* Partridge (*Perdix perdix*)	R B	
* Lapwing (*Vanellus vanellus*)	R B	
* Little owl (*Athene noctua*)	R B	
* Swift (*Apus apus*)	S B	(also urban areas and villages)
* Rook (*Corvus frugilegus*)	R B	

Urban areas and villages

Collared dove (*Streptopelia decaocto*)	R B	(not as common as might be expected in this area)
* Swallow (*Hirundo rustica*)	S B	(also in open country, rivers and open water)

* House martin (*Delichon urbica*)	S B	(also in open country, rivers and open water)
* House sparrow (*Passer domesticus*)	R B	
* Starling (*Starnus vulgaris*)	R B W	(also woods and open country)
* Jackdaw (*Corvus monedula*)	R B	(feeds in open country)

Lowland scrub and carr

Grasshopper warbler (*Locustella naevia*)	S B	
Sedge warbler (*Acrocephalus schoenobaenus*)	S B	
Willow tit (*Parus montanus*)	R B	(occasionally)

Harry J. Scott and The Dalesman

In April 1939, a new magazine appeared on the counters of booksellers and newsagents – largely those in the north of' England, but some through more adventurous agents in other parts of the country. Today the magazine goes into homes in more than fifty countries. It found its way through to the Falklands in the middle of the war with Argentina; it gets through the Iron Curtain into Moscow; it flies to remote islands like Ascension, in mid-south Atlantic, and Tuvalu in the South Pacific; it reaches picturesque addresses like 'Cutter's Corn, Norfolk Island' (midway between New Zealand and the Queensland coast). And it arrives each month at the homes of thousands of countryside enthusiasts throughout Britain and nostalgic ex-patriots living in Australia, Canada, New Zealand and the United States.

The Dalesman magazine is one of the outstanding success stories in journalism of the most wholesome kind.

It started life as *The Yorkshire Dalesman*, created and produced from one room of a house in the pretty village of Clapham, deep in the heart of northwest Yorkshire's limestone country – the inspiration of a man called Harry J. Scott, and indeed it could only have been the creation of a man like him. He was a Quaker, the kindest and most generous of souls, with a gentle humour and a tongue and pen that were incapable of malice. He wrote with love about lovable things, and the greatest of these to Harry J. Scott (after his family) was the limestone country of the Yorkshire Dales. He worked on newspapers in Leeds but yearned for the country life and at every opportunity fled with his wife, son and daughter to a cottage in the Washburn Valley. Since these opportunities occurred only at weekends and in holiday time, they were not enough. In the mid-thirties – not exactly a period of prosperity in the industrial West Riding – he took what was really a dramatic and daring step. He gave up the security of his salaried job on the *Yorkshire Post*, rented an old, stone-built house in Clapham and moved there with his young family. His economic planning had a simple innocence: if he could make £3 a week by freelance writing, they could live well in surroundings which seemed to them idyllic.

And there he could dream, amidst the stream of articles he wrote under his own name and a variety of pseudonyms on every kind of countryside topic, of ultimately pouring all his energy into a magazine of his own, a publication which would reflect the leisurely tempo of life in the Dales, the quality and standards of that life, and at the same time capture the dynamic changes of nature. Quietly he laid his plans and, with his own savings and a little help from friends, *The Yorkshire Dalesman* was launched in the spring of a momentous year – 1939. W. L. Andrews, later to become Sir Linton Andrews, editor of the influential *Yorkshire Post*, was one of those who encouraged the idealistic Scott, and when the first issue appeared he wrote: 'It looks well, contains some good stuff and should make a friendly impression from the start. What a pity the European outlook is so bad. I see no near end to the trouble.' That was, of course, a sadly prophetic view.

Nevertheless, very few people could actually accept war as inevitable, certainly not a member of the Society of Friends. And if J. B. Priestley shared the doubts and fears of Linton Andrews, he pushed them out of sight as he welcomed the first edition of *The Yorkshire Dalesman*. 'I am glad to learn', he wrote in that original issue, 'that our beloved Dales are to have their own magazine.' Priestley went on to recall being commissioned to tramp through Wharfedale and Wensleydale to write a series of articles shortly after the First World War: 'I have never found again – no, not even in the romantic islands of the West Indies or the South Seas, not in the deserts of Egypt or Arizona – the sunlight that set all the dewdrops glittering about my path that morning.' A beautiful recollection of 1919; I wonder if Priestley realized, as he wrote, how close we were to another, even more cataclysmic war which was to involve most of the world. Certainly Harry Scott didn't, or perhaps wouldn't, allow himself to think so. By August 1939, he was enthusiastically writing to potential advertisers: 'Already circulation has reached 7000,' and inviting them to take display advertising space in the magazine at 3s (15p) per column inch. Exactly one month later, the world was at war.

This had the immediate effect of pegging the circulation of *The Yorkshire Dalesman* to the figure that had given Scott so much delight after only four issues. Just about every penny he possessed had gone into the magazine's launch. Now came the problem of keeping afloat amidst the most appalling difficulties, and if Emerson was right in believing that the only reward of virtue is virtue, then what happened next to *The Yorkshire Dalesman* will bear him out. Regular subscribers were asked to return their copies, once read, to that one room in Scott's home, by now named Fellside, where they were recycled, so to speak, and sent to members of the forces. Many of them found their way to ships, airstrips and the battlefields of three continents where the first enemy might well be a German or a Jap or an Italian but the second was most certainly boredom. Scott's little magazine provided the perfect answer to it. In those pages of gently humorous anecdote about Dalesfolk, articles on shepherds and dry-stone wallers, village postmen and farmers' wives, servicemen and women found an antidote to the horrors of war. In the line drawings and photographs and reproductions of watercolours of Dales scenes and characters, they could escape. By the end of the war *The Yorkshire Dalesman* had a new public which might never otherwise have been tapped, and the Dales themselves had a new fan club.

Those who knew Scott well will vouch, to a man, that no thought of this ever occurred to him. He was not the sort who could contemplate his own wellbeing while thousands were dying every day in a war in which he could not take part himself. His simple act of kindness in seeking to offer a little comfort to those who *were* involved quite accidentally assured the success of *The Yorkshire Dalesman*. Virtue had provided its own reward. By 1946 the magazine was on a sound financial basis and expanding in every direction. Those tattered wartime copies which had found their way to the battlefields had not only attracted new readers; they brought an explosion of new contributors, some of them from areas beyond the boundaries of Yorkshire where men and women loved *their* river valleys and high moorlands. *The Yorkshire Dalesman* became simply *The Dalesman*. Later came another magazine, identical in format but catering for those who loved the English Lakes, *Cumbria*, and in their wake a flood of specialist books and booklets covering every possible aspect of country life. The Dalesman Publishing Company Ltd was born. It is still alive and well and flourishing in Clapham.

During those wartime years, Harry Scott, not content with keeping his newborn and much loved magazine afloat, gave a helping hand, in the form of his newspaper experience, to the weekly paper twenty miles away in Skipton, the *Craven Herald and Pioneer*. If that delightful medieval town is the Gateway to the Dales, then the *CH & P* must be the Encyclopedia of the Dales. The hill farmers trace their lost sheep through its columns ('Taken up, horned ewe, red mark left shoulder'); the ratepayers are told in exhaustive detail of the activities, for good or ill, of their elected representatives; whist winners proudly observe their names in bold type; results of every cricket, football, rugby and bowls match are recorded in its columns for posterity. In short, the *Craven Herald* is much like any other weekly paper throughout the British Isles, but it covers a unique area of national parkland and it strenuously resists any form of change to its marvellously traditional appearance, with advertisements covering the front page. Here, during the war, with the staff (like those of other papers) reduced to old men and young boys, Harry Scott met and influenced the lives of a number of embryonic journalists. One was William R. Mitchell, or 'Young Billy', who, after the war, travelled twenty miles up the A65 to join Harry Scott and to become part of the success story of *The Dalesman*.

As the front room of Fellside began to overflow with manuscripts, reference books and typewriters, headquarters were moved – just 100 yards – to the other side of Clapham Beck. The editorial offices are now in what used to be the vicar's coachhouse. Commercial and sales offices are in adjoining buildings of slate and stone which blend perfectly into the village scene. Some of the girls who joined the staff to dispatch *The Dalesman* to all parts of the world are now grandmothers, and perhaps the key to their affection for, and long association with, the magazine is to be found in something Priestley wrote when, after the war, he at last visited the office and heard 'the joyful sound of women singing'.

The publication of books began to grow and David Joy, journalist and son of a journalist with strong Dales affiliations, joined the staff and is now in charge of books. More than three hundred titles are available, ranging from *Countryside Walks around York* to the confessions of a Swaledale poacher, from Pennine birds to Roman forts, brass rubbings to farmhouse recipes, battlefields to watermills, witches to sheepdogs. It's a quite incredible list.

But still, the flagship of the fleet, *The Dalesman*, sails out across the continents and oceans. Mr and Mrs Ashworth, in Port Stanley, Falkland Islands, are subscribers for whom *The Dalesman* staff experienced a special concern in the summer of 1982. When the fighting ended in those far-off islands, Mrs Eileen Plumridge – one of Priestley's 'women singing' – slipped a note into the envelope containing the September edition of *The Dalesman*, anxiously inquiring how many copies they had missed during that brief, sad war. Back came the answer: 'None, thank you – all our copies got through. And by the way, we had a white rose sticker attached to the windscreen of our Land Rover throughout the Argentine occupation.'

There is a sublime wholesomeness about the contents of *The Dales-man* which somehow protects it from the mess of war. It is good for the soul to read a publication in the 1980s which has no reference to conflict, mugging, hooliganism, dishonesty, cheating, lying or deceit. It may not reflect life in general in the world today, but it does reflect those qualities of rural England which it is still possible to find if you search industriously enough – the qualities which Harry J. Scott loved and prized sufficiently to want to encapsulate in one magazine, more than forty years ago. He lived to see his dream come true before he died in January 1978.

Clapham itself is perhaps the most perfect village possible in which to capture and chronicle the story of Dalesfolk. Even the planners were kind enough to divert the A65 around it; if you ring someone there, it's a fair bet that the telephone will pick up the bleating of sheep. And as we walked beside the beck which plunges down from the bare slopes of Ingleborough through the heart of the village, Bill Mitchell reflected, 'When Mr Scott first put the magazine together in his one spare room at Fellside, he loved to hear the calling of the curlews as he worked. We can still hear them as *we* work.'

Moorland sheep

James Herriot

James Herriot is the pen name of a North Yorkshire veterinary surgeon whose stories of life amongst the Dales farmers earned him literary acclaim throughout the western world and whose books, when translated into the BBC TV series 'All Creatures Great and Small', gave the small screen some of its best-loved characters. Herriot is a creation which grew to such proportions that the author found it was taking over the life of the country vet, who then decided, 'Enough.' Above all else he was a man who served his community with the skills of his profession. The Yorkshire vet with a distinctive Scots accent was enjoying a weekly lunchtime visit to a favourite country pub when this conversation took place, in July 1982.

F.S.T. People tend to think that Scotland is not a cricketing country but in fact there is a lot of cricket there – there's a great enthusiasm for the game in schools, colleges and at club level. There has been a national cricket team for years in Scotland and in 1980 they were admitted to the Benson and Hedges Cup competition.

J.H. Yes, I know all about that. I played at school and there was a West of Scotland club and Scotland played a fixture against touring sides, but it is not as fanatical as the following for soccer or rugby.

F.S.T. And there have been some famous cricketers who have come from Scotland – men like D. R. Jardine, Ian Peebles. Mike Denness captained England, as Jardine had done. Did you ever meet Jardine?

J.H. Goodness, no. These were godlike creatures I viewed from a distance. Jardine was a boyhood hero of mine. He could really play the Australians at their own game. He was a bit of an abrasive character, perhaps, but then most Australians are a bit that way, too.

F.S.T. And so the fascination of cricket is really in your blood, then?

J.H. Oh, yes. My game is tennis and I was a fair player when I lived in Glasgow, but I would walk miles to see cricket. Although I *played* tennis, I would rather watch a Test match than watch Wimbledon. My father as an Englishman brought me up in the faith, so to speak, and I have always delighted in cricket.

F.S.T.   What fascinates me is this – your father was an Englishman, you're a Scotsman, you settled in ...

J.H.   Correction. I'm an Englishman. I was born in Sunderland.

F.S.T.   What? So you're a Geordie, then?

J.H.   Well, not quite. I'm a Wearsider. Geordies come from a bit farther north. But I'm steeped in Wearside football as a result, even though I was carted off to Glasgow at the age of three weeks. Since then I've taken on a Yorkshire thing, too, you know? I'm a mongrel – a sort of Glaswegian-Wearside-Tyke.

F.S.T.   And we both end up in the Yorkshire Dales. When I first saw the Dales I just had to stop my car and look, I was so fascinated by the beauty of the countryside.

J.H.   Aye, me too.

F.S.T.   It was around here. On the top of Greenhow Hill. Did you find this strange fascination when you first moved to Yorkshire?

J.H.   Oh, indeed I did. It grabbed me straight away. I was brought up in Glasgow and you have only to drive for half an hour – to Loch Lomond, to the Trossachs – to be amongst some of the most glorious scenery in the world and I suppose I grew up thinking there was no scenery *outside* Scotland. I was amazed when I saw Yorkshire because my impression of Yorkshire was, well, not exactly Coronation Street, but I supposed I might see a bit o' seedy grass between the factories, a few tired Brussels sprouts here and there ... God's truth, when I first went to Wensleydale and Swaledale I couldn't believe it. I had to stop the car. I took the moor road from Leyburn over to Grinton and I stopped and looked down the valley of the Swale and I thought, My God, I can't wait to get back to Scotland and tell my pals just what Yorkshire is like.

F.S.T.   And I don't know whether you have noticed this, but it's a land of moods, too. You see them in the sunrise and you see them when it's setting, and the countryside seems to speak to you. Do you find this?

J.H.   Yes! Every time I go to Sutton Bank, and I must have gone up there in the course of my work literally thousands of times, it's different every time. On a clear, frosty day you can stretch out from the top of Sutton Bank and touch Pen Hill in Wensleydale; other days it's miles and miles away, but different ... always different. As you say, it has its moods.

F.S.T.   It's a different way of life, too. At one time (you can't now, I'm sorry to say) you could drive down the Dales, say from Hebden or somewhere like that, and find a pub with all the lights on and a singsong going on and you could call in and get a drink! Are you a bit like me – hating to see these quarries and things scarring the face of the Dales?

J.H.   Aye, and yet it's wonderful what time can do. One of my great pleasures is walking my dogs and my kids and now my grandchildren over the old mine tracks. Well, *they* were originally dreadful scars, weren't they? Think of the old Gunnerside Ghyll road ... that was an old mine track, but now it's a lovely velvety road which carries you all over the old lead mines. In many places you can see the old scars but they've all been covered over and they've become part of the landscape now.

F.S.T.   And you can stop at farmhouses for bed and breakfast and have a real farmhouse breakfast and it's still inexpensive.

J.H.   I've advertised those folks a bit in my writing and some people have said I have spoiled the Yorkshire Dales with my books.

F.S.T.   *What!* Who said that?

J.H.   Well, various people ... you'll always get someone who takes an opposite view. There was an article last week in the London *Standard*: 'The Dales are alive with the Sound of Herriot ... Herriot has done for the Yorkshire Dales what Stonehenge has done for Salisbury Plain.' It's absolute nonsense.

F.S.T.   It is. I try to sell the Yorkshire Dales all over the world because I'm so proud of belonging to them.

J.H.   That's right. The tourist boards publish glossy brochures which people have to pay for and they are *trying* to get people to come here. Because I write a book, not with that object at all, but because I want to write what I feel about living here, people turn round and say: 'What are you doing bringing all these people into the Dales?' Well, I'm not setting out to bring them in, but what if it does have that effect? As you say, it helps all the little farmers who do bed and breakfast, but I hope it brings people to share the pleasure I feel just by being here.

F.S.T.   And another thing, there are dialects up here that I still struggle to understand. Do you get that?

J.H.   Well, I don't exactly struggle to understand them after all this time, but I can hear the *difference* in the way they speak. Round Thirsk and away on the east coast at Scarborough and then up at Robin Hood's Bay and up the Dales, which I call 'in the Pennines' – they're all entirely different.

F.S.T.   What did you think of 'All Creatures Great and Small' as a television series?

J.H.   Super. Absolutely super. There were two *films* before that series which were very nice but they didn't show much of the Dales. Now the TV series did. There were always lovely shots of some of the most beautiful parts of the Dales which delighted me. I was sometimes a wee bit irritated – they used to send me the scripts to vet (not a bad pun) and occasionally I'd come across a word like 'gradely'. Now that was a script written by somebody who lumped all the north together and didn't know a Lancashire word from a Yorkshire word. You don't spend forty years here without knowing what people say and what they don't. I'd vet that sort of thing, which was presumably why they'd sent me the script, and then no one would take a blind bit of notice! But my wife and I were watching *The Quiet Man* on TV the other night for about the twentieth time and there were these lovely backdrops to everything – every time Maureen O'Hara and John Wayne appeared, there was the beauty all round them. Now in the first two films they did of my books, particularly the very first, there was hardly anything like that. It could have been in the back streets of Wakefield, a lot of it. Great actors – Anthony Hopkins, Simon Ward, John Alderton – I mean, who can you get better than that? But whereas in *The Quiet Man* they didn't miss a trick, in those first two films we got very little of it. So the series of 'All Creatures Great and Small' made up a lot for that – the backdrop of the Dales was there all the time. The Americans and the Canadians loved it and, you know, over there they show it over and over and over again. It's the expatriates, I suppose, who love to look at pictures of countryside and characters they remember with affection.

F.S.T.   In Australia as well, I can tell you. People there have said to me, 'Do you know James Herriot?' and I've always had to answer, 'No, never met him. But some day I'm going to. My wife's met him because he goes to a little country pub run by some friends of ours and one day I'm going there to meet him.' But it's amazing, you know, what you've done for the Yorkshire countryside and Yorkshire people ... a Glaswegian–Wearside–Tyke. I don't suppose you ever thought it would all happen.

J.H.   No ... no. It *was* my ambition to write a book. At school, I couldn't count (I still count with my fingers) but I could make with the words. I could write essays – composition, we called it in the Glasgow schools – and fortunately my father was inclined towards literature and I was born into a house full of books. I soon got over the *Rover* and the *Wizard* and I was reading H. G. Wells, Conan Doyle (still my great favourite), Rider Haggard, as a small boy. I was a big reader and I used to think, 'If only I could write just one book.' I used to dream of it. I could see it in the bookshop windows with my picture on it, and then I'd wake up and find, 'Damn it, I haven't written a book at all.' But I have a bit of a Frankenstein thing, now. I've created a monster and I can't control it. I had fifty people in my surgery yesterday, nearly all Americans, and none of them wanting the services of a vet. And that happens every day.

F.S.T. *Really?*

J.H. Aye. So long as they keep away from my private home...

F.S.T. And how do you feel? James Herriot's not your real name, is it?

J.H. No.

F.S.T. How did you come by your pen name? What made you choose Herriot?

J.H. That was purely by accident. I wrote my books in front of the television because after driving round the farms all day I didn't want to hide myself away at night. I'd never have seen my family. I was desperately looking for a pseudonym since I felt I couldn't use my real name, being a practising vet, but every name I thought of was already in the Veterinary Register. One night I was typing away and watching a football match and James Herriot was playing a great game in goal for Birmingham. It struck me immediately that that was a pleasant-sounding name and there were no Herriots in the Veterinary Register, so that was it.

F.S.T. Oh, I thought it was maybe a family name.

J.H. No, but since then Herriots from all over the world have written to me to say how pleased they were to contact one of the clan and that they were sure we were related because I was the very image of great-uncle Marmaduke Herriot in the family album.

F.S.T. A bit embarrassing, eh?

J.H. Yes, it was and is.

F.S.T. And how do you feel about being called James Herriot? Do you answer to both?

J.H. Yes indeed. James Herriot's a much nicer name than my own, anyway! All my American associates call me James. But I still use my proper name in the town where I live; I'm still the local vet. There's been no difference at all. But it can be a bit embarrassing – all these tourists. It's as if I am some sort of film star.

F.S.T. You are, whether you like it or not; you are now a very, very famous author.

J.H.   In England people have a more sensible view of things. All right, I write animal books – nice, light reading – but over in the States it's a cult. They regard me on a much higher scale, and the most prestigious people write to me from over there, and this is difficult because while I have a system of replying to the hundreds of letters which come in, I have to reply to these people by hand otherwise I annoy them. It's amazing – they want to give me honorary degrees, and they want me to go over and receive plaques and scrolls. The American Veterinary Association invited me to go over and stand up there in front of all the American vets and receive their plaudits. I said, 'I'm sorry. I'm not doing that.' But they came over here, the American vets' president, and we got together with all the characters in the books (who are all real people, of course) and we had a lovely party and they gave me this plaque which is now hanging up in my study. The Americans have been great to me. But there's the other side of the coin. You get nowt for nowt, as they say in Yorkshire, and they come flocking over here, all wanting to take my wife and me out to dinner, and I can't do with that. But, as I say, there were fifty in yesterday, packed shoulder to shoulder, all with their books to sign . . . all nice people, but it really is a problem.

F.S.T.   Do they try to con you by bringing an animal to be looked at or anything like that?

J.H.   Well, no, because if they did I'd send them straight away. I never, never see anyone with an animal who's come to see James Herriot. That would be unethical, d'you see? Those with sick animals come to see the real me, the veterinary.

F.S.T.   It's amazing, where it all started and where it's gone to. Are you frightened of it now?

J.H.   No, not really. I think I am beginning to come to the surface. But with a big success, it's hard to handle at first, isn't it? You've had a long period of it and I suppose it's traumatic. It has its other side, as well, doesn't it?

F.S.T.   Well, in a way I'm like you. This is why I tried to find somewhere quiet to live, to have some peace, because wherever I go, people want to talk about cricket, and wherever you go, I suppose people want to talk to you about your books.

J.H.   Except they don't know me.

F.S.T.   You mean you're not recognized? But you'll know what I mean – people interrupting when you are trying to have lunch or dinner with some friends, wanting either to talk cricket or to get autographs. I will *not* sign autographs for people who interrupt me during a meal.

J.H.   Quite right, too. And that person's cheeky who would do such a thing.

F.S.T.   But the trouble is, they walk away then, and say, 'Oh, he's getting too big-headed' – that sort of thing.

J.H.   Yes. You are in a ten times worse position than I am because I can go all over the country and no one knows me because I am not a well-known face. I might be a well-known writer but, thank heaven, I've got anonymity. You've got as much chance as Prince Charles of getting any peace. What do you do when you want to take your missus out for a meal?

F.S.T.   I usually go to places where I am *well* known and they leave me alone.

J.H.   I see. Well, we can go around the pubs of North Yorkshire and drop in and have a bar snack and no one bothers ... no one knows me. And if I go anywhere local, then there's no fuss again because I'm just the local vet. If there's one thing the Yorkshireman can't stand it's uppityness. You can be anything you like, as famous as anyone, but, by God, if you get too big for your boots they'll never forgive you. I can honestly say that my writing success has not boosted my ego. I still feel that I'm the local vet; I still work as the local vet. And the people I work with and amongst never, *never* mention my books. Around the farms, oh no, *never*. If you've got a sick cow worth maybe six hundred quid you don't want Charles Dickens walking in. You want somebody who can cure your cow, don't you?

F.S.T.   I remember when I got my 250th Test wicket in New Zealand and I came home and the chairman of the Yorkshire CCC said, 'Two hundred and fifty wickets, eh?' and I said, 'Yes. I'm very pleased about it.' He didn't change expression, merely replied, 'Aye, be pleased about it but remember one thing: we *expect* it i' Yorkshire.'

J.H.   And they'd be watching you like hawks for any untoward expression of pleasure in your achievement. I never mention a word about my books. It's nothing to do with the practice, you see.

F.S.T.   There are no stars in Yorkshire.

J.H.   That's right. In my town we've got Graham Fletcher, the famous show jumper. I think that's very much nearer the Yorkshire soul than a writer and at home Graham is very much more famous than me. A cricketer, or a horseman, would always be a much more prestigious person than a writer in Yorkshire. In fact, I think some of them think there's something a bit cissy about being a writer.

F.S.T.   When you are writing a book, do you set it down in longhand, or do you type it, or what?

J.H.   Oh, I type. I'm a brilliant but erratic typist. My handwriting is so bad that when I used to write home, my parents couldn't read my letters. It's always been so bad that years ago Joan [Mrs Herriot] bought me a little Olivetti – fifteen quid she paid for it. This was long before I thought of writing a book, but I'm someone who believes in doing things the right way so I bought a Pitman's book on *Teach Yourself to Type* and now I can type properly with all my fingers. I've tried speaking into a recording machine but it doesn't work with me. I hear Barbara Cartland walks round the room composing umpteen novels a year without ever actually writing a single word. I can't work that way. What I have done is carry a little machine round with me in a car, and as ideas came into my mind on the rounds of the farms I have noted them and then embroidered them afterwards. I speak in the past tense because I don't want to write any more.

F.S.T.   You don't? How many books have you written altogether?

J.H.   Well, not many because, you see, I have been a vet all the time – seven books plus the book on Yorkshire, that's eight, and I didn't start until I was fifty and I'm sixty-five now.

F.S.T.   Are you really a senior citizen? Have you got a cheap bus pass?

J.H.   No, but what I *have* got is a cheap train pass which is going to be a fat lot of good if they are going to abolish the railways! I feel that I've now got to stop the world and get off because I've always had a nice, quiet country life, but I had this compulsion to put something down on paper. I had to closet myself and sit down in a chair and type and I'd never done that before. I'd always had an active life, working outside with animals. Well, I had this compulsion and now I've got rid of it. I've done all that and I just want to get back to my nice, quiet country life as a vet.

F.S.T.   You love all that, the fresh air and the animals?

J.H.   Oh yes! Writing is a solitary occupation. It's lonely and I don't like being alone. I like to be out with the farmers and their animals, and with the cats and dogs in the surgery and with my family in my home. I did write a bit about cricket in one of the books and I got a lovely letter from Sir Len Hutton saying how much he had enjoyed that reference to village cricket. Fred, is it true that when you bowled Polly Umrigar in the Third Test against India in 1952 the bail went almost all the way to the boundary?

F.S.T.   Yes, it went up to the wicket covers, just in front of the sight screen.

J.H.   You've got it framed somewhere, haven't you?

F.S.T.   I gave it to my brother, Arthur. He's got it.

J.H.   I thought it was something like that because I've read all your books and I followed all your career. Do you remember when you felled poor Norman O'Neill and he was sick on the pitch?

F.S.T.   Yes, when I hit him at Manchester.

J.H.   You got his box out and you were hammering it back into shape with the handle of a bat. D'you remember that? He really was ill, wasn't he?

F.S.T.   Aye, but what made it worse was that when he had recovered and put his box back on, the umpire told him he was out, hit wicket.

Sir Malcolm Sargent, 'The Huddersfield' and Handel's *Messiah*

Music

Choirs and Brass Bands

Two of the most significant strands of Yorkshire's cultural heritage developed, indirectly but clearly, from the Industrial Revolution – choral singing and brass band music – and if we seek to illustrate this by taking one example of each of these art forms this is not meant to disparage the many other choirs and bands that thrive in the county. On the contrary, the Huddersfield Choral Society and the Black Dyke Mills Band are the tips of two enormous icebergs, for both traditions of music making have spread far and wide, most notably (as one would expect in cultures born of the Industrial Revolution) in the mill and mining towns of the West Riding. For every Huddersfield, there are fifty choirs, not, perhaps, as famous or as accomplished, but still made up of men and women whose great-great-grandparents had precious little to cheer their lives, and so developed their own simple forms of entertainment. For every Black Dyke, there are fifty bands, most of whom have never won, or ever will win, a national championship, but who play for the sheer pleasure of playing and who give (as their Victorian ancestors did) much pleasure to their fellows. And what is most important of all, both cultures are still flourishing in the streamlined, chromium-plated, neon-lighted jet age of the 1980s. They are part of a tradition, the roots of which were firmly and lovingly planted one and a half centuries ago. They have flourished and multiplied, and Yorkshire is very much the richer because of them.

John Wesley, the mendicant evangelist, played a major part in establishing choral singing by bringing in a form of Christian worship that had an instant appeal to the working class of northern England – passionate preaching and fervent singing. Apart from his Christian message, Wesley gave his new Wesleyan chapels hymns that he or his brother Charles had written, hymns with stirring words and rousing tunes like 'Before Jehovah's awful throne', 'Oh God, my God, my all

Thou art', 'Father of all whose powerful voice' – and with a powerful voice indeed they were sung!

Sunday services in Wesley's Nonconformist chapels became more than an act of worship. There was a great deal of personal joy to be experienced in singing well-loved hymns, and they were – still are – sung with fervour. And as the early nineteenth-century home crafts of spinning and weaving were swamped by the advancing tide of industrial mechanization, so workers were thrown together in ever-increasing numbers. They sang together on Sunday and worked side by side during the week. Why not combine the two and *sing* side by side *during* the week?

And so the first choirs were born. As oratorios and other forms of sacred music filtered into England from Germany, repertoires became more ambitious, even though a pitiful few of those early choristers can have had any formal training in reading music. If they had a voice, they learned to use it by standing next to a singer who *knew* the music, and they learned every note, every cadence, every inflection, every rhythm, every tempo, simply by listening. Music was precious and a printed score in the hands of one who could read it opened up new vistas of delight to his choir. There is a story of a man from Bacup, in Lancashire, who walked to Manchester and back (a round trip of nearly fifty miles) simply to *look* at a copy of *Saul* in the window of a music shop.

This, then, is what music meant to the mill-working, chapel-going populace of the industrial north in the nineteenth century. It gave them beauty to brighten a drab existence; it has given us magnificence to enrich our more sophisticated society, and I hope we are all grateful for it.

The Huddersfield Choral Society

In 1986 the Huddersfield Choral Society will celebrate – and I mean celebrate – 150 years of singing for the sheer joy of singing. A new history will be produced and its author will be Bob Edwards, a first tenor in the choir, so the Huddersfield will follow a tradition of keeping it in the family. But there will, of course, be a 150th anniversary concert, and what, I wonder, will that be like? What *can* the choir do that it has not already done? How can it climb higher than the highest peak? How can it sing any better than it has done, with incredible consistency, for so long? But it will, somehow. Nothing is more certain than that.

How, then, did it all begin, this creation of a sound which in its full, disciplined volume can make the hairs stand out on the nape of the neck, and then be hauled down from those soaring heights to a pianissimo 'above which the ticking of the clock can be heard'? The phrase is that of Sir Henry Coward, the man who really shaped the singing of the society as it is today. It represented the discipline he demanded – and got. But the Huddersfield Choral Society had existed for sixty-five years when Coward took charge. Its beginning was as unlikely as anyone can imagine. When Wesley first visited the area in the middle of the nineteenth century he described the local populace as 'a wilder people I never saw in England'. But he left behind his Nonconformism and from those Wesleyan chapels and Anglican churches came sixteen men, on the evening of 7 June 1836, to meet in the Plough Inn, in Westgate. It was an occasion which, nearly 150 years later, brings a chuckle from Bill Drake, who has been singer, librarian, choir secretary, general secretary, vice-president, president: 'Can you imagine it – sixteen teetotallers (as they would have to be as nineteenth-century Methodists) meeting in a pub? I wonder what they drank?' Well, they weren't all TT, but soberly they drew up a 'Preamble' establishing a musical society and ordaining that the first meeting was to be held in the Infant School Room, Spring Street, on Friday, the 15th day of July 1836, at eight o'clock in the evening. The succeeding meetings to be held on the Friday on or before the full moon in every month. That designation of practice night sounds a little bizarre, but it was essentially practical: full moonlight was rather necessary to find one's way home over unlit roads!

From the first there was a discipline which we see reflected in the present-day rules. Late arrivals for practice were fined 3d (just over 1p at today's rate), 6d if they were more than fifteen minutes late or absent altogether, and here you see the sound commonsense of it: if you are going to have a choir, the absence of even one voice can affect the balance of its singing. Today, the members register their attendance at rehearsals (rather in the manner of clocking-on at the mill) and those who do not make the required number of appearances meet a fate far worse than a 6d fine – they are dropped until they have been re-auditioned. That could mean missing a concert which, to a member of the Huddersfield, is the most condign punishment of all. So the basic disciplines are still there; they merely take a different, and more practical, form.

One tradition which is not maintained – at least not in anything like the same form – is the provision of three gills of ale and bread and cheese for each member at practice night. (A gill, by the way, pronounced jill, is the word still used by many Yorkshiremen for a half pint, so there was no real danger of alcoholism at these rehearsals, but I wonder what the pastor would have said, back at the chapel?) Lady members did not have to pay for their refreshments – a nice touch of gallantry, I think. The men's were paid for from their subscription of half a crown (12½p) per six months. After the first six months of the society's existence, there were fifty-four men but only eight 'female performers', a balance which is greatly changed today, but it was essentially a form of self-entertainment in that no public concerts were given. The first conductor was Henry Horn, who was organist at St Paul's parish church, so he was one of the founders who was not from the Nonconformist fraternity, and his principal lieutenants were twin brothers, James and Edward Battye, librarian and secretary respectively. James Battye was a particularly accomplished musician and some of the glees and anthems he composed are still sung. Perhaps his finest epitaph lies in a minute of the society for 20 November 1848: 'Resolved that a selection from the works of Handel, Haydn, Mozart, Battye, etc., be performed ...' That's what I call moving in distinguished circles.

By 1842 the society was ready to give its first public concert because at last a suitable hall was available – the Philosophical Hall, which was hired for four 'quarterly meetings'. Hiring fees might have presented a problem, but not to a group of Yorkshiremen accustomed to watching their brass carefully. The choir simply gave one extra concert, in December or January, to pay the rent!

And now we find 'Subscribers to the Society's funds' beginning to appear in the records. Today that tradition is maintained and subscribers come from as far away as London, Richmond, Nottingham. There is even one from Fowey, in Cornwall. The three subscribers' concerts which are given every year fill Huddersfield Town Hall's 1200 seats and there is a waiting list of a hundred or more to become subscribers. Two performances of the *Messiah* are given in winter, one for subscribers and the other for the public. Within an hour of the box office opening, all seats for the public performance are sold. And if you have ever heard the society sing the *Messiah* you will know why that is. In a recording it is truly magnificent; in the flesh, so to speak, it is awesome.

By the middle of Queen Victoria's reign the society was firmly established and its concerts had become major musical and social events in the growing textile town. Choir practice took precedence over everything short of family bereavement – and the fact that this tradition has been maintained – even strengthened – amidst the sophisticated counter-attractions of the 1980s is something which I find particularly endearing. It is not difficult to imagine members, sometimes the conductor, getting carried away by their own enthusiasm from time to time. One nineteenth-century conductor, searching for even greater passion in the singing of a chorus from 'Hymn of Praise', is reported to have snarled at his forces: 'Damn your eyes ... *praise* to the Lord.' There was the thunderous bass who was gently admonished by a more kindly conductor: 'Now, William Henry, a little less bass, please. We want to hear the other parts.'

It's a proud choir, perhaps at times moved to arrogance by that pride, at least in the view of a member of the BBC Northern Symphony Orchestra: 'They're a right bloody awkward bunch. We were playing with them and some of us in the brass section were stationed amongst the singers. I was directed to a place already occupied by an old bugger who flatly refused to make room.

'Now, as you can see, I'm a six-feet four-inches, seventeen-stone rugby forward, but this little old lad didn't turn a hair. "I've sat here for forty-two years and I'm not moving for thee," he said. So I'd had enough. I stuck my trombone on his lap and said, "Right, you *sit* there then – and play *that*."'

Susan Sykes, the daughter of a Brighouse gardener, was found to have a remarkable singing voice as a child. She first sang in public at the age of fourteen and at nineteen she married a local butcher to become Mrs Sunderland; to this day, in Yorkshire music circles, the name has a regal ring to it. It is perpetuated by the Mrs Sunderland Musical Competitions, held annually, which have started many singers on their careers. So great were her natural gifts that by the time she was twenty-three she was giving recitals in London. Queen Victoria was a staunch admirer, and after one of her many private concerts at Buckingham Palace, the Queen handed Mrs Sunderland her own autographed score of the *Messiah*, with the tribute: 'I am Queen of England, but you are Queen of Song.' And for ever afterwards, Mrs Sunderland has been known as 'Yorkshire's Queen of Song'. Yet for all the fame her superb soprano voice brought her, Mrs S., *née* Susan Sykes, sang for twenty years as the Huddersfield Choral Society's principal soprano – without a fee.

Yet despite those palmier days, the society had serious problems in the 1870s. Its concert hall had been converted to a theatre and there was no other suitable building in which to perform before the public. Naturally enough, support drained away. Fees for guest soloists were getting higher, income from concerts lower. The Dark Ages of industrial change were receding, illiteracy was less prevalent, and Novello's music-publishing company was making available scores which hitherto had been unknown to choral societies – the works of Brahms and Berlioz, Verdi and Wagner. At the same time, Parry, Sullivan and, later, Elgar were writing choral works of great beauty and, I suppose, the society found that in a number of ways the pace of change was too swift for it. Yet there was enough perspicacity in the membership to ask, when Huddersfield was about to be incorporated as a borough, to be allowed to collaborate in the design and construction of the first Town Hall. When it was opened, in October 1881, it included a concert hall and an organ.

So what better way to open the building than with a three-day Musical Festival?

The choral society, more than 250 of them, assembled in their serried ranks and for three days and nights the music poured out of Huddersfield's brand new Town Hall – Mendelssohn, Berlioz, Spohr, Rossini (the *Stabat Mater* – nothing frivolous, you understand). World-famous principals were called to Huddersfield for those three days of song, singers like Albani and Maas and Santley. Sir Charles Hallé brought over his orchestra of growing reputation (once referred to by a mayor of Wigan as 'Sir Charles 'all and 'is Ally Band!' – a digression, but I love it) and at the end of the Festival said, 'I have conducted many choruses but have never found a better, or, indeed, one so good. For refinement, perfect truth of intonation and expression, and especially for power, it cannot be surpassed or equalled for the same number.'

The 'Huddersfield' was back on course after a few troubled years and, what was more, it had now found a true home. Even while the choir continues to travel the world and to startle new ears with the sound Hallé admired so much, Huddersfield Town Hall has remained its spiritual home. Joshua Marshall was the conductor through the period which the society itself refers to as its renaissance. John North took over and saw the membership rise to 450. For the next ten years they were conducted by John Bowling; and then came the new century and a new era for the society when, in 1901, Dr Henry Coward became the conductor. Coward, who was later knighted, was not only technically brilliant as a musician; he was a man of vision, imagination and sensitivity. 'Under him,' wrote Sidney H. Crowther, in an early history of the society, 'rehearsals became not merely formal practices but occasions of valuable education, both vocally and intellectually, which no one wished to miss.'

Coward took a choir with a reputation for immense volume ('Sledge-hammer singing', according to London critics) and revolutionized its style. The famed – perhaps notorious – lung power of the HCS was taken and shaped into a whole new range of sounds, tender and delicate. Remember – many of those 400 voices belonged to men and women who spent their days in spinning and weaving sheds. Any kind of conversation at all between workmates had to be conducted at full fortissimo to be audible above the rattle of the looms. There was no great need to develop voice production amongst Coward's cohorts. He had the base material and he worked on it. With the expansion in vocal technique came the ability, now, to extend the repertoire. By 1907 the society was being invited to join the London Symphony Orchestra in Bach's B-minor Mass at the Queen's Hall. Four years later it was an English representative choir at the International Music Congress. It was conducted by Elgar, Parry, Walford Davies, Coleridge Taylor, Bantock, Vaughan Williams and Hamilton Harty in their own works. Coward remained with the Huddersfield Choral Society for thirty-one years and the value of the association is incalculable.

He was succeeded by Malcolm Sargent, who was to become the much loved 'Flash Harry' to a future generation of final-night Promenaders. So came another golden age for the Huddersfield. Sargent worked on Coward's 'flexible instrument', refining its already splendid qualities until that pianissimo moved critics to a new extravagance of description: 'In *The Dream of Gerontius* the choir could give a diminuendo so delicate that it was difficult to decide where the tone ended and the silence began.' Sargent took the society to Vienna, Berlin, Brussels and the United States. Austria found their *Messiah* to be 'sensational'. Magnificent recordings flowed from the presses – *Messiah*, *Elijah*, and *Gerontius* ... If any had doubted the international reputation of the society, these recordings alone would have dispelled the doubts, but Sargent marched his choir around the world as if to establish that the acclaim was not due to the skill of recording engineers.

Sir Malcolm Sargent was followed, relatively briefly, by John Pritchard who took over at a rather anticlimactic time for the society. He brought with him Douglas Robinson, from Covent Garden, as chorusmaster and together they established a happy rapport with the choir until the pressure of Pritchard's growing commitments forced him to end their association.

Then came the dynamic and imaginative Welshman, Owain Arwel Hughes, with a briefcase full of new ideas. One of these has proved outstandingly popular – the Workshop Weekend. Off go all the current 228 members to a big, seaside hotel to refresh themselves, to concentrate hard on their music making, and also to enjoy something of the good fellowship of an artistic association which is not always possible back in Huddersfield.

What is it that creates the unique Huddersfield sound, the sound that soars and shimmers and hovers and then flies to join the angels from whom, it seems, it must have come in the first place? It is not mere quality which marks it as different. The 'Hallelujah Chorus' of that incomparable 1958 recording of the *Messiah* is as distinctive, musically, as the Taj Mahal is architecturally. Sir Malcolm Sargent is reputed to have explained it thus: 'Northern people are accustomed to speaking their minds. They are not afraid to open their mouths to report what is in their hearts and the singing of the Huddersfield is an expression of their thoughts and feelings.'

But how do you equate that with the view of a lady member of the Huddersfield who outraged a few million Celts by offering the view: 'The Welsh sing with their hearts; we sing with our heads'? From Arnold Harrop, the longest-serving member of the society, came this explanation: 'It's something to do with the moors, the wide open spaces which surround us. You can go up there and let rip as loud as you like to develop the voice. A Welsh rugby player called Arthur Peck came north to play Rugby League in Huddersfield and he joined us as a tenor. He used to go out onto the moors and sing away as loud as he could.'

Arnold Harrop joined the society in November 1929. He is now seventy-four and the speaking voice is still the rich, dark, velvety instrument he uses in the ranks of the basses. Across the table from him sits David Platts, aged seventeen, who joined the society in June 1982, inspired by a musical inheritance from his mother and the society's performance of the *Messiah* in 1981. As we have seen, tickets for those performances are like gold, but when a friend telephoned to say, 'I've got a spare ticket for tonight. Can you be ready in an hour?', David was ready. And he came out of Huddersfield Town Hall with a new musical ambition – to help make that glorious sound.

'I was on the committee when David came,' mused Arnold Harrop. 'We could tell the voice would develop, even though he was very young. I stand in the next row to him when we sing and I can keep a fatherly ear on his progress. He'll be all right.'

Arnold himself is part of the Nonconformist tradition of entry into the HCS, 'graduating' from the Mount Pleasant Wesleyan Methodist chapel at Lockwood. His greatest memory of singing with the society? Performing Verdi's Requiem in York Minster under Victor de Sabata. But fifty years of membership in that great vocal orchestra have given him a thousand other memories: 'When Sir Henry Coward was our conductor he told us of an instrumentalist in an orchestra he was rehearsing who had a 340-bar rest. He used to leave the platform, go out to the pub for a drink, and so good was his knowledge of the score that he would be back at exactly the right moment to play his next note.

'Before recordings were made on tape, each piece had to be recorded in sections of four and a half minutes to fit onto one side of the old 78 r.p.m. discs. We often did it as many as eight or nine times before we got the perfect fit – and, of course, the perfect sound.

'We went to Liverpool to record *Belshazzar's Feast* with Sir William Walton conducting his own work for the first time. In fact, he had never conducted before, I think. So we had to show him how to conduct us before we could get on with the recording. Now the last bit of *Belshazzar* is rather tricky and we couldn't quite get it right. Over and over again we sang and each time Walton was dissatisfied. So were we if *he* wasn't happy. After all, he had written the piece. But our last train back to Huddersfield left at 6.25 and by this time we were singing with one eye on the score and one on the clock. At last, we got it just right. Walton slumped over his stand and gasped, in sheer relief, "Good." And on the original pressing of that recording of

Belshazzar's Feast the composer/conductor's expression of satisfaction is the last sound that is heard.' Arnold Harrop – a man with a lifetime of precious musical memories.

There are not so many Arnold Harrops around these days. Often where there were once three Methodist chapels there is now one – and in some places none at all. Those stately buildings have become school annexes, builders' offices, even car showrooms; the voice of their choirs is stilled and one great area of recruitment to the Huddersfield Choral Society is gone for ever. Sue Green, the society's publicity officer, says sadly, 'Churches, chapels and their choirs are no longer the centre of community life. They may need to reinforce their choirs at festival times or perhaps join forces to stage a music production. There is a noticeable shortage of young people, though, and it looks as though the process of learning to sing by induction – alongside enthusiastic and experienced singers – is no longer valued.'

Mrs Green, the fourth generation of her family to sing with the society, is head of a primary school and sees the danger presented by modern tastes (and technology). 'Young children have not changed; they sing spontaneously and with obvious enjoyment. But teachers report that children become increasingly embarrassed and self-conscious and reluctant to sing, especially in mixed groups, as they grow older. There is a shortage of attractive music, too. Pop music is a great challenge to music teachers. In some schools, music has become an examination subject for the academically gifted. In others, teachers have developed guitar groups or brass and reed bands, to replace their school choirs. But young people *can* be persuaded to sing with their friends, if the music is right and the teacher is popular.

'These changes in music making become apparent when we hold auditions for our choral society. For people with little previous experience our test can be quite a trial: an ascending and descending scale, two sets of sight reading (chosen at random from a selection closely guarded by the choir's secretary) and a carefully rehearsed art song are required. However, there is a steady flow of applicants and membership is still highly prized.'

Mrs Green reports gratefully that there is a growing interest amongst young professional people and, as the standards and reputation of the society hold firm, many members now travel long distances (without having to wait for the light of the full moon!) to Friday-night rehearsals, drawn by those standards and stirred by the challenge of the audition. If they are admitted, they will still face a test every five years because those standards are closely and lovingly guarded. When you think about it, that velvety bass of Arnold Harrop must have been tested now ten times, but I am pretty sure that when the time comes for him to step down, no auditioning committee will need to tell him. He'll know. And then he'll look round for another way in which he can help the choir in which he has sung with such pride and pleasure for fifty years. The president, George Slater, sings second bass; the general secretary, Richard Barraclough, is a first tenor. And we've seen Bill Drake take on one office after another and Sue Green follow the family tradition. That's the way the Huddersfield works and it's a bit like cricket. When something has given you an immense amount of pleasure you should be prepared to put a little bit back into it.

The Black Dyke Mills Band

At the top of the bare wooden staircase hangs a print which I dare say epitomizes the archetypal Yorkshireman – at least to a lot of the southern gentry. He sits, eighteen stone of him, in shirt and trousers, a plate bearing the remains of his evening meal in front of him, with the mandatory dish of pickled onions and a pint bottle of stout.

A thin, blue woollen curtain covers the entrance to the next room from which comes subdued conversation of a technical nature. 'I think that's a B-flat at bar 27, Ian ... yes, well, it must be a misprint in the score, then. Will you alter it to B-flat, please? Right. Let's try it again.' There is the light tap of a thin baton on a music stand. You know that music is about to be made. But no way in the world are you prepared for what now comes surging through that thin blue curtain, swelling through the stout gritstone walls, rolling and roaring around the rafters. It is a juggernaut of sound, picking you up and tossing you like matchwood in an Atlantic gale. You are carried away on a sea of molten brass. It dies away to a tender pianissimo, held just on the boundary of credibility ... gently, delicately, tremulously held. And then, with an upward sweep of an unseen, baton-clutching hand, away we roar again. In the concert hall the sound of the Black Dyke Mills Band is majestic, imperious; here, at rehearsal in the bandroom which just finds room for the twenty-six players and their former Mosquito-pilot conductor, Trevor Walmsley, it stuns the senses. And yet for all the sheer volume of sound, it is controlled, ordered, disciplined – and magnificent.

Four miles down the hill the Brighouse and Rastrick Band will never forgive me for saying that the Black Dyke symbolizes the great tradition of brass band music in the West Riding. There will be rumblings, too, in Shipley (Hammond's Sauce Works), in Leeds (Yorkshire Imperial Metals) and in the coalfields to the south (Grimethorpe Colliery and Carlton Main/Frickley Colliery), for they too are superb examples of brass band music making – names which you see high up on the list of contenders in any contest. But for me there is one name which always stands out: John Foster and Son Ltd Black Dyke Mills Band. And this is for two interrelated reasons: the sublime quality of the sounds it conjures up; and the fact that second, or any lower place, is no good at all to 'the Dyke'.

The band won the first Crystal Palace contest ever held, back in 1860, and it has been used to winning ever since. Its record in the National Championships shows wins in 1902, 1928, 1947, 1948, 1949 (after three successive wins the Dyke had to miss the 1950 contest), 1951, 1959, 1961, 1967, 1972, 1975, 1976, 1977 (another year's exile for another hat trick), 1979 and 1981. Eleven second placings, nine thirds and three fourths are regarded as unworthy of mention. The band won the European Championship in 1978, 1979 and 1982 and were World Champions in 1970. And for good measure Black Dyke were the BBC's Band of the Year in 1967, 1970, 1975, 1976 and 1979. So it's not difficult to see why, to me, they are the foremost representatives of a form of self-entertainment which grew from the poverty of Victorian England.

Perhaps I should make that 'Victorian Britain', because the first known all-brass band was formed at Blaina, in South Wales, in 1832, an area where the poverty of the working class was just as grinding as that of the West Riding. The delicate touch required for stringed instruments was not a natural attribute amongst the manual workers of these industrial regions and, apart from that, they must have found the playing of brass a braver, more stirring experience, than scraping a violin. Consequently, the brass band became to the horny-handed sons of toil what the string quartet was to the occupants of stately homes.

The origins of the town band can be traced back to the 'Waits' (a term more usually applied today to carol singers), small groups of musicians who wandered the streets. As long ago as the 1820s there was a group of four in Bradford, all of them blind, and together they found their way through the streets tied to a pole. A brass band in the early nineteenth century would have been incapable of making any-thing like the sort of sound a modern band makes because the brass instruments of those days had no valves, so the range of notes was limited. Repertoires were extended by adding reed instruments like the clarinet, flute and piccolo, giving greater range, but there were few working men who played woodwind. Army units were able to train musicians to play them, however, and today a combination of brass

The uniforms may have changed but not the sound of 'The Dyke'. John Foster and Son Ltd Black Dyke Mills Band then and now

and woodwind (with percussion) is still called a 'military band' as distinct from the brass band, which has no woodwind. It was the perfection of the valve, to develop the range of brass instruments, which played a major part in establishing the brass band tradition of the working man's music making.

Queensbury, which straggles over a high ridge between Bradford and Halifax, was a tiny village called 'Queenshead' when Peter Wharton formed a brass and reed band there in the year that Wellington and Bonaparte were having their little ding-dong on the fields of Waterloo. Eighteen years later the village got its second band, still a 'military' combination, with a French horn player called John Foster in its ranks. Foster owned the local woollen mill and he bought a set of brass instruments to form a band for his workers in 1855 and the Black Dyke Mills Band was born. Its players today are no longer mill workers. They range from a senior lecturer (Phil McCann, principal B-flat cornet) to an unemployed victim of the recession, from an Australian scholarship winner to Salford College of Music (David King,

solo cornet) to John Slinger (second baritone) who is a school caretaker and, after thirty-two years, the longest-serving member of the band. But John Foster's company still gives financial support to the band and in return the players carry the name of John Foster and Son Ltd all over the world. (Mind you, the fine mohair suitings the mill turns out do their bit as well.) Without financial backing, no great band could exist independently today because the instruments alone cost around £30,000 and, ideally, they are replaced every ten years. A B-flat bass, for instance, costs £2000, a euphonium £1400. The Dyke's principal euphonium player is John Clough and he's an organ builder by trade. I wonder how the cost of one of his organs compares with the price of his euphonium!

Fred Ellis is secretary and treasurer of the Black Dyke and a former player. His pride in his association is manifest but, just like the current players, the first thing you notice about him is that he radiates a sense of enjoyment in his work. Personal pleasure – joy, even – filled that rehearsal room as the music had filled it a moment before. It communicated itself powerfully and I felt good – a sense of being close to something cheerful and wholesome. Black Dyke take their pleasure, and their music, to fifty concerts a year. They have toured Europe and the United States. They have broadcast well over five hundred times and made forty records. They have played for the Queen, the Duke of

Edinburgh and Prince Charles. They have been conducted by Edward Heath and backed a 'single' by Paul McCartney. They have played in Henry Wood Promenade concerts and staged a BBC 2 Television 'spectacular'.

Yet their enjoyment of their own music making never seems to flag. Perhaps it comes from a sense of release from the tensions of the two great contests a year – the British Open, formerly held at Belle Vue and now in Manchester's Free Trade Hall, and the National Championships in London.

'Everyone wants to knock Black Dyke off their perch,' says Fred Ellis. 'We don't listen to the other bands. If we are drawn to play early, we do it and then disappear until the adjudication. If we are late in the draw, we get back into the bus and go for a drive into the country until it's our turn. No, not to a pub. There's no drinking *before* we play. Afterwards? Ah, well, we might relax a bit then. But we generally know when we've won without waiting for the results.'

How can that be if they don't listen to the other contestants? Well, here we find the natural confidence of men who know quite simply that, in top form, they are the best. If they have played well, they know it. And they know that at their best they are unbeatable. I like that.

Fred handed me a cassette of their latest recording (Russian music – Shostakovich, Rachmaninov, Mussorgsky, Rimsky-Korsakov, Prokofiev, Glinka, Borodin, Tchaikovsky) and a car sticker proclaiming me a 'Pondasher' of the John Foster and Son Ltd Black Dyke Mills Band. 'Pondasher' was the pseudonym of a *Sunday Times* writer who produced an article on the band and they delightedly seized on it as a generic term for their aficionados.

There can be little doubt about the identity of Dyke's No. 1 Pondasher. He has got to be Frank Dean who, as a youngster in Pateley Bridge – forty miles or so from Queensbury and about as different in character as it is possible to get – was regaled with stories ('brainwashed', he calls it) of the famous band by an old village bandsman called Frank Watson. It was, I suppose, rather like youngsters like me being reared on stories of Herbert Sutcliffe, Wilfred Rhodes and George Herbert Hirst, as members of the great Yorkshire teams in cricket's golden age. Well, the tales certainly fired young Dean with enthusiasm because he started travelling all round the country to hear Dyke play. His regular support was noticed by the band and it was one of the trombonists, Grenville Richmond, who invited him to a rehearsal in the early 1960s. Within a few months the resident conductor, Geoffrey Whitham, took Frank Dean's breath away by suggesting that instead of wandering around the country on solitary pilgrimages he should travel with the band in their coach.

Frank Dean's hero-worship developed into near-idolatry and in 1980 he put his gratitude into written form by publishing at his own expense a beautifully produced little booklet in which I was rather pleased to get a couple of mentions. Frank quotes a *Financial Times* correspondent who described the preparation of an article on the band as being 'like interviewing twenty-five Freddie Truemans'. And talking about the band's wonderful record in contests, Frank himself writes: 'When Black Dyke come second, they have lost. In true Freddie Trueman and Harvey Smith fashion, they see second as failure.' Well, I'll go along with that, and I know Harvey will as well. It's something I can quickly identify with because in my days with Yorkshire cricket we were always expected to win the county championship as of right and if we achieved anything less than top place in the table we certainly regarded the season as a failure. And yet, just as we never forgot how to laugh, even when things were going wrong, so the Black Dyke never lose sight of the fact that there is a lot of fun in their lives and that making great brass band music is not only a pleasure, it's a privilege.

Like Yorkshire's cricketers down the ages, they have accumulated their own folklore, usually born of their sense of fun, and the world of brass is indebted to Frank Dean for recording some of it – stories like these:

Major C.H. Jaeger, one of the band's line of distinguished professional conductors, was due to rehearse with them, as a test piece for the National Championships, the Berlioz overture, *Carnaval Romain*, but on the weekend before he arrived in Queensbury, the players learned that he had been promoted to lieutenant colonel. Rehearsal night arrived and the conductor didn't waste any time. 'Straight down to work, gentlemen – *Carnaval Romain* and here we go ... one, two ...' The band gave him a spirited opening of ... *Colonel Bogey*.

A bit of pressure had been brought to bear upon a teenage trombonist to conform to the band's image of dignity by having his flowing locks cut to a more acceptable length. The tonsorial operation complete, the youth arrived with a radically changed appearance. The E-flat bass, with an air of mock mystification, looked around his colleagues and asked, 'Who's the new trombone?' The trombonist accepted this with a grin, only to be told by the bass, 'Well, it's to be hoped tha' can play better than t'other bugger.'

A coach driver who seemed to be dawdling on his drive to a concert was instructed, 'Get your foot down, driver. All t'flies and insects are running into t'back window.'

On journeys which took the band through Halifax, they noticed over a period of time that renovation work on a churchyard seemed to be taking ages to complete. This brought a comment from one player – 'They're taking their time' – and from the back of the bus the explanation was roared, 'They've only got a skeleton staff at weekends.'

So there is a lighter side to this life of music making which springs, I think, from the strong sense of camaraderie which exists in all great bands, as in all great teams. But there is no frivolity in Dyke's approach to playing. They set their own standards and they have to live up to them every time they play, as Frank Dean discovered after hearing an outstanding solo performance by a sixteen-year-old cornettist.

The lad rightly got a tremendous ovation from the audience, but Frank was intrigued to notice that none of the other players in the band joined in. He asked a senior bandsman about this and was told, 'No. Why should we? He wouldn't be in t'Black Dyke if he were not capable of playing to that standard. If you really want to help him, tell him to get in a lot more practice when he gets home.'

Now, that's an attitude I can understand. That tells me more about Black Dyke's greatness than anything else.

The band is a Yorkshire institution, as much as cricket and fish and chips and Ilkla Moor and batter pudding. Wherever music is played in the world, they've heard of the band from that windswept hilltop of Queensbury, but let's leave the last word to Frank Dean, who wrote this of the band: 'A slip or a "fluffed" note is a national crisis and there are no allowances for reasons and certainly no place for excuses. They aim higher than is possible to achieve and usually arrive at a point which is as near perfection as human frailty will permit. When a collection of plumbers, joiners, teachers and clothworkers can assemble and produce the sounds which Dyke do, then there has to be a God and most certainly they at times produce the sounds of a minster organ.'

And when a Pondasher can produce a tribute like that, Mr Dean, he's indeed a man who loves his music and his band. Black Dyke represent the best of a great Yorkshire tradition and I too am proud of them.

Elizabeth Harwood

Just as the choirs were born out of a need to create one's own entertainment, they in turn produced men and women with outstanding
voices to be the soloists at their concerts. Many of these went on to
win international reputations on the concert platform and the stage.
But there were also those who were quite simply born to sing, whose
natural gifts were developed through private tuition and training in
the great musical academies of the north of England. One such singer
is the soprano, Elizabeth Harwood.

Strictly speaking, Elizabeth Harwood is not a Yorkshire lass at all –
but it would not be advisable to give her an argument about it. She
was, in fact, born in Barton Seagrave, Northamptonshire, the daughter
of a 100 per cent thoroughbred Yorkshireman, who moved back to his
native county when his daughter was just five months old. Sydney
Harwood was a Scarborough-born local government officer and in
1938 he became Clerk to the Skipton Rural District Council. So the
young Elizabeth spent the whole of her childhood in the Gateway to
the Dales.

Elizabeth has that serenity and gentle confidence which invariably
comes from a happy and secure family background. More than that,
she was brought up in a home filled with music, so much so that there
was never the slightest doubt in her mind that music was to be her
life. Father was a chorister, a gifted natural tenor with perfect pitch,
for whom music was a hobby – a dearly cherished hobby, true, but
one that enriched his life rather than taking it over. Mother (Constance
Read in her professional life) was a beautiful soprano, the daughter of
a talented contralto and sister of yet another singer. Miss Read, against
her father's wishes, enrolled at the Royal Academy of Music, took her
LRAM in singing and teaching, and performed as a soloist in the early

days of broadcasting. And after the family had moved to Skipton - their home was actually in the village of Embsay-with-Eastby, just outside the town - Mr and Mrs Harwood (tenor and soprano) teamed up with their friends Dr and Mrs Merlin (baritone and contralto) for Sunday musical evenings in that delightful Edwardian tradition. And so for the young Elizabeth began a life of music.

'I remember those Sunday evenings of singing, all through the war. They were wonderful. And, of course, with Mother teaching, there were always pupils in the house waiting for lessons when I came home from school. Mother tells a lovely story about one of them - a very pretty girl who took a long long time to learn.

'She had a very high voice, a very pretty voice, but it took her a long time to sing the aria properly. And Mother tells the story of trying to teach her pupil this bit of *The Magic Flute* while she could hear me, upstairs at the age of four, singing it perfectly. So it was all being taken in. I was learning music, absorbing it, becoming steeped in it, at that age.'

Elizabeth went to the kindergarten department of Skipton Girls' High School and as she moved up to the senior school she learned the piano, the violin and the double bass. She was always 'going to do something in music - there was never any doubt about it'.

'The physical act of singing is, in itself, wonderful, of course, but more than that, it's what music does to me, not just my own music but music of every kind. It's the most important thing in my life and something I could not do without.'

At seventeen she took a West Riding County major scholarship to study in London but Mrs Harwood (who had now been teaching her daughter for several years) urged her instead to join the Northern College of Music in Manchester where there were first-class teachers and a great tradition of producing singers of high quality. There she was taught, first by Frederick Cox, the principal - 'a marvellous man, absolutely unbelievable, he had such an influence on my life' - who, in her first term, put her into an opera. The young student reacted with a prima donna's flash of temperament. 'I'm not going to sing in an opera. *I'm* not an opera singer. I'm an oratorio singer.' Mr Cox smiled disarmingly. 'Right,' he said. 'There are to be three performances of the opera. You do just one performance and I'll find another girl to do the other two.' Mr Cox knew his psychology. 'Certainly not,' snapped his first-year student. 'If I am going to sing it once, I'll sing all three performances. I'm not having another girl come in and take over my part.' And perhaps it was in that moment that an operatic soprano was born, because, while Elizabeth Harwood has never lost her love of oratorio, and she finds the experience of singing in a great cathedral more moving and more stimulating than any other, it was in those days at the Northern College in Manchester, with its operatic traditions, that her love of the stage began to develop.

Her next teacher was Elsie Thurston, who taught Marjorie Thomas and many other famous singers. In her nineties, she still writes to Elizabeth in a firm hand every Christmas as she no doubt writes to singers all over the world. But it was before she had gone to Manchester, in fact while she was still at Skipton Girls' High School, that Elizabeth first met Sir Malcolm Sargent.

'This is a story about the self-confidence of youth. I joined a country-dancing class in Skipton and met a boy who was away at school but whose father was Captain Fordyce, agent for the Skipton Castle estate, and his mother was, for a while, secretary to Sir Malcolm Sargent. John was home from school and asked me if I would like to go to a concert Sir Malcolm was giving in Leeds. I leaped at the chance because I had never been to anything like that, and at the concert John sent a little note round – written on Skipton Castle notepaper, which had the desired effect – asking if we could meet him. The conductor replied that he'd like us to have dinner with him afterwards at the Queen's Hotel in Leeds and I couldn't believe it. I had to pinch myself. I was no more than sixteen but I remember telling Sir Malcolm that I was going to be a singer and he patted me, metaphorically and indulgently, on the head and said, "Of course you are, my dear." I insisted, "Yes, I am. I know I am going to sing with you, one day," and he again indulged me, very pleasantly, thinking, I'm sure, The poor little thing doesn't know what it's all about. Five years later I went to London after winning the Kathleen Ferrier Memorial Scholarship and in fact Sir Malcolm gave me some of my first big chances, to sing at the Royal Albert Hall and in the Proms.'

Elizabeth's first operatic role was with the Buxton Opera Group, while still at college. She sang Micaela, in *Carmen*. In 1961 she joined the Sadler's Wells Company and her first role was Gilda in *Rigoletto*. 'I went in head first, but that's been the story of my life. I did my first "Countesses" in Salzburg with von Karajan. I've always pitched myself headlong into things because, having a mother like mine, bless her, she would say, "Go on. You can do it." It hasn't always come off, but fortunately it has most of the time.'

Elizabeth was still only sixteen when she sang her first *Messiah*, hence, perhaps, her conviction when she went to college that she was to sing oratorio rather than opera. It was an engagement her mother was due to fulfil in one of the villages near Skipton – 'I think it was

Beamsley but Mother says it was Bradley' – but Madame Read went down with a cold and sent her daughter instead. The fee was to be one guinea but Elizabeth was given 25s 'because she showed a lot of promise'.

In 1965 she went to Australia with Joan Sutherland and a company of singers, some of whom were just beginning, some already well-known names. La Sutherland wanted someone who could take over her roles when she went into a new one, so Elizabeth found herself listening to the great Australian soprano singing *Lucia di Lammermoor* for a week, then taking over the part herself. They performed six or seven operas, including *Lucia*, *L'Elisir d'Amore* and *La Traviata*, with practically no rehearsal at all, and once again it was a case of the youthful Miss Harwood being thrown in at the deep end. 'I'd find myself on stage, looking round and thinking, Ah, yes – the fountain's over there, so that must be the door where the tenor comes in. It was a bit like rep opera. But it certainly helped you find your feet very quickly . . . or else!'

Amongst that company was a young tenor called Luciano Pavarotti. 'He was marvellous. It was at a comparatively early stage of his career but you knew he was going to make it. There was never any doubt about that. I did a lot of my first performances with him and I had a habit of singing to the gallery, looking up to the higher reaches of the theatre, so that my head was always tilted upwards. Luciano used to say this was bad for me because you have to use this column in singing and how could I do it with my head stretched upwards? I remember singing love duets with him in *Lucia* or *Sonnambula* with his hand on the back of my neck, trying to keep my head down. I didn't know these sort of tricks at the time but he was absolutely right, of course.

'He was also very fond of cooking. He was always cooking pasta and spaghetti which were very, very bad for us all, never mind him, and he put so much butter in his spaghetti – a pound at a time! Then *he* would take his little liver pills so that he was all right. But he was a great character.'

Like her father, who died seven years ago, Elizabeth Harwood is a great animal lover. At home in Essex, which is now her base, her two cats are never far from her side; outside on the lawn squirrels frolic and pheasants stalk their arrogant way around the hedgerows. She loves her home, even though she misses the hills of the Craven countryside, and has found a country lane where she watches the corn ripen and where she used to exercise her dog, Spiro, before he died at the ripe old canine age of seventeen. Spiro joined the family as a direct consequence of Elizabeth's meeting with her husband, Julian Royle the sixth generation of a family of fine-art printers and publishers in London. She was called at short notice to travel to Cardiff to stand in for Sir Geraint Evans in a television performance when the great Welsh baritone was taken ill. Into her compartment of the train strode 'this very dishy young man' with a tiny poodle in a red, knitted jacket, reasoning (as she learned later) that a young lady was less likely to object to the presence of a dog than other passengers. They talked about music most of the way to Wales but at the end of the journey they went their separate ways and it took Mr Royle some time to track her down. His quest was not helped by the fact that Elizabeth, then with the Sadler's Wells company, had a colleague called Julian *Moyle*. So whenever her mother reported that the young man had phoned, Elizabeth assumed that it was the other Julian calling about rehearsals. However, the persistent Mr Royle was eventually successful in making contact and within a year they were married.

'Seven or eight months later my mother-in-law's poodle sired puppies and she arrived one day with one of them and told me, "This is yours." I said, "I don't want it. I don't like poodles, really – they're soppy dogs." Anyway, we kept the poodle in the end and within a matter of months I had become completely obsessed by him. I had never met such an adorable dog, especially when I found that every time I went into the drawing room to practise he'd follow me, his little throat would go up and he'd sing with me and – blow me if he didn't get a better top C than I did! He'd quite a loud voice, too. A favourite aria? Not really, so long as it was high, he loved it.

'He was called Spiro because when he arrived we had recently been in Corfu and Spiro is the local equivalent of Tom, Dick or Harry. It seemed a handy name to call him – Spiro-o-ooo – spiralling up the scales. Anyway, soon he had been in all the dressing rooms with me. At Glyndebourne it was virtually in the contract that Spiro came with me. Covent Garden ... all the dressing rooms in the British Isles. Of course, I should never really have had a dog because I went away so much, but when he travelled with me – well, I grew to love him so much and he became part of the company wherever we went.

'The time came when I went up to Scotland to do a charity gala performance with Scottish Opera and during rehearsal they asked if I could do something "a bit daft" as an encore. I said, "I'm not very good at turning cartwheels or anything like that – but I have a dog that sings." Well, they fell upon this and asked if I would bring Spiro if they paid his first-class return fare up to Glasgow. "Of course," I said, and made a beautiful bow out of the same coloured material as my lavender dress and took Spiro off to Glasgow with me. I sang my two lieder and then told the audience, "I've brought somebody with me who is desperately anxious to make his public debut with Scottish Opera. His voice isn't quite what it used to be because he's every bit of fourteen and he's getting a bit grey about the whiskers but he does so want to sing for you." Everyone wondered what was coming next and I went off and brought back the little chap. Well, the audience, all two thousand of them, fell about. At first I thought he wasn't going to perform, so I picked him up, sang a high scale and said, "Come on darling." He had a look round the theatre, saw all the people there and, bless him, he threw back his head and sent a scale soaring right up to the gallery. And then another, for an encore. After the show we went down to the bar and someone filled an enormous stein with water for him. I'll bet it's the first time a little dog has had that sort of treatment.'

It's hard to pin Elizabeth Harwood down to one favourite opera, possibly because of her passionate love of music as a whole, but she will concede a special affection for *Don Giovanni* and *La Traviata*. Really, she loves whatever she is doing at the time. She will, however, accept that Mozart is her favourite composer. Her husband is not musical in the active sense but is devoted to the art simply as a listener. Their teenage son, Nicholas, has a good voice and sings in the school choir but is keenly interested in school drama. He's good at picking up accents and dialects, which pleases his mother because she is proud of her Yorkshire vowels and happy to lapse into them when off duty.

The strains of life as an international operatic star are considerable, not only because of the separation from one's family, or in meeting the demands of a most demanding art, but in terms of self-discipline and, indeed, self-denial. Diet has to be very carefully watched, hair can never be completely let down at a party and late nights have to be rigorously rationed. Yet, mercifully, there is always time for a laugh, even – perhaps especially – at oneself.

'I remember on the way out to Australia, we went via Singapore and Joseph Ward insists that one of the funniest sights of his life is seeing Monica Sinclair and me in a cycle-rickshaw being transported by a poor little man with spindly legs. I am not what you would call large but I've never been exactly sylphlike and Monica has rather a large BTM so it must have been quite a sight. But that tour was a marvellous early insight for me into what an opera singer's life has to be – watching Joan Sutherland work, day after day. And I think that tour helped to whet the appetite of Australia for opera, and with Joan and her husband, Richard Bonynge, now based out there, it really is very popular in Australia. It's nice to think I had a little part in all that.

The girl who lived
in a house filled
with music –
Elizabeth Harwood

But how has Miss Harwood been able to divide her life between a career in music which has taken her to just about every corner of the earth and being a wife and mother?

'It hasn't been easy, and having the right husband has helped. Julian has always encouraged me to sing. He's said, "Darling, if you want to do it you must do it." And again, my parents came to live with us twelve or thirteen years ago and a lot of that time, when Nicholas was young, I could close the front door and know that things would be looked after at home while I was away in Berlin or Vienna or New York. They would bring Nicholas out to me during the school holidays, and Julian would come whenever he could, not out of a sense of duty but so that we could be together and because he wanted to hear the performances. I'd ring him up from Belgium and say, "I'm singing tonight in a lovely chateau. It's tiny and all candlelit and the champagne's flowing and we've got the King and Queen of the Belgians here and you've just got to come. It's going to be a wonderful evening." And he'd get on a plane about five o'clock and he'd make it by seven. He'd always be game to make it if he could.'

Mrs Harwood, at seventy-seven, looks twenty years younger than her age. She has eight pupils who go to her regularly for lessons, and every Wednesday morning twenty members of the local Women's Institute choir arrive for rehearsals. She runs a harvest festival concert, compering the hour-long show herself. She has an incredible zest for life. Perhaps that's the secret, the unbroken link, spanning the years since she and her husband sang in the chapels and village halls of Beamsley and Hebden and Giggleswick and Appletreewick. For her daughter, too, those days are fresh in the memory – Mother pedalling away at a little harmonium and joining Father in a duet, 'Love Divine, All Loves Excelling', and the harvest festival days with suppers of 'wonderful Yorkshire cooking and baking'.

The remarkable Mrs Harwood, *née* Constance Read, still loves to accompany her daughter whenever possible. 'She came four times to the opera with me last week.' The bond between mother and daughter is strong, very strong, created out of natural family affection and increased by their involvement in music which is difficult to put, succinctly, into words. In fact, the words tumble out, cascading in a way which provides its own descriptive quality so that a formal arrangement of the phrases would seem superfluous: 'I took my LRAM very early, when I was about seventeen, and my parents realized then that I had something. My mother tried to put me off a bit, to say, "Look, it's not going to be easy." But the music was so strong, the love of, the sheer love of, the sound of the music, what it did to me, what the Bach B-minor or *Messiah still* do to me this day ... Do you remember Eric Robinson and those "Music for You" programmes? I often used to appear with him – he and Sir Malcolm did a tremendous amount for me in those early years – and I'd hear a lot of singers on his programmes and they'd impress me so much and I'd think, I can sing that, and I'd go away and learn it and ... Elsie Thurston tells me that, at college, I'd go in and say, "Oh, I've just learned the Constanze arias for *Entführung* or the Zerbinetta," which are lethal things to sing at that age, so she'd say, "Good morning, dear. Have we got Brünnhilde this morning?" She'd really take the mickey out of me, because the ability of my voice to sing things was way ahead of my understanding of them, and my understanding of what I was doing. It was a natural voice, I suppose, but then difficulties with that sort of voice come later because you've got to learn exactly what you are doing and to get a basically good technique.'

Elizabeth Harwood has sung in nearly every major opera house in the world except South America. She has had triumphs at La Scala and with the New York Metropolitan, sung her beloved Mozart to eight consecutive Salzburg Festivals, lunched at Buckingham Palace and dined at Windsor Castle. Has she, then, still any unfulfilled ambitions?

'I say to myself, "I'm going to make myself do that one of these days." I'd love to have time to read more, I'd love to have time to visit places without having to sing there. There will, of course, be many years when I can do those things, but at this moment I am looking forward to my son's future, and I love doing things with my husband connected with *his* work, nothing to do with *my* work ... being involved in his interesting side of the arts. But so far as my personal ambitions are concerned, nothing really musical, unless I get the opportunity to do things again. If I am able and fit and the voice is up to it, I'd love to try and do them better. But then, that's not always possible. For instance, Janet Baker, a great friend of mine, was out here recently and I said, "I've got a tape of our *Rosenkavalier* – shall we listen to it?" And we listened for a while and Janet said, "No, Lizzie, I don't really want to hear it ..." because she knows that that time will never come again. She's on to the next thing. I can remember Maestro von Karajan saying, as we talked after a performance was finished, "No, I've forgotten about that now. We are on to the next thing." He never looked back; he was always looking forward to the next thing. Now I'm not so good at that. I love to look back. I love memories. I treasure so many of my memories. They're so real. And so many of them are of Yorkshire ... the happiest of childhoods with the music that my parents gave me. I miss the Yorkshire people; I miss their warmth. I used to walk a lot at home in Yorkshire and I love the seclusion of being alone. This is actually what I call therapy. When I go back north, to Ilkley, I've got to go on the moors, just up to the Cow and Calf Rocks. It's sheer therapy and nothing can take its place.

'You can have all the Swiss mountains in the world, but to go up onto the Cow and Calf ... the sheer beauty, the marvellous air ...'

There's really no need to supply a formal ending to a sentence like that. Anyone who has climbed up to Ilkley Moor will know exactly what she means. So that is Elizabeth Harwood, a lovely lady who bubbles with life, and joy and happiness because that is what her whole life has been about, a lifetime's love affair with her art which, in turn, carries the incomparable privilege of giving pleasure to others.

Ian Carmichael

Ian Carmichael, after a life that involves nearly forty years of stage, film, television and radio experience and almost six years of soldiering, lives in a romantic cottage with a salmon pool at the bottom of his garden in a peaceful corner of the North York Moors. His acting career has been a series of light, frothy, engagingly silly-ass roles, which have given endless pleasure to audiences, listeners, viewers and cinemagoers. His private life has been that of an endearingly nice man whose courtship and marriage followed a story line which no writer would have dared offer to a publisher. It would have been denounced as too perfect. He lost the girl he adored just six weeks before we met in the enchanted garden they had built together: August 1983.

F.S.T. This is a very beautiful spot you have found, but it must seem a bit remote after so many years spent in London?

I.C. My wife and I never lost touch with Yorkshire because holiday visits to stay with relatives have always been very much a part of our lives. My first memories of childhood in Yorkshire are happy ones and they have grown and grown over the years.

F.S.T. You obviously love the countryside and the coast, but you were born a townie, weren't you?

I.C. I was the eldest child of one of four brothers who formed a luxury-goods business in Hull after the First World War. I was born in a street called Sunnybank, but when I was about ten my father 'bettered himself' (there's a good bit of Yorkshire, right at the start) and we moved to a beautiful country house at Elloughton, beside the Humber. It is now a very large complex, with a Hawker Siddeley factory there and it's not as pretty as it was when we lived there.

F.S.T. What do you remember about your childhood?

I.C. Oh, difficult ... so many things – an orchard full of plums at my widower grandfather's home ... his housekeeper's home-made toffee ... the church bells tolling for Evensong at the end of a peaceful Sunday afternoon. My grandfather Carmichael died from a heart attack suffered on the eighteenth green of a golf course. I suppose he must be said to have died a happy man. My mother's father was 'in glass'. I remember his house as being full of sunshine and fresh air but his office always smelled of cigar smoke. Between eight and thirteen I went to Scarborough College and then to Bromsgrove School where I completed my formal education preparatory to going to the Royal Academy of Dramatic Art. I think I had done a couple of terms there when war broke out and I went into the Army.

F.S.T. I remember your film role as Private Stanley Windrush. Was the Army anything like that for you?

I.C. Not quite. I was in the Royal Armoured Corps. Now people say glibly, 'Oh, the tanks.' That's quite a different thing, really. The RAC was the Royal Tank Regiment plus all the cavalry regiments and I was in a brand-new cavalry regiment which was formed in 1940 called the 22nd Dragoons, having gone first to Catterick Camp for initial training as a trooper. Then I went through Sandhurst and was commissioned into the 22nd Dragoons. It all brought me back to Yorkshire very quickly.

F.S.T. How was that?

I.C. I joined the regiment at Whitby, which was good. There had never seemed to be time for ambitious family holidays when I was younger. We always seemed to go to Hornsea or perhaps Bridlington. Being in Whitby was extending the repertoire a bit.

F.S.T. The Dragoons sound rather glamorous. How did you come to be in something of a crack regiment?

I.C. Well, I had started out as a trooper in the RAC, so towards the end of my officer-cadet training at Sandhurst I was interviewed by a Regular Army cavalry officer who seemed to be a sort of casting director. Which regiment did I want? The only cavalry regiment I had heard of was the local Territorials at home, the East Riding Yeomanry. Some of my Hull friends had joined the ERY so I plumped for that. 'Full up,' I was told. 'Have you another preference?' And Windrush-like, I asked mildly, 'What other regiments have you got?' This, fortunately, did not provoke the explosion which might have been expected. Instead, I was given a big sales pitch for the 22nd Dragoons.

F.S.T. So you went to Whitby as a cavalry officer – what was it like?

I.C. Well, I was twenty when I emerged from Sandhurst (and immensely proud to have been through the Royal Military College, I may say) and I think I looked about sixteen. The regiment had been formed from a nucleus of officers and men from two long-established units, the 4/7th Royal Dragoon Guards and the 5/6th Royal Inniskilling Dragoon Guards, and it was round this core of seasoned professional soldiers that young men like myself were to be built into a regiment of the line. My first night in the mess was just a little nerve-racking with my seniors clanking about in spurs, drinking large pink gins and referring to girls as 'fillies'. Three nights later, a fellow second lieutenant called Haddock (and inevitably known as Fish) took me down to the Spa where an all-ranks dance was being staged. Before the end of the evening we spotted two 'fillies' who turned out to be cousins, recently out of school. I grabbed the taller one, a blonde who was sensationally pretty, and whisked her off to dance to the strains of the current hit song, 'Amapola'. After the last waltz, my filly (who had her mother's Morris Eight for the evening) ran us back to the mess – all of 500 yards – and after a brief and entirely chaste snog, I went in and Fish asked, 'What was yours like?' 'Oh,' I replied, 'I intend to marry mine.' I did. Her name was Jean Pyman McLean – Pym – and she was eighteen and very lovely. Pym died from cancer in the summer of 1983 and left the most appalling gap in the life we had shared for forty years.

F.S.T.   Yes, I know how deeply attached you were to each other ... everyone did.

I.C.   The regiment moved from Whitby to Helmsley, still in Yorkshire, where we preceded Brian Johnston's mob (the Grenadier Guards) and spent nearly two years at Duncombe Park and then about nine months before D-Day they turned us into a highly secretive unit with lots of highly secretive equipment which was used to storm the beaches of Normandy. Troops of my regiment landed at H-Hour on D-Day on the Normandy beaches, using tanks equipped with flails to explode mines.

F.S.T.   So you were one of the first men back into Europe?

I.C.   No. My role was at brigade headquarters and I followed several days later. Because we had this special equipment we were in almost every offensive right through until VE-Day and moved up and down the various fronts, through the British, American and Canadian armies – we joined whichever unit was carrying out a particular assault to clear a way through the minefields.

It was some time after VE-Day that Brian Horrocks, who was a particularly enlightened general, decided that we had to entertain the troops in Germany because not sufficient entertainment was coming out from the UK. A pool was formed of all available artistes, irrespective of rank, and when I went for an audition I found it was being conducted by a chap called Richard Stone who had been at RADA with me. 'Never mind the audition,' he said, 'come and sit here.' He was my agent for twenty years after we had both left the Army.

F.S.T. So you returned to take up your professional life as an actor ...

I.C. On 8 July 1946, I walked out of a demob centre in Leeds with a certificate granting Major I. G. Carmichael eighty days' leave and releasing me from military duties on 26 September. Having trained at RADA I had gained a little bit of stage experience in the twenty-two months between leaving school and joining the Army but for the next five years and ten months I had been a soldier. I was frightened when I looked at my future.

F.S.T. Frightened?

I.C. Yes, very definitely frightened. You see, I had lost the years between twenty and twenty-six in terms of living my life. Lots of other people did. Some obviously were profoundly affected by this, others perhaps not quite so much, but it must have affected everyone who experienced it in some sort of way. I wasn't sure exactly what I was going to do next. Pym was now my wife and we had a daughter, Lee.

F.S.T. Before we go on to your career, could we talk a little about your Yorkshire associations and memories?

I.C. Well, I suppose we were a rather insular family because although my father was relatively well off, there never seemed to be a lot of money to spare. I think it was possibly that he put everything into making sure his children had a good education. After prep school in Scarborough (which I loathed – we'll come back to that in a minute), I went to Bromsgrove and my sisters went to Harrogate Ladies' College. And then my father was bound up in his work and by taking holidays somewhere close at hand like Hornsea and Bridlington, he could drive to his office when necessary. The first time I went abroad was when I landed in Normandy. I think they were happy enough as holidays, but Hornsea, you could say, lacked glamour and the same, I suppose, was true of Bridlington. But it had the Spa, with a big ballroom, and Herman De Rewsky's Band used to play there. I used to go to *thés dansant* and watch him play and watch the drummer at the back. I remember the whole family got whooping cough, which is not the best disease to get when you are on holiday.

Scarborough, a little farther north, was a place I didn't really know until I went to school there. I was deposited on the doorstep with a tuck box and a trunk and I was not eight years old until a few weeks later. I absolutely hated and loathed the whole blooming situation. I loathed being away from home, I hated Scarborough College – it was a Dickensian sort of school – and Scarborough, to me, meant everything that was absolutely awful. When I left, at the age of thirteen, I just hoped I would never see Scarborough again. I never wanted to go back there in my life. Well, I went back with the Army and things were entirely different. Scarborough seemed the only civilized place on the east coast. Tom Laughton's hotel was going, the Pavilion, and before we were married I took Pym over there a lot. Then I was on a course there and suddenly what had been an awful town became absolutely marvellous. There was something about it that was terribly glamorous. Later we spent the first part of our honeymoon there and by now the memories were all the happiest, happiest, happiest memories. In February 1983, I took my wife back to Scarborough, to the Belevedere Nursing Home, with what turned out to be cancer and I had four agonizing months until she died in June.

During those last four months I said to her, 'It is absolutely astonishing that, although neither of us has ever *lived* in Scarborough, what a monumental part in our lives the town has played ... the graph going up down, up down.'

F.S.T.   How did you come to decide upon acting as a career?

I.C.   I suppose I wanted to show off, really. At first I couldn't decide whether I wanted to be a musician and run a dance band, or whether I wanted to act. I was a mad fan of all the dance bands in the thirties. I ran a small band in Hull in my late teens, not very successfully because I didn't know anything about music, really. I knew a little – I played the saxophone, I played the drums – but I didn't know enough. And I thought that, to become a top musician, it meant hard work, really hard work, so I decided to go to the RADA and become an actor. Or rather, I persuaded my parents to send me there. They were very tolerant because they wanted me to go into the family business, but once they decided my mind was made up they were very helpful. It was just something I wanted to do. I remember doing little plays and things in the nursery at Elloughton with my sisters, rigging up curtains and stages.

F.S.T.   So what was your first professional part?

I.C.   It was as a robot in a play called *RUR*, written by a Czech called Karol Kapek. It ran for a week at the People's Palace in the Mile

Ian Carmichael in his enchanted garden with a salmon pool

End Road, Stepney. The cast included six robots who were extras, and they went to the Royal Academy to engage six students for the parts. I was paid 10s 6d (52p) for the week's work.

F.S.T.   So how did you progress from there?

I.C.   Well, I hadn't done anything like enough before the war to become in any way established so it was a matter of starting all over again. I did all sorts of little bits and pieces around the club theatres of the West End and someone from BBC Television, then at Alexandra Palace, took a shine to me. The result was that I then did an awful lot of musicals from AP. None of my family had ever seen television. I wasn't well enough off to own a set and Pym used to go and sit in some soul-destroying viewing room in Broadcasting House to watch them, or to someone who *had* a set – my agent, for instance. So I did an awful lot of musicals on TV when no one could see it outside the London area. Then I got into big touring musicals – *The Lilac Domino* and *Wild Violets*, which gave me such invaluable experience in the late forties.

Between 1951 and 1953 I went into revue, which was the vogue at the time, and graduated from what is called the wines and spirits (the also-rans in the company) to top billing with Hermione Baddeley and Dora Bryan. So – people say to me occasionally, 'D'you mean to say you sing?' And the whole of my early years were spent in musicals! Then I went into a straight play in the West End and in 1955 the Boulting Brothers put me under contract and I did five years of movies with them. I'd done movies before but not in big leading roles.

F.S.T.   So in musicals you were doing the Bobby Howes roles, that sort of thing?

I.C.   Yes. If you look at some of the old 78 r.p.m. records with the Columbia label it says, 'Fred Astaire (light baritone) singing "Night and Day" from *The Gay Divorce*'. I was, I suppose, 'light baritone'.

F.S.T.   So what was your first film?

I.C.   The very first one of all was practically a walk-on part, virtually a one-liner, in a film called *Bond Street*. It was, as I remember, an episodic picture about different people in that street. I was a maître d'hôtel and the film was made in Welwyn Garden City, at the studios there. I used to have to get up about 4.30 in the morning to get there by public transport. I didn't own a car until I was about thirty-five. I couldn't afford to. And I didn't get home until nine at night.

F.S.T.   How many films have you made?

I.C.   I can't answer that because frankly I am not a statistics man. I don't think it's a very impressive number. When I started making movies they were all crammed into a very short space of time – they keep coming up on TV all the time, don't they, in black and white? Old movies. I think a lot of people think I only make old movies! But they were all over a six, seven, eight-year span. And then I went back to the theatre again.

F.S.T.   Which film have you most enjoyed making?

I.C.   Well, that's asked a lot and it's difficult to answer. The Boultings sent me two scripts and said, 'This will be your first film and the other will be your second.' The first was *Private's Progress* and Stanley Windrush was such a marvellous part. It might look a little dated on telly, these days, but it really was a marvellous part. It wasn't as broad as the 'Carry On' series. It was full satire, part of a whole new cycle of films poking fun, sending up institutions. The second one was the part of Roger Thursby, the young, greenhorn barrister, in *Brothers in Law*. I am very hard-pressed to know which of those I like better. Certainly I liked *Private's Progress* because it was something brand new and it was fresh and it was a big starring part and it was a wonderful part. So I couldn't dislike it. I think, possibly, Roger Thursby just had the edge on that one. Then, of course, there was *Lucky Jim*, which was Kingsley Amis's sock-hit best-seller, but there were troubles on *Lucky Jim*. It wasn't as smooth a ride as the others had been.

F.S.T.   What about *I'm All Right, Jack*?

I.C.   Ah, yes. Now the Boulting Brothers always liked to write their own scripts and they had the idea of a film bringing in all the main characters from *Private's Progress*, now back in Civvy Street, and so they went to Alan Hackney who wrote the original book of *Private's Progress* and commissioned him to write *another* novel. They didn't want a film script. They wanted to do that themselves. So they asked for a novel and Alan wrote one which he called *Private Life*. The Boultings then wrote the script of *I'm All Right, Jack* from that novel. What I am a little disappointed about is that Alan later wrote yet another novel, a sequel to *I'm All Right, Jack*, and this time it was the whole lot again, ten years on, by which time Kite, the shop steward (the Peter Sellers role), had become General Secretary of the TUC, but the Boulting Brothers never made that into a film, which I am rather sorry about.

F.S.T.   What was Peter Sellers like?

I.C.   Mercurial. When I knew him he was still up and coming. I believe he became quite difficult towards the end of his life but I saw none of that – no temperament. He was certainly mercurial – a very Goonish character. In a way there was a certain flamboyance with it, especially so far as spending money was concerned – new cars every five minutes. I got on extremely well with Peter. He was very – what's the word I'm looking for? – impromptu, in a way. If he had to do too much rehearsing or too many takes, that worried him. He thought he had lost his flair. He liked the early ones with the spontaneity to them.

F.S.T.   You have close connections with cricket. How did you become involved with it in the first place?

I.C.   I learned it at school and I enjoyed my cricket. At Scarborough I played for the prep school. When I went to Bromsgrove I played for the Junior Colts and the Colts. I don't think I ever turned out for the Second XI; I certainly never turned out for the Firsts but by this time I was getting older and my interests were altering. In my mid-teens I was much more interested in dance bands and music rooms and things like that. Between eight and thirteen I was a seamer (if you can bowl seamers at such a tender age), and when I went to Bromsgrove they tried to turn me into a wrist-spinner. I took quite a number of wickets but I can never remember having turned a ball in my life. And I really took no active part in the game until the war was over. We had found a home near to Lord's and a number of actor chums used to go there when they were out of work and watch cricket from the Tavern. It cost 2s entrance fee for the whole day and that, of course, is where the Lord's Taverners started. I suppose I got back into the game playing in charity matches for the Lord's Taverners and for various beneficiaries amongst county players. I was Lord's Taverner No. 367.

F.S.T. So you were in very early . . .

I.C. Well, it didn't seem like it at the time. I kept trying to become a member and people kept saying they would put me up and forgot about it. It was ages before I got in. There were an awful lot of good things then which have gone by the board now. I suppose the great excuse now is that they are making so much money for charity and I know that pretty well excuses anything, but in the early days it was not allowed to excuse anything. For instance, no one was allowed to buy himself into the Taverners, no matter how much money he promised to donate if he were admitted. Also, it's interesting to look back now at the rule which said no professional cricketer could be admitted to membership while he was still playing the game professionally. We elected a Cricketer of the Year every year and he was admitted to *honorary* membership, like, say, D. C. S. Compton, but that was the only exception. I remember trying to get the Bedser twins in as a pair – you can't separate them, can you? – and I was told quite categorically, 'No, and not until they have finished playing.'

F.S.T. Have you a favourite cricketing memory?

I.C. From a personal point of view I had two analyses – 5 for 27 in a Ken Barrington benefit game at Esher, and 3 for 17, which was, I think, in a J. T. Murray benefit game at Totteridge, but I'm not absolutely sure. I did the hat trick at Welton with the aid, I believe, of some skullduggery behind the stumps by Clement Freud. As for watching professional cricket, I am very, very proud to have been at a practically empty Lord's when Willie Watson and Trevor Bailey saved the day (30 June 1953) against the Australians. Willie got 109 and Trevor 71. And I was in the crowd at the Oval in 1956 when J. C. Laker took all 10 Australian wickets for Surrey.

F.S.T. How involved have you been with Yorkshire cricket?

I.C. Very little, strangely enough. As a schoolboy, I went to the Scarborough Festival. Since I came back to live in Yorkshire, noises have been made suggesting I should become a Yorkshire member, but I don't get many opportunities to make the pilgrimage over to Headingley to get, frankly, value for my money. I *am* a Yorkshireman, after all! Already I pay a vast amount of money to be a full member of MCC and during the five or six years I have been up here I haven't really been able to get the full benefit of *that* membership. So I'm sure you'll understand that I don't want to pay out any more money when I cannot get full benefit for it. I am a York-shireman to that extent.

F.S.T.   Of course I understand. Now, when and why did you come back north to live?

I.C.   I have always said that in 1941, when I was posted by the Army to Whitby, I fell in love with a girl and I fell in love with the area. I have always *adored* Whitby and the surrounding countryside. I always have got on terribly well with my in-laws, who live in the Esk valley, and we kept coming back, as a family, for holidays. My children also got on very well with my in-laws and they developed a love for the area as well. So I said to Pym, 'Look – your parents are not getting any younger and if they die we may never come back to this area again.' And we didn't like the idea of that at all. So we started looking round for a place of our own. I was very selfish about it, I admit. Pym didn't want to come back, although it was very much her part of the world; she felt she was being separated from her children and grandchildren. But, like a dutiful lady, she came along and for six years she made an absolutely super home for me. We have loved it and I still love it. I adore it.

F.S.T.   Did your wife come to love it, too, despite her misgivings about coming back?

I.C.   Yes, she did, and in some ways it was fortunate that we had returned north because for the first three or four years her mother needed a lot of care and attention which Pym would not have been able to give her if we had stayed in London. When we talked about such things, however, she would say, 'If you go first I am not going to stay up here. I shall go back to London.'

F.S.T.   Have you a favourite part from the many you have played?

I.C.   This is terribly difficult because I tend to enjoy most the part I am playing at the time. Also, one changes these things about a bit in one's mind. When I went back to the stage after playing in all those movies I had an absolutely marvellous part in a play called *The Tunnel of Love* which I think I quoted in *Who's Who* at one time as my favourite. Then in something like 1964 I had another absolutely cracking part in a play called *Say Who You Are* at Her Majesty's (the same theatre), written by Keith Waterhouse and Willis Hall. I then did a musical – a wonderful, wonderful musical, which was crucified universally by the English press – called *I Do, I Do* at the Lyric in 1967. It was a musical version of Jan Herzog's *The Fourposter*, only two people in it. The story of a marriage from the altar to middle age when the children have grown up. On Broad-way it was done by Mary Martin and Robert Presten and was a very big success. It was a marvellous, marvellous, marvellous piece, choreographed and directed and everything else by Gower Champion. That I adored. The English press condemned it universally as being 'hideous, sweet, gooey, American saccharin, bearing no relationship to married life', which was totally untrue. It might have been saccharine sweet but it certainly bore *every* relationship to married life. It was no consolation to me when, ten years later, Rock Hudson and Juliet Prowse came back to do a limited revival of it at the Phoenix and it received exactly the same critical reception.

F.S.T.   Did you enjoy playing Bertie Wooster?

I.C.   Yes, I did. I turned it down, once. It was quite extraordinary. It was a period of my life, my early forties, when I was having trouble finding suitable new material and my agent suggested Wooster. I thought about it and I'd been having a rather dull patch for a couple of years. Somehow I felt it would accentuate the passéness I felt about this dull patch if I had to go back to the 1920s for new material. So I forgot about it until a year later when a BBC TV director called Michael Mills brought it to me. He fired me with enthusiasm for it and made me change my mind. But after that came Lord Peter Wimsey and that was very much *my* baby. It took me about six years to get anyone to do it and then, when someone finally did it, he didn't want me in it. Oh, it was quite a saga, but it was a role I think I coveted almost more than Bertie.

F.S.T.   Have you any ambitions left to fulfil?

I.C.   Any ambitions? D'you know, I don't know about that now. When I left London and decided to come back to Yorkshire I was about fifty-eight, I think, and my eldest child was sixteen before we ever had a holiday together away from home – that is away from my in-laws – the first time we had been to the South of France together. And I think we only went together twice because I had left it too late. I thought this was awful. I had been too busy working all the time. And at about fifty-eight I decided there were two philosophies by which a man could live in late middle age. One was that of the man who wants to die with his boots on, and the other was that of the chap who says, 'Get out and enjoy yourself, it's later than you think.' I decided I would subscribe to the second policy. I didn't want to work as hard as I had been doing. I didn't want to have to go to the theatre every night. I wanted to be able to go out and have a meal and to have one too many to drink without having to worry about the next day. When I came up here I said, 'I don't care if I never pass through a stage door again as long as I live. I want to do a little bit of work to earn a bit of money but I can do films and I can do television and I can do radio … from here.'

Now that my wife has died I have, of course, formulated no plans, no views. Everyone says, 'Bury yourself in work,' but that would be a tremendous upheaval. I would probably have to quit here; I don't know that I want to quit here. I don't know what I want to do. I think I would like to continue in the lifestyle that I have settled into, really, which is sort of semi-retirement. That's a cliché, but I can't think of any other way of putting it. Just picking and choosing. If they don't come to me, they don't come to me – that's all.

F.S.T.   Finally, would you say you have had a happy life?

I.C.   Oh, certainly. Yes, of course. I couldn't say anything else. I have had an *extraordinarily* happy life … I have had an extraordinarily *lucky* life and luck plays a tremendous part. Yes, I have no complaints. But to go back to your initial reason for coming to talk to me, I still feel very much a Yorkshireman. I still love Yorkshire and I still want to live in Yorkshire.

I went to London last weekend to see my children, the first time I had done so on my own, and it was rather an emotional occasion and I was thrilled to see them … but having seen them I couldn't wait to get back. Now that's no criticism of them, nor is it unfeelingness on my part. I adore them. I adore the grandchildren. It opened up questions like: 'Are you going to live nearer to them, now? You're sixty-three, you know … I don't want to live down south, if I can avoid it. I want to live in Yorkshire.

England *v.* Australia, 1936. Hedley Verity (England) bowling to Chipperfield during the First Test match at Brisbane

Sport

Yorkshire Cricket

The early years of Yorkshire County Cricket Club were, in many ways, as stormy as those of the 1970s and 1980s. A hundred and twenty years ago the Yorkshire character and temperament was as blunt, obstinate and uncompromising as it is today. Spades were called bloody shovels; fools were never suffered gladly; nothing was ever swept under the carpet; and, to complete the metaphorical sequence, a lot of dirty washing was aired in public.

The county club was formally constituted on 5 January 1863, in Sheffield, with a minimum subscription of half a guinea a year. It would, therefore, have been something of a gentleman's club or at least a club for those who, if not perhaps gentlemen in the MCC's interpretation of the word, had a bit o' brass. Half a guinea in 1863 would buy a lot of material possessions and membership of a county cricket club would not rank very high in a working man's list of priorities. The first committee consisted entirely of Sheffield men and there was immediate bridling in such areas as Bradford and York where, it was felt, there was an equal, if not greater, right to speak in cricketing terms for Yorkshire. As early as 1864, the Kent secretary, in trying to arrange fixtures, was uncertain as to 'who were the proper parties to get up Yorkshire county matches', according to J. M. Kilburn (for so long the distinguished and scholarly cricket correspondent of the *Yorkshire Post*). And by 1865 there was a massive fallout between the members of the first county side, brought about by north-south rivalry within the county. *Plus ça change, plus c'est la même chose!* That first county side, which played against Surrey at the Oval on 5 and 6 June 1863, included three players from Sheffield and three from Huddersfield, but two from Bedale, in rural Wensleydale, and one from Ripon, the tiny cathedral city in the North Riding – unlikely bedfellows. And it was ill feeling between the different factions that led to George Anderson declining the committee's invitation to captain the side in 1865, and to four other players – G. Atkinson, R. Iddison, J. Rowbotham and E. Stephenson – also refusing to take part. Two years of depression followed until the Victorian rebels were persuaded to return to the fold.

It is something more than depressing to realize how the wheel has turned full circle in just over a century. Let's hope that the mid-eighties bring Yorkshire cricket the same glory as that healing of the breach in the 1860s.

The two years of eclipse (1865–66) saw the emergence of a great pair of bowlers, George Freeman and Tom Emmett, and in seven matches of the 1867 season Freeman took 51 wickets at 7.4 and Emmett 30 at 5.2. Freeman was the greatest fast bowler of his day, according to the two greatest batsmen – W. G. Grace and Richard Daft, of Nottinghamshire. While these two bowlers were proving the irresistible force, Ephraim Lockwood and his uncle, John Thewlis, were setting themselves up as immovable batting objects, and Yorkshire cricket was established as the force which, with a few lean years, it remained until 1970, although it took more than twenty years for them to win their first county championship. Emmett perhaps goes down in history as one of the first characters of a game in which much of the folklore has been based on the dry one-liner – like Emmett's comment after a day in the field against Gloucestershire with 'W.G.' in full cry: 'It's Grace before meat, Grace after meat and Grace all bloody day.' And it was Emmett (again, according to Jim Kilburn) who complained to Lord Harris after a bad crossing of the Bay of Biscay en route to Australia, 'I don't think they've had the heavy roller on, my lord.' I'd have been proud of both remarks!

George Ulyett was the great man of the 1870s, starting as a bowler and developing into an all-rounder with hard-hitting batting as his strong suit. And by now the great dynasty of slow left-arm bowlers, which was to be Yorkshire's pride for the next hundred years, had been established. Edmund Peate averaged 7 wickets a match over three years in the 1880s and had, according to Lord Hawke, 'the most perfect action of any man'. He was succeeded by Bobby Peel, who topped the 100 wickets' mark in nine successive seasons – seasons in which far fewer matches were played than today. The 1890s saw the arrival of George Herbert Hirst, with 125 wickets in 1893, and, with two other bowlers doing even better, Yorkshire won their first county championship – the first of thirty they were to win up to 1968. It was an early and clear illustration that bowling and fielding win championships, a lesson that Yorkshire were never to forget. They developed a system of specialist fieldsmen and even if some of the positions seem unlikely in the 1980s (Hirst at mid-off, for instance), it was a system that brought great rewards in the years to come.

If 1893 had been the bowlers' year, 1895 was certainly the batsmen's, highlighted by a score of 887 against Warwickshire at Edgbaston. Peel made 210, Lord Hawke 166, Wainwright 126 and F. S. (Sir Stanley) Jackson 117. George Hirst went in at No. 10, made 85, shared in a ninth-wicket partnership of 136, then bowled 40 overs and took 8 for 59. That total of 887 was made in less than eleven hours. But the year of the batsman still produced a new Yorkshire bowler in Schofield Haigh, who took 8 wickets against the touring Australians at Park Avenue. The following year saw the introduction of winter pay for the professional players, who consequently became established as men with financial security as well as tremendous kudos in the county.

A Yorkshire player was by now something of a demigod. There was no television to bring the great players under the close scrutiny of every household in the country, no cult-of-personality writing in the newspapers to detail the most personal habits, hobbies or outside interests of the players. They stood or fell by their achievements on the field while retaining a general anonymity off it. Relatively few of the cricketing public 'knew' players as they do today. There was, in consequence, a marvellous mystique about the great ones and the idolatry that their talents induced was good and wholesome. Yet even in this era – perhaps *especially* in this era – the public image had to be maintained with dignity. When Bobby Peel's fondness for the tipple was somewhat ostentatiously manifested, Lord Hawke sacked him, for all his greatness. It was well for Yorkshire that a ready-made replacement was waiting off-stage in the one and only Wilfred Rhodes.

Now when people talk about the great all-rounders of the 1980s – Ian Botham, Imran Khan, Kapil Dev and Richard Hadlee – or about those of the recent past like Gary Sobers and Keith Miller, I raise my cap, as I happily do to all great players of any generation. But I think I raise it just a little higher to Wilfred Rhodes, a marvellous old man as I was privileged to know him until his death in 1973. Rhodes's career spanned the whole of cricket's greatest golden age. He bowled at Grace and he bowled at Bradman. He shared a record first-wicket partnership for England and another for the last wicket. He scored 1000 runs in a season seventeen times and took 100 wickets in a season twenty-two times, twice topping the 200 mark. He bowled unchanged through a match on six occasions, three times with George Hirst and three with Schofield Haigh, did the hat trick against Derbyshire in 1920 when he was forty-three, and he gets no fewer than fifty-two entries in the Yorkshire CCC handbook under the heading 'Exceptional Bits of Bowling'. Rhodes played in fifty-eight Tests for England over a thirty-one-year period, scoring 2325 runs at 30.19 and taking 127 wickets at 26.96. For Yorkshire he scored 31,156 runs at 30.10 and took 3608 wickets at 16. Now that's what I call an all-rounder.

Wilfred was not a colourful character in the way that Sobers or Botham or Miller can be called colourful. He was, in many ways, the epitome of the dour Yorkshireman. He was not a gentle, kindly man in the way that George Hirst and Maurice Leyland were gentle and kindly. He was not a man to lose graciously. On the contrary, he *hated* to lose, as he hated inefficiency in any form of cricket. The ground was his battlefield and while the Hawkes and the Whites and the Burtons and the Wilsons and the Luptons might be the generals, Rhodes was the sergeant major, the leader of the fighting men, the man who made things happen. Neville Cardus in his autobiography has described Rhodes's bowling in one of the finest pieces of prose in the whole of cricket's considerable literature. It was written reflectively, with hindsight, and while it is a beautiful, brilliant piece of writing, it gives us perhaps an over-romanticized portrait. Cardus as the cricket reporter, on the other hand, working in a contemporary situation, provides a more realistic picture of Rhodes as an operational slow left-arm bowler. From the *Manchester Guardian*, Yorkshire *v.* Lancashire, Bramall Lane, 1919:

Rhodes was easily the best of the Yorkshire bowlers. In his 42nd year, Rhodes has recaptured a characteristic which made his bowling unique 20 years ago. There were slow bowlers before Rhodes who had his enormous finger spin, but they could only get it to operate on the average wicket by tossing the ball well into the air, which had the defect of giving quick-footed batsmen time to jump in and drive. Rhodes seemingly set a scientific principle at defiance by spinning at a tantalisingly slow pace, yet with the low flight of the medium-paced man. The result is a twisting ball that defies the offensive tactics best calculated to cope with it and one has, perforce, to wait for the ball and allow the spin to come off, which, of course, is the very thing one wants to prevent.

This combination of a characteristic of the slow bowler with one belonging definitely to the medium-paced bowler got Rhodes his wickets yesterday, three of them significantly lbw. He is a delightful bowler to watch even when he is working destruction against Lancashire.

I have gone on at some length about Wilfred Rhodes because, although he was in teams which had many other great players, somehow he seems to me to sum up more completely than anyone else the essential character of Yorkshire cricket in its greatest days. There were

Yorkshire under Lord Hawke and an original caption which clearly distinguished the officers from the other ranks. *Back row*: Turner (scorer), Wardall, Whitehead, Mr Dodworth, Mounsey, Draper (umpire). *Middle row*: Tunnicliffe, Peel, Lord Hawke, F.S. Jackson, Wainwright. *Front row*: Brown, Hunter, Hirst

more accomplished batsmen (though never a greater bowler), more athletic fieldsmen and more picturesque personalities. There were grim and gritty men in abundance and there were droll and whimsical players, lovable and heart-warming players. But Wilfred Rhodes seems to have embodied just about everything that set Yorkshire cricket apart from that of other counties. There were the Tunnicliffes and the Browns, the Hunters, Kilners, Sutcliffes, Huttons, Veritys and Boweses, all great men and great, great players. But if the county decides some day to put up a statue at Headingley inscribed simply 'Yorkshire cricket', then I think it would have to look like Wilfred Rhodes.

But let us not neglect some of the others who helped to win those thirty championships, starting with Lord Hawke, the most notable non-Yorkshireman to play for the county. He was born Martin Bladen Hawke in 1860 at a time when his father was rector of Willingham, in

Lincolnshire. But that father was a proud Yorkshireman and the family estates included the battlefield of Towton where Edward IV destroyed the Lancastrian forces on Palm Sunday, 1461. And you can't get much more Yorkshire than that! The rector inherited the title and young Hawke lived at Wighill Park, near Tadcaster, for fifty years from 1874, and he led Yorkshire from 1883 to 1910 (he was also president of the county for forty years from 1898 to 1938). His background – Eton and Cambridge University – could scarcely have been in greater contrast to that of the forces he commanded and yet he probably did more than anyone else, before or since, to give stature and standing and dignity to the professional cricketer. And he did it in what was the age of the gifted (and not-so-gifted) amateur.

George Macaulay was a bowler whose sustained aggression towards, and blatant hatred of, batsmen would have earned him high marks from me every time. Jim Kilburn wrote of him:

Batsmen, temporarily, and groundsmen, permanently, were Macaulay's sworn enemies and he never dissembled. He wanted to be taking wickets all the time from half-past eleven to half-past six and he resented the interruptions of luncheon and tea. He once caught Lancashire on a crumbled wicket at Old Trafford and when he had bowled them out twice in a day regretted they could not be given a third innings. On an occasion of sunshine after rain at Hull, when there was a delay until the storm waters soaked through, Macaulay was observed pacing the pavilion enclosure in an agony of impatience. 'Seven left-handers,' he was muttering. 'Seven left-handers in the side and I can't get at them.' If you did not know Macaulay except by reputation, you soon recognized him.

Macaulay played from 1920 to 1935 and by then we had seen the development of Bill Bowes, my coach and my friend after the Second World War, and Hedley Verity, the next of our marvellous slow left-armers who, so sadly, did not survive the war. He died of wounds sustained in the landings in Sicily when he was a captain in the Green Howards. But these two, in their contrasting styles of bowling, were the Yorkshire spearhead through the 1930s when the county won seven championships in nine seasons, and counted their third place in 1936 and their fifth in 1934 as wasted years. Verity first played in 1930 and had a return of 7 for 26 against Hampshire before he was fully established in the side. In 1931 he took all 10 wickets against Warwickshire for 36 runs and finished with a haul of 169. In 1932 he took a total of 146 wickets, including that never-to-be-forgotten 10 for 10 against Nottinghamshire, like his first all 10, at Headingley. From then on, until the war put an end to county championship cricket, he took

Yorkshire in 1923. *Back row*: Leyland, Macaulay, Waddington, Kilner (N.), Sutcliffe, Ringrose (scorer). *Middle row*: Dolphin, Rhodes, F. Wilson, G. Wilson, Robinson, Holmes. *Front row*: Oldroyd and Kilner (R.)

successively 168, 100, 199, 185, 185, 137 and 189 wickets. To my very great regret I never saw him play but Jim Kilburn has summed him up for me:

He looked his part. At first glance he was obviously a student of something, and he loved his art. He thought about it, talked about it, experimented with it and was never happier than when a bowling problem was set before him. The problem, indeed, was more important to Verity than the solution accomplished.

The minor batsmen he dismissed summarily; to the great opponents he paid the tribute of his greatest skill. He was tall and his arm was high in an admirable action. From these native characteristics he derived an asset not available to all slow left-handers (though it would perhaps be true to say that his pace was nearer to medium than slow): he could make the ball lift as well as turn. This faculty made him a bowler to be feared when the wicket was soft but not sticky and provided hundreds of catches just behind or in front of the bat. Every now and then he bowled a faster ball which was far above medium pace and which very rarely failed in accuracy of line and length. During his run-up to bowl this batsmen's surprise, the wicketkeeper (Arthur Wood) would stretch out his hand and back would scuttle the slips and gulley. Dozens of spectators, players and critics watched for years to discover the signal between Verity and Wood but the secret was never known until after Verity had been killed. Wood then confessed that there had been no secret at all. 'I just sensed it,' said Wood.

Now, Bill Bowes I did see play but obviously not at his greatest. Like Hedley Verity, he had fought in the war and while he was fortunate enough to survive, years in prisoner-of-war camps wrecked his health and he was never really a *fast* bowler when he returned to play Yorkshire cricket again in 1946 and 1947. But I have spent hour after hour yarning with Bill, both as a Yorkshire coach and later as a very shrewd cricket correspondent of, first, the *Yorkshire Evening News* and, when that paper ceased publication, the *Yorkshire Evening Post*. He has always been an essentially modest man, particularly about his own achievements, but he has a superb memory and a great gift for describing cricketing occasions, like the time he bowled Bradman for a duck at Melbourne in 1932:

The crowd applauded him all the way to the wicket. It was deafening. And just as I started to run in, the applause started up again. He walked away from the wicket and I stopped. Just for something to do while the noise died down I waved the deep fine leg to come up closer. There was nothing clever about it, no deep-laid plot. But when the applause started once more, again, for something to do, I waved the mid-on to move in a bit closer. And at last the clapping stopped. I started to run in. Suddenly I sensed that Bradman expected me to bowl a bouncer. As I got near the wicket I saw him start to get into position to hook and I bowled a ball of full length. He saw it and tried to get back into position. He was so good that he nearly got there and just got the faintest nick on it before it hit the stumps. Well, the silence . . . it was something you could really feel. It was awesome. You could hear the rattling of the trams down in the middle of Melbourne. And as Bradman started to walk slowly back to the pavilion just one spectator started to applaud him. Just one. It was a woman and we could see her out of all the vast crowd.

It's a marvellous story – as any account of Bradman bowled for nought has to be – but the thing is really to hear Bill tell it himself. You can feel that silence as he and Jardine's touring team experienced it in Melbourne.

Bill, though very much a Yorkshireman, came to the county XI from the unlikely training ground of Lord's, where he was on the ground staff at the age of nineteen. He took 40 wickets for the county in 1929 and from then until the outbreak of war he was Yorkshire's first-

A young
Don Bradman
with Maurice
Leyland
in 1930

choice opening bowler. He made the ball move both ways in the air, could make it deviate off the seam, and with his height (over six feet) he seemed always to get bounce on the most docile wicket. If it started to break up, or if it had moisture, he could be unplayable. He was a very complete bowler indeed. His Test career paralleled that of Bradman, so he was always up against it at a time when England played more Tests against Australia than anyone else. He missed the Don's 334 at Headingley in 1930, but four years later led the England attack on the same ground when Bradman scored 304 – bowled Bowes, who had 6 for 142 after 50 overs of hard labour, 5 of them clean-bowled. The part played by Verity and Bowes in those seven championship wins in nine prewar seasons is best understood when you look at the figures: Bowes 1351 wickets at 15.68; Verity 1558 at 13.71. What a pair! They were backed up by men like Frank Smailes and Ellis Robinson, and by marvellous catching close to the wicket by such specialists as Arthur Mitchell and Brian Sellers. The 1930s was indeed an outstanding decade in Yorkshire's history.

It was, too, the period which saw the rich maturity of Maurice Leyland and Herbert Sutcliffe and the start of Len Hutton's career as the greatest batsman I played with. Herbert Sutcliffe was probably the greatest player on bad wickets that Yorkshire and England have ever known. He was, of course, a magnificent batsman on *good* pitches, but eminent critics have long felt that he came into his own when batting was at its most difficult. He became a great friend in his later years – especially when I retired from cricket and he retired from the Yorkshire committee. There had been, you might say, a personality clash on one or two occasions when we were both in office! But afterwards, particularly when he lived in a nursing home near my home, he used to join us regularly for Sunday lunch and we spent hours talking about his cricketing days and mine.

In an entirely different way from Lord Hawke, Herbert Sutcliffe made an immense contribution to raising the status of the professional cricketer. Lord Hawke did it by exercising a kind of patriarchal benevolence; Herbert did it by example. His kit was always quite immaculate; he was the very model of what a well-turned-out cricketer should look like. His brilliantined hair remained as unruffled as his temperament at moments of crisis.

Cardus wrote of Herbert Sutcliffe that he could play at and miss six balls in an over, then lean nonchalantly on his bat at the end of it as though he had middled every one. This infuriated Herbert when he read it. 'Never,' he exploded, 'never did I play at and miss six balls in an over in my entire career.'

He died in January 1978, and mercifully was spared the worst of Yorkshire's internal warfare. It would have broken his heart, for his love of Yorkshire and its cricket was as passionate as his pride in it. His opening partnership with Percy Holmes was immortalized by the record 555 at Leyton in 1932, but let's not forget that together they had three other first-wicket stands of more than 300, fourteen others of more than 200 and fifty of 100 or more. Percy Holmes had not the style of Sutcliffe, either on the field or off it. He was very much more

The greatest
opening pair –
Herbert
Sutcliffe and
Percy Holmes

of a homespun character than his dapper and dignified partner. But
each had a deep – and, in its way, affectionate – appreciation of the
other.

Len Hutton was dogged by poor health in his teens and, although
a strong family background in cricket plus his unmistakable talent had

brought him to the notice of Yorkshire when he was little more than a boy, he was nursed rather gently into the first team. Indeed, he had won his regular place only two years before he startled the world with 364 against the Australians at the Oval in 1938. In a game which started at 11.30 on a Saturday morning, he batted until half past two on Tuesday afternoon in the timeless last Test of the series. It was an unprecedented piece of concentration and, quite apart from making him every Yorkshire schoolboy's hero, it established him as Public Enemy No. 1 with succeeding generations of Australian bowlers. It was as though the Millers, the Lindwalls and the Johnstons were imbued with a missionary zeal to exorcise the indignities heaped upon their predecessors over 13 hours and 20 minutes on 20, 22 and 23 August 1938.

During the war, Hutton – an Army physical-training instructor – suffered a broken left forearm which healed only slowly, painfully and never entirely satisfactorily. With this disadvantage (and five years out of his sporting life) he carried on a career which brought him eighty-five centuries for Yorkshire and a total of 24,807 runs (average 53.34). He scored nineteen centuries in his seventy-nine Tests, in which he made a total of 6971 runs (average 56.67), and in 1952 he became England's first professional captain. In Yorkshire cricket terms, Leonard was a captain in the Illingworth mould rather than that of Brian Close. He believed less in inspiration and flair than in ruthlessly eliminating (or at least minimizing) the possibility of error. England won eleven Tests under his captaincy, drew eight and lost only four. My relations with Len as a Test captain were not the most cordial but my respect for him as a player has always been, and will remain, boundless.

Much has been written by me, and others, about Yorkshire's post-war years and there is little point in repeating it in a book which is not primarily a *cricket* book, but one character must certainly be mentioned in this chapter. Arthur Booth, a left-arm spinner, had waited patiently in the shadow of Hedley Verity throughout the 1930s with very little opportunity to show what he could do. In 1946, at the age of forty-three, he played his first full season of county championship cricket. It was a wet summer and, with wickets uncovered, provided conditions much to the liking of spin bowlers. Little Arthur Booth – he was a tiny fellow with a wry sense of humour – took 111 wickets which brought his career haul (and remember it spanned 1931 to 1947) to just 122. He later did some coaching, but then became a member of the *Lancashire* CCC committee. It's a career worth remembering.

The end
of Hutton's historic
innings at the Oval
in 1938

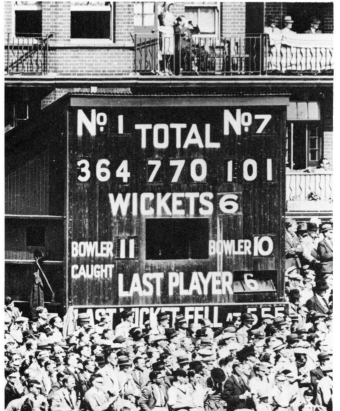

After winning the county championship immediately after the war, Yorkshire shared it with Middlesex in 1949 and then had to wait ten long years for their next success, partly because Surrey, with the marvellous attack of Lock and Laker, Loader and Alec Bedser, Surridge and Eric Bedser, dominated the competition almost throughout the fifties, and partly because Yorkshire, despite a tremendous playing strength, did not always pull together. I had come on the scene in 1949, together with Brian Close and Frank Lowson – we all made our debut together against Cambridge University – and over the next twenty seasons I was to take 1745 wickets for the county at 17.13 and score 6852 runs. During that period I very proudly played sixty-seven times for England, taking 307 Test wickets at 21.57, held sixty-four catches and scored 981 runs. It doesn't need me to tell anyone that those were the happiest days of my life, and the proudest of all came at Sheffield, the ground which had played such a part in my cricketing life, in 1968, when I led Yorkshire against Bill Lawry's Australians. I was thirty-seven years old. I had bowled as if I hated all batsmen for twenty seasons and although I would have killed anyone who suggested it, somewhere, perhaps deep down in the subconscious, a little voice was saying, 'It can't go on indefinitely.' Three years earlier, during the series against New Zealand, I had played my last Test. My mind wouldn't really accept that a part of my life which had meant so much to me was over. And so, at Bramall Lane, Bill·Lawry's men represented the Last Enemy, and my friend John Arlott captured the atmosphere of battle:

He performed his first duty satisfactorily, won the toss and gave Yorkshire first innings which Boycott, Sharpe and Padgett cautiously developed to 271-4 on the first day; thereafter, with defensive field-placings, Illingworth, with a late flourish by Trueman and Stringer, pushed up to 355 for 9 before Trueman declared.

So he gave himself and Hutton nearly half an hour's bowling before lunch and reserved a modicum of shine for the afternoon session. He himself opened the bowling with the most hostile field yet seen in the match. His first ball was a beamer which hummed passed Lawry's nose, and then in the same over Binks, standing back, was hit on the arm by another full toss. This was a fast bowler. Redpath tried to glance him, did not middle the stroke, and Binks, throwing himself a long way on the leg side, took the catch. Trueman maintained the pressure, regardless of runs edged through his close field, and a few minutes before lunch Walters, playing a hesitant back stroke to Hutton, got an edge and Trueman, remarkably athletically for a man of thirty-seven, dived far to his right from second slip to catch him one-handed; 36 for 2 at lunch. Bad light and then a storm (the wicket was covered) delayed the restart but soon Trueman caught Sheahan at slip and ran out Chappell with a fast return from extra cover. Illingworth dealt with Inverarity and Taber and Lawry who, at last erring in his selection of the leavable and the playable ball, nudged him to Trueman in the gulley. Gleeson and Connolly held up Yorkshire for a little until Trueman came back himself and, with all his old killing certainty, removed them both. When the ninth wicket fell and the groundsman's assistant came out to ask him which roller he wanted, he waved him imperiously away to make the inquiry of Lawry. He duly took the last wicket; had 3 for 32, three catches and a run-out to his credit in the innings; and asked Australia, 212 behind, to follow on. They had twenty minutes of their second innings to run that evening. Trueman rolled back a year or two and began bowling off his long run but it was Richard Hutton who gave him not simply a wicket but the one wicket he wanted. An overpitched ball swung in to Lawry and hit the foot of middle and leg. The Yorkshire players leaped in the air and the crowd cried its sight of the triumph to come.

Next morning Trueman, asked his forecast of the day, said that Yorkshire would win by half past three. Hutton again took an early and valuable wicket when Redpath moved across so far to an inswinger that he was lbw when it hit him on the back of the leg. That started the main stand of the innings, between Walters and Sheahan. Although Trueman pressed them with close fieldsmen they made 50 together in an hour with an ease and security that exhibited the truth of the wicket. It was a humid day and Trueman, short of a bowler – Stringer, who had damaged a groin muscle – switched the remainder rapidly to keep them fresh. Eventually, he came back himself in much of his old pomp: first he plucked out Sheahan's middle stump; then, with a ball he had been striving to bowl all morning, he pitched fractionally short of a length to Walters, straight enough to compel a stroke, made it leave the bat and Illingworth took the catch in the gulley.

The rest was a matter of tidying up, carried out mainly by Illingworth, though Trueman intervened to remove McKenzie. The match was won – at half past three, as predicted. Yorkshire beat Australia, for the first time since 1902, by an innings and 60 runs. It was a highly efficient performance; some fine catches were held and none dropped and Trueman had directed the entire operation with imagination and maximum effort. He never bowled quite so fast again. He did, though, at Scarborough in that season, run out Keith Fletcher with a return, on the run from long-off, which amazed not only the batsman.

That year we won our third successive championship and I retired a very happy man, if a part of me was still just a little frustrated. It wanted to go on playing in matches like that for *another* twenty seasons! Sixteen years later every part of me is glad not to be involved. I am appalled by what has recently happened to Yorkshire Cricket Club, and the many good and decent men who have given so much time and effort to the county. I wait for the day when our great club recovers its pride and dignity.

Yorkshire members at Headingley on the day Bradman scored 304 runs

Cricket Grounds

It is not widely known outside Yorkshire, and a surprising number of people within the county don't seem to realize it either, that the County Cricket Club does not have a ground of its own. A fee is paid for the use of each ground whenever Yorkshire play a game on it. Even Headingley, for so long the scene of Test cricket – and what marvellous Test matches we have had there over the years – belongs to the Leeds Cricket, Football and Athletic Club, or, to give it its more recognizable title, the Rugby League Club, which operates on the other side of the great back-to-back stand on the southern side of the cricket ground. And, to be absolutely fair about it, that ground has seen a lot of historic thirteen-a-side rugby played there, too.

But, since the 1890s, Headingley has been the very heart of Yorkshire cricket even though it was not until the county club had been in existence for a hundred years that the offices of the administrative staff were moved from Park Row, in the centre of Leeds, to the new building on the cricket ground at Headingley. In fact Centenary Year, 1963, was the last year in which correspondence went out under the old letterhead: 'Old Bank Chambers, Park Row, Leeds 1'. From 1964 the address became: 'Headingley Cricket Ground, Leeds 6'. And the story of cricket there is an integral part of the history of the game. Going back a mere fifty odd years, we have the immortal Bradman hitting over 300 in a day on 11 July 1930, after going in at 2 for 1 wicket, against the bowling of Larwood, Tate, Geary and Tyldesley, with dear old Maurice Leyland called up in desperation to bowl his Chinamen. It was a historic innings in many ways by the Boy from Bowral – 105 before lunch, 115 in the middle session and 89 between tea and the close – 309 runs in a day. It has never been equalled and with the present-day over rates it is never likely to be, either! His final score of 334 remained a record for eight years until (with Bradman doing his damndest to prevent it) our own Len Hutton topped that at the Oval

in 1938. Before that, Bradman had returned to Headingley in 1934 to score another triple century, a mere 304 this time, and on his next visit, in 1938, I suppose you can say he failed with only 103 (out of a total of 242!).

It was at Headingley that a man who was to become a dear old mate of mine and one of the finest left-hand batsmen of all time, Neil Harvey, scored a century in his first Test against England and, incidentally, took one of the finest outfield catches the ground has ever seen, to dismiss Cyril Washbrook. Here it was, in that same game, that Australia hit 404 for 3 in the fourth innings to win the Test, and the Don, on his last appearance there, made 173 not out – against the clock. Sir Donald Bradman will never be forgotten as long as the game is played but nowhere will he be better remembered than at Headingley.

Dickie Moulton, the groundsman in the forties and fifties, was a magnificent preparer of wickets. Not for Dickie the lavish application of marl or use of scientific aids. He believed in watering and rolling in

Ian Botham (left) on his way
to 149 against Australia at
Headingley (the 500–1 Test win) ...

... and Bob Willis (far
left) polishes off the
Aussies with the help of a
wicketkeeping record
for Bob Taylor

his delicate quantities of natural fertilizer – cowdung. You could *smell*
Headingley wickets, quite literally – and you didn't bother to lick your
fingers when bowling. There is now a car park where the old bowling
green used to stand, formerly a pleasant place to relax with a pint
after a day's play. And the old pavilion, at long-on, had an atmosphere
which has never been recaptured by the more utilitarian structure at
mid-wicket. Here, the physiotherapist (we called him the masseur in
those days), Bright Heyhurst, reigned supreme – probing and kneading
at tired muscles, massaging weary bodies and dispensing homespun
philosophy. It was always accepted that visiting teams tipped Bright a
few bob in acknowledgement of his labours, so there was a great deal
of sympathy when he strode into the England dressing-room at the end
of a Test against West Indies, brimming with righteous indignation.
'I rubbed yon lot till they shone like ebony,' he muttered, 'and they
haven't left me a ha'penny.' A comment which today would be more
likely to incur the wrath of the Race Relations Board than a
dressing-room smile perhaps.

Of course, I was always going to have the fondest personal memories of Headingley from the moment I made my own Test debut there on 5 June 1952, against Vijay Hazare's Indian tourists. England had a professional captain for the first time in Len Hutton and I was on leave from the RAF at Hemswell, between Lincoln and Gainsborough. My pals who couldn't get to the Test settled down in front of the TV (the transmissions then just creeping up the country into the Midlands) to watch young Trueman in his first Test match and the damned telly broke down. They were a bit sick down in Hemswell. It was on the third day that my memorable moment arrived and the Headingley scoreboard read: India 0–4. Four wickets fell in the first fourteen balls of the Indians' second innings and when Hazare played and missed, coming in at No. 6, I was deprived of a hat trick in my first Test by nothing more than a cat's whisker.

Headingley in
1926 and 1983

That apart, I used to get weekend leave from the RAF to play as professional for the Leeds Cricket Club for £10 a match, which was a bit more than I got for a week's duty as a serviceman, though I would not in all conscience claim that my Air Force duties were especially onerous. It was here that I met two great men of Rugby League, Arthur Clues, the Australian second-row forward, and Bert Cook, the New Zealand fullback, and through them I conceived an affection for the game which has remained with me.

Headingley is not the loveliest of grounds and it is not the best equipped, but it has a north-country character of its own, a very clearly defined personality. The line of tall, elegant trees (debates on their origins and their species take place in our BBC commentary box during every Test there) which stand sentinel along the northeastern perimeter are as well known a landmark as the gasholder at the Oval

and a good deal more attractive. The red-brick pavilion still stands, now divided into many uses, as a reminder of the more gracious days of cricket. The severe, workaday lines of the rugby football stand were at last relieved in 1983 by the opening of the streamlined Sir Leonard Hutton Bar for Yorkshire members. And to the west there are the wide open spaces of the 'popular' side terraces from where many a pungent comment on the day's activities is bellowed across the green acres. The slope, from northwest to southeast, is pronounced and the wicket is on something of a plateau so that for fast bowlers in particular a familiarity with the terrain brings an advantage in establishing rhythm of approach. On Test match days, as with Roses matches of yesteryear, the atmosphere in the ground is vibrant. Somehow, everyone feels a part of the game and, indeed, everyone is.

There will always be a soft spot in my heart for Bramall Lane, Sheffield, because it was there that I took my first steps along the road to first-class cricket. It was here that I came under the wing of Cyril Turner, a great friend and teacher, who had been a Yorkshire all-rounder before the war and was now responsible for developing the young talent of South Yorkshire and directing it towards the county side.

As Headingley is owned by a Rugby League club, Bramall Lane belonged to the Sheffield United Football Club, which has known great days in the Football League. The club has featured many great foot-ballers, of course, but perhaps its greatest days are highlighted by the happy philosophy of Sheffield members: 'Hutton all summer and Hagan all winter.' I shall be eternally grateful to the football club for waiting until after my retirement in 1968 before deciding that the development of the ground as a football stadium was more important than retaining the century-old tradition of cricket there in summer. It enabled me to enjoy the greatest day of my life - leading Yorkshire to victory over the Australian tourists.

I suppose it can be argued that the ground was neither one thing nor another, the footballers playing with one touchline bordering on the open space of the cricket area and bowlers and fieldsmen having to move about the lusher grass of the football area when their turn came round in summer. But somehow this never mattered to players (to cricketers at any rate) and it never seemed to matter to spectators. They had grown up with both games played in these circumstances and they simply accepted them. True, Bob Platt, Mick Cowan and Tony Nicholson, to name but three of my opening partners, used to have something to say about continually having to run up to the wicket through the football grass, but we all had our moans about one aspect or another of every ground.

The fact remains that to these unique characteristics of topography, Bramall Lane could add one of the most colourful and knowledgeable crowds anywhere in the world. They addressed all Yorkshire players by their first names, bellowing across a hundred yards of sward as though engaging in intimate personal conversation. I am convinced this was done not so much out of any presumptuous familiarity as from an intimacy with the game in all its nuances which extended to its practitioners. The opposition were not accorded the same courtesies and the crowd was quick to seize on any name which might lend point to their collective or individual wit. Thus, Bernie Constable of Surrey, playing resolutely up and down the line with one eye on the clock as it approached 6.30, was informed: 'Constable – you'll be back on't beat tomorrow.' The pun was as popular as the double entendre. Winston Place, as representative of the mortal enemy (and nowhere was the Roses rivalry more fervently expressed than Bramall Lane), was exhorted to 'get back to t'fish shop'. And even remarks intended to be sympathetic were invariably barbed. Mick Cowan, who was in the middle of a bad trot with his bowling, found himself called upon to field for Northamptonshire when the visiting team ran out of substitutes and had the supreme misfortune to drop Closey when he hooked Frank Tyson. 'Well done, Mick lad,' came the commiseration from the terraces, 'tha's not takken a wicket but tha's saved one.'

The greatest of cricket reporters, Sir Neville Cardus, seems to have had a love–hate relationship with Bramall Lane. His partisanship in Roses matches is forgiveable (in retrospect, at least) for the sublime quality of his prose and the brilliance of his observation. He was the first to suggest (light-heartedly, of course) that the steelmasters of Sheffield stoked up their furnaces when Lancashire were batting to impair the quality of the light! And I've seen the suggestion repeated in recent times at Bradford when an allotment holder decided to burn some rubbish. The sincerest form of flattery? But Cardus was, of course, unique, and bless the *Guardian* for agreeing to the publication in book form in 1982 of his Roses match reports in the years between the wars. It gives us the opportunity once more to savour the great literature of cricket: 'Once again comes the ancient feud and the scene this time is the bleak wastes of Bramall Lane, Sheffield, a place where the sun seems to shine only as it shines on a withered heath, putting all things in an inimical light.' That was in 1922. Three years later Cardus was not only re-emphasizing that particular point but giving an impression of that particular crowd which sums it up beautifully: The ancient feud broke out again on Saturday, this time in the cockpit of Bramall Lane. Low clouds and dim light suited the play; the smoke that hung here and there over the field might well have come out of the slow, smouldering fires of the match. A crowd of 25,000 watched the cricket – a crowd which, true to Sheffield, was full of character. It was an honest multitude, unashamedly partisan and yet not blind to merit in the enemy's ranks. Makepeace was cursed by thousands between noon and evening on Saturday, cursed for his stubbornness in the teeth of Yorkshire's attack; but even while passionate men from Sheffield wished him in the bottomless pit, they vowed in the next breath that "E's a reight plucky little owd —— is Makepeace.' The Sheffield crowd is constantly getting into the bad books of the game.

Nonetheless, I confess I would not have it lose its own true heart, temper and vocabulary. It is better that we should have authentic character in this world of the North, rather than those good manners which make for dullness of spirit.

That was Bramall Lane as I knew it, described in the words of a master craftsman.

Bradford's ground at Park Avenue is homely and lovable rather than majestic and historic. It was also, for almost the whole of my playing career, a very happy hunting ground indeed. It could rain all day Saturday (as it frequently did) and we would still get a result on Monday and Tuesday. The pitch changed character with a suddenness that was unaccountable, giving us dramatic and breathlessly entertaining cricket. This again was a ground combining cricket with association football but, unlike Bramall Lane, soccer languished and finally died here. When the football stand was finally pulled down at the beginning of the 1980s, a view of Bradford, hitherto unseen, was suddenly opened up. A little of the character of the ground went with the stand because hitting a six into the weed-strewn reaches of the football field no longer gave aesthetic pleasure to the striker or dramatic emphasis to the watcher. Here there is a 'popular' side bordering Horton Park where the wiseacres have offered their advice and comment from time immemorial. Here it was that Norman Horner, after a two-match career with his native county in 1950, played in the colours of Warwickshire on his first return to Park Avenue and fielded on the boundary. A shot climbed high from the bat towards Norman as the umpire's cry of 'No ball' echoed round the field, unheeded as it happened by two venerable observers close to its point of arrival. Norman let it bounce in front of him and threw back to the wicketkeeper as the two watched in mystified silence. Finally, one turned to the other and asked, aghast, 'Did tha see that?' 'Ah did.' 'What's tha mak on it?' Long deliberate pause for reflection, then, 'Well it *were* our Norman. Ah suppose blood's thicker na watter.'

At Park Avenue it was, in the days before the First World War, that Alonso Drake bowled to Jack Hobbs and was struck for 6 into the face of the football-stand clock with such force that the hands stuck at three o'clock. Ruefully the bowler lamented to his team-mates, 'Ah wish 'e'd knock it to 'arf past six.'

I had my enjoyable moments at Park Avenue, like the reaction to my sending a middle stump rocketing out of the ground against Derbyshire – applause which, said Alan Revill, the non-striker, was as if I'd scored the winning goal at Wembley. And I've had a different reception, too, like the time I had to stay at one end until close of play on a Saturday evening. Carefully I put a straight bat to ball after ball until one exasperated spectator yelled at me, 'Are you cummin' back 'ere on Monday, Trueman, 'cos if you are, *Ah'm* not?'

The pavilion end was my beat at Park Avenue, the end where the high wall which protects county members from straight drives of low altitude provides the backdrop for the fast bowler's approach. Although the football end is not noticeably upward-sloping (and many fast bowlers opt for it these days) we rated bowling there in my day as the equivalent of running up the cellar steps with a barrel of beer on the back. Some of my partners have sworn that bowling from the football end took five years off their lives. It was at Park Avenue in 1962 that Hampshire, needing 163 to win, reached 156 for 5 – and lost by 5 runs. It was here that George Tribe took 16 Yorkshire wickets for Northamptonshire and ended on the losing side. It was here that Dickie Bird hit 180 not out for Yorkshire against Glamorgan and was dropped for the next game. Park Avenue celebrated a hundred years of cricket in 1981 and I hope it gets another century.

Like Headingley, the Fartown ground at Huddersfield has long been shared with Rugby League, a game which was played brilliantly there before the war and again in the 1950s. Sadly, rugby has had no success for a long time and cricket, in recent years, has been limited to one-day matches, but Fartown certainly has its place in Yorkshire's cricket story. The one criticism I would level against those who first developed the ground is that they designed the pavilion for midgets. If a side with six big chaps wanted to change there, the other five would have to stand outside! But it was the scene of a breath-stopping tie in 1954 when Johnny Wardle ran out Leicestershire's last man, Terry Spencer, with the scores level. And off his own bowling, as well.

But perhaps the game which has lived longest in Yorkshire memories of Fartown was the county championship match against Essex in 1935, when Yorkshire were bowled out, quite inexplicably, for 31. Yorkshire were on their way to their eighteenth championship and their fourth in five years. Just three years earlier they had run up 555 for 1 declared (Herbert Sutcliffe and Percy Holmes) against Essex, who were not unreasonably regarded as something of a chopping block. The story goes that one member, arriving a little late, glanced up at the scoreboard which read 29-9 and inquired, 'Who's bowling 'em out – Bowes?' 'No,' came the reply from a gloomy and incredulous watcher who had been there from the start, 'he's *batting.*'

That does not stand as Yorkshire's lowest championship score, however. That particular little jewel is reserved for a team of which I was a member and provides an outstanding memory of the Acklam Park ground, at Middlesbrough. It has been a good ground for me, and for Yorkshire generally, since we first started playing there in 1956. But the events of the morning of 20 May 1965 are so difficult to explain that most of us who figured in the game have to laugh. It's a bit of an embarrassed laugh, true, but no one can really account for what happened. Frets from the North Sea kept descending upon the ground and livening up the wicket and it seemed, throughout, that while Hampshire played and missed a lot, we got nicks and the catches stuck. The conditions at the start were just right for a bowler like Derek Shackleton who, from a gentle medium pace, always swung the ball and moved it off the seam as well. A dangerous bowler when conditions were right was Shack. Every batsman in the game respected him; some feared him, but top-class players reckoned they could cope if all things were equal. At Acklam Park, in May 1965, they were *not* equal. 'Butch' White, who had genuine pace, was taken out of the attack after 7 overs and the less fiery Bob Cottam was brought in to partner Shack. We were 47 for 7 when I went in and the first gentle delivery from Shack hit me on the shoulder! So there was only one thing to do – swing the bat. And swing I did to take three sixes in one over from him and score 55 out of our total of 121. Hampshire got a first-innings lead of 3 and we went in again on the second morning. This time the top scorer was Don Wilson, at No. 10, with 7 not out, and five batsmen finished with ducks. Our total was 23. We had lost by 10 wickets by one o'clock on the second day.

There are happier personal memories of the game against Frankie Worrell's West Indian tourists in May 1963, when we beat a side whose batsmen included Worrell, Sobers, Kanhai, Nurse, Butcher and Solomon, by 111 runs before lunch on the third day. I had 10 wickets for 83 in the match and recall it with considerably more affection than John Hampshire, who was hit by Charlie Griffith on the head and carries the memory of the blow, if not the scar, to this day, and Doug Padgett, who was felled by Griffith in the second innings.

At Acklam Park, cricket shares the ground with Middlesbrough Rugby Football Club which has produced many fine players for Yorkshire Rugby Union. It has a slope from the rugby end which is not sufficiently steep to spoil a bowler's rhythm but pronounced enough to have a psychological effect upon any batsman with a dislike of really fast bowling when he stands at the bottom end. I had an enjoyable morning there against Warwickshire in 1967 with figures that read 5–5–0–3; I was a bit quick that day. Neil Abberley was an interested bystander at the top-end wicket and he stayed there for so long without getting to strike at the other that the umpire, George Pope, inquired conversationally, 'Don't you fancy it down there, then?' Neil's reply was something in the nature of 'Are you kidding?' and he played quietly on against the bowling of Richard Hutton, operating up the slope. Now, in case this seems to be getting a bit immodest, let me say it is Don Mosey's story. He was broadcasting from a point at the bottom end of the ground and watching me run in from the top. When Abberley eventually played a ball from Hutton in the air towards mid-wicket, he cantered resignedly down the pitch in the certain knowledge that he was going to be caught out. Of all people, Don Wilson put the catch down and over the effects microphone (which picks up the sounds of the crowd and the cricket) came an agonized cry of 'Oh shit!' The single took Neil to 'my' end and, next over, c Hutton, b Trueman, thank you very much. However, that missed catch apart, Don Wilson will remember the game with pleasure because he took over from Hutton at the bottom end and returned 6 for 31, followed by 7 for 21 to give him career-best match figures. And as he had already got the first of his three hat tricks for Yorkshire at Acklam Park in 1959, his memories of the ground will be rather pleasant, too, I imagine.

St George's Road, Harrogate, is the smallest of the Yorkshire grounds and one of the most pleasant. It is ideally suited to the Festival atmosphere and I have always thought how marvellous it is to see the Festival developing there in recent years, while almost all the traditional end-of-season seaside gatherings have gone. Scarborough is the only real exception and that is not quite what it used to be. The people at Harrogate are different, too, 'involved' in their cricket in quite a different way from those at Leeds, Bradford and Sheffield. We had to beat Glamorgan there in 1962 to win the championship and the supporters drove up and turned on their car headlights so that they could work through the night before the game, helping the groundsman to get the pitch ready after a lot of rain. They were rewarded with a much interrupted, low-scoring game which ended in breathless excitement on the third day with a 7-wicket win for Yorkshire to send Vic Wilson into retirement. The highest score in the game was 67, made by Ken Taylor, who was, nevertheless, the third victim in a rather strange hat trick for Jeff Jones of Glamorgan. He bowled only fifteen deliveries in our first innings and only twelve in the second, but the last two of that first stint dismissed Don Wilson and Mel Ryan and, when Yorkshire batted again, needing 66 to win, he bowled Ken Taylor with his first delivery.

But Harrogate, for most Yorkshire cricket lovers, is synonymous with the name of Maurice Leyland, one of our greatest players ever and most lovable of personalities. He had a quiet humour all his own; he was a master of the understatement, reflecting his own modesty; he could produce the perfect throwaway line, as at Melbourne in the Third Test of England's 1936-37 tour. England in their second innings had to score 668 to win and were not making much progress in this direction when R.W.V. Robins joined Maurice as the No. 8 batsman. He had not scored in the first innings and immediately set out to remedy this by calling for ones and twos at breakneck speed. In fact with fifteen minutes of the penultimate day to go, he just about lapped Leyland going for a second; this caused Maurice to cast a whimsical eye at the scoreboard and administer the smiling admonition, 'Steady on, Robbie. I don't think we'll get 'em all tonight.' The book shows that England finished 365 runs short of the impossible target, but M. Leyland was still there, 111 not out.

Maurice's Test debut was against the West Indies at Lord's, in 1928, and in his only innings (because England won by an innings and 71 runs) he joined that distinguished band of great players who have failed to trouble the scorers on such an occasion. He was comprehensively bowled by one H. C. Griffith who knocked two stumps clean out of the ground. Before departing for the dressing-room, Maurice took out the remaining stump and laid it reverently beside the other two. His captain, Percy Chapman, was not amused and demanded an explanation for the eccentric gesture. 'I thought it looked a bit lonely standing there all by itself,' replied Leyland and immediately established himself as one of the game's endearingly whimsical characters. He had the great gift of inspiring affection in all who knew him, not only in his playing days but as a Yorkshire coach handling postwar generations of players.

My abiding memories of the Circle Ground, Hull, are associated with water. It always seems cold and windswept at the best of times (and if the wind was out of the southeast it invariably wafted with it a pointed reminder of the fish docks in my day), but I seem to remember the ground for rain, rain and more rain. In 1958, Ronnie Burnet and Reg Simpson surveyed a ground under four feet of water. Yorkshire and Nottinghamshire might have arranged a swimming gala, but there was not the slightest chance of playing a game of cricket there, even two days later. They went off to ring Lord's about an immediate cancellation and were told there was no precedent for abandoning a match on the first day. So while the rest of us went home, the two captains booked into an hotel for the night so that they could return solemnly next morning and formally call off the fixture.

I recall a young left-arm spinner, a bit quicker through the air than most, arriving in Hull for the first time with the Kent team. His name was Derek Underwood. And I remember one or two personal duels with my old mate, and great adversary, Bill Alley there. It was at the Circle Ground that we witnessed one of the great kamikaze operations of our suicidal captain, D. B. Close, as we raced against the clock to bowl out Surrey. Younis Ahmed struck a ball from Don Wilson violently against the shin of Closey, standing (as usual, whether the wicket was doing anything or not) about six inches from the bat. We could see the blood pouring down into Closey's sock and Wilson stood aghast, unable to bowl, until the captain swung round and snarled at him, 'What are you waiting for? We've only got twenty minutes left to get these buggers out.' We got them out.

And so to Scarborough, where the Festival was Mecca for so many supporters of the game – and for one or two players, too, who looked to complete their 'double' of 1000 runs and 100 wickets in a season in those closing days of the summer. It was a great social cricket occasion, the games played with something less than the grim intensity of county championship matches and the evenings enlivened by a round of parties. The crowds had their favourites and, going back to prewar days, the greatest of them all was Patsy Hendren, that much-loved Middlesex batsman who is a cricketing legend more than twenty years after his death and will remain so for all time – more than 57,000 first-class runs and 755 catches ... 3311 runs in the 1928 season ... two separate hundreds in a match four times – he was the darling of the Festival crowds. On the final day of his last appearance at Scarborough, the spectators crowded outside the pavilion to give him a last farewell and Patsy wept. Like most Festivals, Scarborough's lost some of its glory when players' sentimental attachment to it began to wane in the face of financial rewards to be gained elsewhere but, I am proud and happy to say, Yorkshire flatly refused to let it die as others had done. With the help of sponsorship, and under the presidency of our 'Test Match

Special' colleague Brian Johnston, a revival began in the 1980s and long may it continue.

Apart from the Festival in the early days of September, the North Marine Road ground has also traditionally staged a county match in the height of the holiday season when thousands of holidaymakers have flocked to the resort during the traditional 'feast' weeks in the industrial areas of the county, and it was there in 1955 that I came within a hairsbreadth of a double hat-trick which must have gone down in the records as unique. In the first innings, against Nottinghamshire, I had Ron Giles c Binks when he was 17, Freddie Stocks c Wilson first ball, and Cyril Poole c Lowson, also first ball. Hat-trick. In the second innings I bowled Giles when he had reached 30. In came Stocks on a king pair and bagged 'em, c Illingworth. So who should come to the wicket, also on a king pair, but Cyril Poole? I bowled, the ball hit his pad, I screamed an appeal for what would have been a hat-trick in each innings of the same game with three identical victims in the same order. Paddy Corrall, the umpire, turned it down and I am certain to this day that he was wrong. Who is to say that my enthusiasm carried me away at the thought of that unique feat? And by the same token, who is to say that Paddy wasn't wrong for once? What might have been lingers in my mind to this day, and it always will. Did Paddy know just what was at stake? If so, he was in a roughly parallel situation to that confronting that great umpiring character, Alec Skelding, when he was called upon to adjudicate in the case of the first all-lbw hat-trick of all time by Horace Fisher, for Yorkshire against Somerset at Sheffield, in 1932. But Alec was a whimsical character with a strong sense of the dramatic. Folklore hands down to us the report that the first appeal brought a formal reply of 'That's out' and a simple, symbolic raising of the finger. The second evoked, 'And *that's out*.' But the third ... what was there to say? Alec, on the threshold of history, felt something much more than a straightforward response was called for. He drew a deep breath, raised his eyes to the heavens and delivered himself of the historic judgement, 'As God is my judge, that's out as well.' Ah well. What a pity Paddy Corrall, a wonderful personality behind the stumps for Leicestershire, had not the same theatrical flair twenty-three years later.

Scarborough has seen all the great personalities of the game, all the great touring sides, Gents *v.* Players, the marvellous eccentrics and benefactors of the game who hired their mercenaries for the end-of-season fireworks. It has seen mighty hitting like the straight six of Cec Pepper which cleared the boarding houses – sorry, private hotels – at the seaward end of the ground and landed in Trafalgar Square. It has seen annual gatherings of friends who came together just once a year for t'Festival and departed swearing undying brotherhood, to meet again in a year's time. And it has seen the greatest emphasis of all on the axiom that, in the last analysis, cricket is meant to be fun. It is as if Yorkshiremen, at the end of a season in which they have been locked for four months in the decidedly grim business of competitive cricket – from their county side down to the humblest of leagues – have come together to let their hair down at last. Only for a day or two, you understand.

Scarborough Festival, 1928. MCC – Macaulay, Leyland, Geary, Chapman, Hammond, Duckworth, Tyldesley, Sutcliffe, Hobbs, Hendrew, Tate

Rugby League

Rugby League is a game which was conceived and born in the north; it is played at professional level almost exclusively in the north and, as befits a contest so utterly northern in character, it came into existence because of a row with them fancy fellers down south. And while we cannot claim it exclusively as a Yorkshire game, it was certainly founded here and its headquarters have always been here. It was in the George Hotel, Huddersfield, that Rugby League started life on Thursday, 29 August 1895, and the circumstances which created it have not, when you come to think about it, changed all that much over the years. The game of Rugby Union then, as now, was played right across the whole spectrum of society – but some parts of it were more equal than others. In the north it was (as it is now) generally believed that southern clubs were made up of more affluent members, men who didn't have to work too hard for a living and were substantially better paid. In the north (where they still tend to believe that everyone living south of Birmingham is a banker, a stockbroker, an accountant or a lawyer), rugby was played by working-class men from working-class homes, side by side with teams of grammar school old boys and university graduates. And those working men – from textile or engineering factories, or from the mines – worked a hard, five-and-a-half-day week of long shifts for an average wage of 26s (£1.30) a week. They quite simply could not afford to lose their pay for a shift on Saturday morning when they were required to travel to an away fixture. But the very nature of such men prevented them from giving up the game when it came to a choice between work or play. They loved their sport; they played it with immense enthusiasm and a tremendous sense of rivalry. And many employers, equally enthusiastic, were (there can be little doubt) willing to give a bit of a helping hand, when it was required, to star players. Thus, certain natural suspicions grew in the minds of southern clubs and administrators that the purity of rugby as an amateur sport was being tainted by 'broken time' payments to some players in the north.

Allegations were flung and denied; the row simmered for several years, just below boiling point. Much, I think, of north–south rivalry in sport, where there is more than a touch of bitterness, can be traced to this period and the breach that followed. It was the northern clubs which finally took the initiative and broke away from the Rugby Football Union, in 1895, as the Northern Union. It operated games on a competitive basis with Senior Leagues in both Yorkshire and Lancashire. In its second season of existence, the Northern Union introduced a knockout competition for the Challenge Cup and the first final, on 1 May 1897, was watched by 13,490 spectators who paid £624 to see Batley beat St Helens by 10 points to 3 at the splendid new stadium built at Headingley by the Leeds club. The Challenge Cup that year, and those that followed, saw many stirring encounters between the best clubs of Yorkshire and Lancashire, which otherwise did not meet each other with any regularity, and gradually the clamour grew for a Super League of the top sides from each county. This, not unnaturally, caused dismay amongst the less successful clubs, which relied on fixtures with more glamorous sides for their best gates – they still do, eighty or ninety years later – but the proposal to form a Northern Rugby League, composed of the twelve best clubs, was accepted by a meeting, again in Huddersfield, in 1901. In the 1902–3 season there were now two divisions of the Northern Rugby League, each consisting of eighteen clubs with a two-up, two-down promotion and relegation system, but it was disastrous for the smaller clubs in Division Two. Some went to the wall and after three years the League reverted to one division of thirty-one clubs, with each club compiling its own fixture list, much as Rugby Union clubs had always done *without* a formal competition for any championship. The Leigh club topped the table and were rewarded with a contemptuous sneer for allegedly rigging their fixtures to include all the weaker sides! This resulted in a play-off being arranged for the top four clubs on a knockout basis and that formula, with certain extensions and refinements, is still used today.

From the first, the Northern Union placed strong emphasis on the more attractive elements in the game. If they were going to be professional, then they needed income and to get that they had to draw in crowds, as Association Football did. Spectators seemed to want the game to flow; they wanted strong, fast running and expert passing of the ball. Mauling in the mud was all right for the chaps who played

in front of two men and a dog for the sheer love of mauling in the mud, but the Northern Rugby League was going to be dedicated to more attractive stuff than that. In 1906 the step was taken that separated the game utterly from Union – the number of players in a side was reduced from fifteen to thirteen. Which two positions to eliminate? That was the problem. But, logically at that time, the League decided to dispense with the wing forwards, arguing no doubt that the role of those two gentlemen was (a) to block the scrum half; (b) to bury the stand-off half; (c) generally to prevent the ball reaching the fleeter members of the side by any means at their disposal. In short, their job was to spoil. So out they went and for the next sixty or seventy years League was indeed a much more fluent, spectacular and entertaining game to watch.

I find it a touch ironical that the wing forwards, retained by Union, are today a major factor in *creating* attractive rugby, which is, of course, technically a very much more advanced game than it was in

A game for MEN. The 1982 Challenge Cup final replay, Hull *v.* Widnes, at Elland Road, Leeds

1906. And by adopting a rule change from League just a few years ago, Union took a major step forward in opening up *its* game. By eliminating kicking direct to touch in the middle of the field (between the two 25-yard lines, or 22 metres, if you want to be metric), Union followed League in creating running, rather than kicking, fullbacks and provided a platform for a game in which there was more emphasis on open, handling rugby. Perhaps the time has come for League now to take a tip from Union by tidying up and disciplining the scrummaging which, for most of the time, is a travesty.

Nevertheless, it is a game for MEN, and I really mean those capitals. The 1982 Challenge Cup final replay between Hull and Widnes was played on the soccer ground at Elland Road, Leeds, and for sheer, total commitment it must rank as one of the great finals. The few fans who were normally soccer spectators watched in something like awe and I heard one say to another, 'I've seen more effort in five minutes than I see from Leeds United in a whole season.' Then came the

Australian tourists in the autumn of 1982 to add yet another dimension to the game. For speed, and sheer physical strength and fitness, no one in this country had ever seen anything like it.

Why, then, has the game of Rugby League never caught on in a real sense outside Yorkshire, Lancashire and Cumbria; even Workington, Whitehaven and Carlisle were, to varying degrees, latecomers? It was tried in South Wales in 1907 with clubs at Merthyr Tydfil and Ebbw Vale; the following year Aberdare, Barry, Mid-Rhondda and Treherbert joined, but the venture did not survive even until the outbreak of war in 1914. True, these were esentially working-class communities with great sporting traditions, but Rugby Union has a hold on the Welsh heart which nothing will ever break – not in the Harlequins, Wasps, Rosslyn Park tradition of devotion to the code, or even that of Coventry and Northampton. Rugby Union in Wales owes nothing to the old-boy network but everything to the passion of national pride. Another attempt was made to establish League in the valleys shortly after the Second World War but again it soon foundered (perhaps to the relief of northern fans who had a hell of a time trying to say 'We're playing Ystradgynlais next week'). More recently it has been tried once again, at Cardiff, but this is partly in the nature of an economic move – using a soccer ground which would otherwise be empty every other week while rates and other overheads have still to be paid. A similar adventure at Fulham was started with a certain degree of success, and at Carlisle, where they fairly quickly ran into trouble. Between the wars it was tried, without gaining any hold on public affection, in London (Acton and Willesden, Streatham and Mitcham) and in Newcastle-upon-Tyne – perhaps the most rabid soccer area in the country at that time!

No, it never really developed as a game or exercised an appeal to a wider public until after the Second World War. Until then it was just a quaint northern ritual observed by those quaint northern peasants. I'm sure it was regarded in Maidenhead and Bognor Regis and Cheltenham and Bournemouth as a twentieth-century re-enactment of some tribal rite from the Dark Ages. It got no coverage in the London-printed editions of national newspapers except once a year when the Challenge Cup final took the wild northerners to town to let blood at Wembley Stadium, where the final was first staged in 1929 (Wigan 13, Dewsbury 2, with 41,500 people paying £5614). Even then it was usually a patronizing piece written more with condescension than with knowledge of the game, but no one could ever say there was hooliganism or crowd misbehaviour. Rugby League fans have always been and still are fanatically proud of standards of conduct which are fit to set

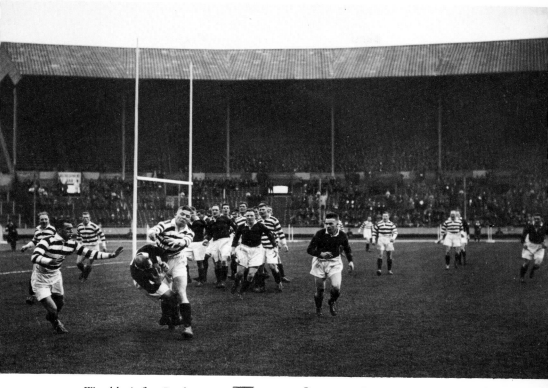

Wembley's first Rugby
League Cup final, Wigan
v. Dewsbury, 1929

before a Queen or a Princess or a Prime Minister who accepts an invitation to be a guest at the final. London hoteliers and even the hard-to-please cabbies will tell you they look forward to that modern Rising of the North. The League fans are not afraid to spend their brass without feeling it necessary to kick in the front door.

But the game as such failed to spread around the country, I think, for at least a couple of reasons. Because national newspapers in the south ignored it for fifty-one weeks a year, a very large percentage of the country's population knew nothing at all about the game. And this was a two-edged sword because the best of northern writers tended to drift to London. The game has never had a Brian Glanville or a Brian Moore or a Hugh McIlvanney to write about it and to give it the literary dignity they have given to Association Football. It has always had a quiet honesty and integrity of its own but it is still, nearly ninety years after its inception, written about within a limited framework of clichés. For example, very rarely do you find a forward pass described simply as a forward pass – it has to be *palpably* forward. Rarely is a long kick to touch simply that – it is a *raking* kick. Around twenty such phrases form the basic description for most games and this goes to explain the oddity of David Oxley, the secretary of the Rugby Football League, who is an MA (Cantab.) in English, summarizing during a TV commentary in phraseology reminiscent of the Crowthers of Bankdam. This will not, I hope, be taken as gratuitously offensive to David, who is a charming and engaging chap. Together with David Howes, his publicity officer, he has done an immense amount in the last decade to improve the image of the game. But the prose in which any game is described, verbally or in print, has not changed much in the twentieth century. Perhaps it adds, somehow, to the appeal of the game.

Another reason why Rugby League has not the widespread appeal of soccer is that the players are part-timers who thus are always somebody's next-door neighbour in a way that soccer players are not. Not for the RL man the detached villa in Collingham, Linton or Harrogate, with a half acre of land. His home is more likely to be in a terrace of miners' cottages in Castleford or Leigh. There is a story of a hooker from Featherstone, thirty years ago, who was transferred from his club in the little mining town to the wealthy Leeds club and given a club house (a rare luxury in RL circles). Hearing a dressing-room conversation in which one of his new team-mates – a big Australian who used to do a bit of all-in wrestling – was complaining that he was losing engagements because he couldn't get a telephone installed, the hooker took him on one side and said, 'Hey, Mac. I've got one of them things in my new house. I don't know owt about it so if it's any use to thee, come ower and tak it.'

George Philpot was a referee in the fifties who worked at a large engineering works in Leeds. One Saturday he felt obliged to send off the Featherstone Rovers' loose forward and then face with some trepidation his return to work the following Monday morning where he would meet his foreman – the Featherstone Rovers' loose forward!

These are stories I find delightful sporting folklore but they do not help to create a mystique surrounding RL players such as the soccer blokes enjoy. *They* are rarely *anybody*'s next-door neighbour; certainly if any of them had a foreman, he would be a very impoverished foreman by comparison. But there *is* a warmth, a homeliness about the game which is infectiously endearing. There are the hard men, there are the head-hunters, and everybody knows them. But the paramount sentiment amongst players is, I think, one of mutual respect. If a 'softie' somehow strays into the game, it shows in about thirty seconds flat. There is an immediate mistrust of any Union player who turns professional for a big fee and he is watched with the keenest critical attention until he has proved himself. David Watkins, a talented Welsh international stand-off half, was reported to have received the astronomical figure in the 1960s of £13,000 to 'come north' to Rugby League. In his first game he was an obvious target for the opposition and he was hit hard and floored time and time again. He recalls with a grim smile dragging himself wearily to his feet for the umpteenth time as one of his own supporters bellowed the advice, 'Never mind, Watkins. 'it 'im with yer wallet.' Yes, it's a hard life, but even in the grimmest moment will come one of those flashes of light relief.

Oldham were playing Hull in a vitally important cup tie and, with a good team in the 1960s, one of their most potent weapons was the goal-kicking boot of Bernard Ganley – 200 a season he used to belt over the crossbar. Now Bernard was an extremely handsome chap, film-star profile and all, and would never have claimed that tackling was the main strength of his game. The team accepted this and as long as Bernard was popping over the points they were content to arrange their game so that a little bit of extra cover was always available. By one of those accidents which sometimes upset the best-laid plans, a huge Hull prop forward, Mick Scott by name, found himself through the cover and lumbering on with only fullback Ganley to beat. It presented a dilemma for both men: Ganley had never in his wildest dreams thought of having to tackle someone of Scott's bulk; Scott was not entirely accustomed to being out in the clear, with no one to pass to, faced with the prospect of running something like 25 yards. Ganley was the first to act. He moved close to Scott and hit him smartly on the point of the jaw with a right hook. It is difficult to imagine which of them was more surprised. Scott, it is said, shook his head in perplexity, rather than agony, and with a deeply pained expression, stopped dead and inquired, 'Why did you do that, Bernard? Whatever came over you?' The referee was Eric Clay, one of the greatest officials and an equally great character. Almost choking with laughter, he rushed up to prevent possible mayhem, gasping, 'Eee, Bernard, lad, you'll have to go, you know. You did it in front of everyone.' And the handsome but apprehensive Ganley, thus free from any possibility of retribution, just managed to resist the temptation to shake 'Sergeant Major' Clay gratefully by the hand. 'Thank God for that. Thanks, Eric.' And with a light-hearted tread, he departed to an early bath.

Which brings us, of course, to Eddie Waring. More than any other individual, he drew attention to the game through his commentaries on BBC Television and created a public which had never existed before. His tortured accent and fractured English made him a cult figure. An Eddie Waring Impersonation Club even sprang up. His style did not make him universally popular in the areas where the game is played. Indeed, a St Helens-based group lobbied Broadcasting House in London, in an effort to have Eddie removed from commentaries. But his supporters within the BBC were staunch and his fan club around the country far outnumbered his critics in the north, even if they felt they had legitimate grounds for complaint. The argument against Eddie was that his extraordinary style stamped the game with a sense of the ridiculous, and there is no doubt that this school of thought had a point. Although they never knew it, these critics had rueful allies amongst succeeding generations of TV directors within the BBC who groaned in despair at Eddie's refusal (or inability) to achieve programme requirements by following instructions. He was always liable to digress into pigeon fancying or the contents of a letter from South Wales as a winger was screaming down the touchline en route to a spectacular try. Indeed, when the BBC, in response to a clamour from devotees of the game, tried to mount a Try of the Month sequence (to match goal-scoring spectaculars in their soccer coverage) they found that a remarkable number of tries had been televised with no identification of the players involved! It drove the purists mad, but it seemed to endear Eddie more and more to a huge band of followers in the southern areas of the country and perhaps it was this, more than anything else, that augmented the anti-Waring faction in the north: he was painting a picture of the north as southern people wanted to see it, a picture of quaint, uncouth, unlettered barbarians performing one of their quaint, barbaric northern rites. But Eddie retired in his own time, with legions of fans in unlikely places. We shall never know how many laughed *with* him and how many *at* him. But there can be no doubt that his commentary was unique.

Media coverage of the game has thrown up many characters, almost all of whom had a devoted allegiance to the club they followed and wrote about week after week. There was dear old Bert Foster who travelled far and wide with York just after the war as Rugby League correspondent of the *Yorkshire Evening Press*. The club was in a sorry state at the time and heavy defeats followed one after the other. It was this, I think, that prompted the paper to put the result (in Bert's Monday review of Saturday's game) at the end of the article, arguing perhaps that the scoreline would deter even the most hardened reader from pursuing the report further. Thus Bert's pieces used loyally to begin, 'York were distinctly unlucky to lose at Wigan on Saturday ...' Then would follow around 800 to 1000 words of eulogy before the stark last line was reached: 'Wigan 54, York 2.'

From the *Yorkshire Evening Post*, Phil Brown sallied forth to chronicle the deeds of the Leeds club and chauvinism landed him in trouble on the windswept heights of Watersheddings, where Oldham play at a considerable altitude. With twenty minutes of a cup tie gone, Phil rattled out his first 500 words for the Saturday 'buff' and handed the copy to a local man to telephone to Leeds. The messenger disappeared and Phil sat back to compose the next stanza, punctuating it with colourful epithets ('He's playing like a blind Girl Guide with wet knickers' was a favourite). But five minutes later his telephonist returned to announce that he flatly refused to send Phil's copy because it was 'too bloody biased'. Patriotism transcended professionalism.

The economics of Rugby League are something to marvel at. Regularly, something like one third of the clubs play before home crowds of fewer than 1000, yet they soldier on, Huyton bravely flying the flag in the most fervent of soccer citadels – Liverpool – and Doncaster, against impossible odds, chalking up defeat after defeat in the sporting wasteland of the Yorkshire–Nottinghamshire border. It is difficult in the extreme to see how clubs like these, and Rochdale Hornets, Bramley, Keighley, can remain in existence. But they do. As one board of directors succeeds another (retreating, impoverished, to lick its collective financial wounds), hope springs anew that *this* time the success which has eluded the club throughout its entire Rugby League history is just over the horizon. At the other end of the scale it is, of course, a different story and there is nothing quite like seeing an entire town shut up shop and set off for Wembley at the beginning of May.

Hull FC, to give it its formal title, provided the success story of the early 1980s, when, just seven years after it faced extinction, it was involved in two successive Challenge Cup finals. Hull's turnover in 1981–82 was £650,000 and, the following season, threequarters of a million. More was paid to the Rugby League in levies on its gate receipts than clubs like Huyton and Doncaster take, in aggregate, in a whole season. As the soccer club, half a mile down the road, teetered on the brink of total insolvency, Hull FC at the Boulevard was building a new stand, bringing over not one, not two, but *three* players from New Zealand, and when a rather tatty French team played in an ill-tempered international match there, relieved only by the most dazzling try imaginable from a winger called Patric Solal, the Hull directors immediately set out to try to bring him into their ranks as well.

Hull had had great sides before, in prewar days, and in the fifties and sixties, but around 1976 they had reached just about rock bottom. Playing strength was, to put it mildly, modest; gates had dwindled and the finances were in a truly terrible state. In fact, one new director put it like this: 'If we had known then what we know now, we would never have taken office.' But they *didn't* know, and they *did* go in and the city, reeling under the burden of its unemployment figures and the murder of its centuries-old fishing fleet, came to sporting life. In the northeast of Hull, the rival club, Kingston Rovers, was already enjoying a degree of success and together they went to Wembley, with families divided and father shouting against son. The rivalry between Hull and Hull KR has always had a unique edge to it. My old mate, Jimmy Binks – that marvellous wicketkeeper who was with Yorkshire from 1955 to 1969 – was a Rovers supporter and the mere mention of Hull was enough to bring a black frown to his face. And so it was throughout the city.

The renaissance of Hull coincided with the retirement from first-class cricket of another pal of mine, Mike Page, who was a very much better batsman for Derbyshire than many people (including himself) gave him credit for, and a damn fine short-leg fieldsman into the bargain. Mike had put his benefit money and his savings into a little business supplying office furniture and equipment. I am delighted to say that it prospered and, as a young man with sporting interests and a bit of brass, Mike was invited to join the Hull board of directors. Seven years later he confessed to enjoying the role even more than he enjoyed his cricket. I found him like a dog with two tails as his office phone rang ceaselessly – half the callers wanting electronic gadgetry, the other half pleading for 1983 Cup final tickets. 'First of all, it's a great game,' he said, 'one I've always loved. Then, it's great to be associated with success on the scale that we've known it here for the past few years. And there's no reason why it should just disappear as it has before, in Hull, and as it does with so many clubs. If the planning and organization are right, success can be a continuing process.'

The club secretary is Mike Dooley, who moved to Rugby League from soccer (he had experience 'in the office' with Leeds United and Sheffield Wednesday). He had been with Hull only a few months but had obviously got caught up in the buoyant feeling of optimism which success brings. 'Directors of Rugby League clubs are so much more interested and knowledgeable than football directors,' he claimed. 'I have been in soccer boardrooms where the directors were watching a rugby match on TV while their own game was going on outside.' And after years of involvement with soccer's fight against football hooliganism, he positively purred with delight at rugby's good-boy image. 'D'you know – we had a letter last week from the landlady of a pub in Lancashire thanking our supporters for their good manners after they had collected the glasses and taken them back to the bar?'

The team manager is Arthur Bunting, a shrewd, witty character, whose laidback, laconic approach to his job disguises a very thorough grasp indeed of what it takes to make a successful club. He was a scrum half with Hull Kingston Rovers, so his crossing of the River Hull to lead the arch-rivals to glory is looked upon with more than usual disfavour in the northeast of the city. This, however, merely intensifies the regard of Hull fans, who look upon the move as 'Arthur getting some sense finally'. He feels that the M62 motorway, which has Hull on one end and Liverpool on the other, should be renamed the Rugby League Way because it links most of the great traditional centres of the game. He believes the game has made a lot of progress in recent years – 'There are a lot more thinkers in it today.' He not only has to get his own players to peak fitness and form, he has to anticipate and counter the tactical thinking of other very shrewd operators in the game. Even after casting a sympathetic eye towards the Doncasters and Huytons, Bunting feels that the game is very much on the way up. 'Just remember how strong it is at amateur level,' he points out. 'BARLA now has member leagues all over the country, not just in the north. There are Rugby sides in universities, and there's a club in Kent trying to get admission to the professional levels of the game. Oh yes. The game is strong – and getting stronger all the time.'

Hull have sixty players on their books – miners, plumbers, car salesmen, a welder, an insurance man, carpet cleaners – and 'six or seven hundred more who want to get in'. It's good to get into this atmosphere of enthusiasm and drive and optimism. It's infectious and you come out of it with a spring in the step. But then you think about what a different atmosphere it must be down at Tatters Field, Doncaster, and the thought is sobering. And then you think again – not trite, platitudinous thoughts like 'If there are winners there have got to be losers', but that there is a sort of heroism in the existence of Doncaster Rugby League Club. It came into the game with nothing but hope and it still has nothing but hope around thirty years later. Generations of players have come and gone, conditioned to accept defeat as virtually inevitable, yet still driving themselves to play their guts out. The Hulls of the world still play it just as hard against Doncaster as against Widnes or St Helens or Wigan or Leeds because amongst players throughout the game there is mutual respect. It's a man's game.

Burnsall, high on the list of England's prettiest villages

Rainbow over the high moors

The majestic ruin of
Bolton Abbey beside
the Wharfe

The Ure at Aysgarth

Cottage beside the infant River Aire, Malham

Crag and Fell country

Fountains Abbey, built in 'a fitting lair only for wild beasts'

Above: Huddersfield Choral Society sing in York Minister. Principals (left to right):
Stuart Burrows, Elizabeth Harwood, Norma Proctor, John Shirley Quirk
Below: Trainer Michael Dickinson with first five horses in the 1983 Cheltenham Gold Cup:
Bregawn, Captain John, Wayward Lad, Silver Buck and Ashley House

Above: Scarborough cricket ground during Festival Week
Below Left: F.S.T. with Don Bradman
Below Right: Barney Colehan, the man who created 'The Good Old Days'

The Railway
Children's personal
line – Worth Valley
Railway

The Nidd at
Knaresborough

Dick Williamson

He was born in an October snowstorm at Queensbury, which is about the highest point reached by the road from Bradford to Halifax. He hated one of his schoolteachers, vowing to catch him some dark night after leaving school – and then discovered that the man was the best friend he ever had. And there you have a neat encapsulation of the character of Dick Williamson, one of the craggiest personalities sporting journalism has produced, a man who has never moved from his native West Yorkshire but is known to football and cricket writers all round the world. It is a safe bet that at some stage of any overseas cricket tour one or other of the press party will start a conversation, 'Do you remember when Williamson . . .?'

His conversation crackles like a machine gun and can be just as wounding if he has been offended. It sweeps over you at something like 250 words a minute, incorporating elegant phrases from journalism of another (and more gracious) age, switching to dramatic figures of speech, punctuated with 'just a minute, just a minute' as his victim essays an ineffectual defence before rushing onwards, engulfing, brushing aside all attempts to counterattack.

To the new and unwary visitor to a Park Avenue or Headingley press box the approach is more subtle. It starts by being elaborately oblique – a monologue, a soliloquy addressed to no one in particular and yet delivered just within earshot of the new boy. 'It passes belief and human understanding . . . no, it can't be correct – and yet can it? I would say it can't, but then who am I to question matters which are as sacred as Holy Writ.'

It is an irresistible line of patter, worthy of the greatest door-to-door salesman who ever lived. Despite his better judgement, despite the warnings of more experienced colleagues, the newcomer is drawn in and the first timorous inquiry is received with courteous, avuncular benevolence. 'Oh hello. Your first visit here? I'm Dick Williamson. I was just musing, thinking aloud really, about ... well, *you* tell *me*: do you think there is the remotest possibility ...?'

A response at this stage is permitted. Then, 'You really think so? Well, *I* don't know but if you really think it's possible.' (Big pause, big intake of breath, final decision, magnanimous offer.) 'Go on. I know I'm throwing money away, but just for the hell of it I am willing to wager a modest crown that you are wrong.'

The new man is hooked – and in the same moment he is lost. Our Richard knows with 101 per cent certainty (as everyone else in the box knows) that the 'modest crown' is as safe as the Bank of England. Everyone else has suffered, and paid, at one time or another and it is a point of honour that no one interrupts the foreplay. Being taken for a crown or two is part of the apprenticeship in cricket journalism on the Yorkshire circuit. There are not many newspapermen unaware that Dick Williamson has the finest collection of football and cricket records in Britain, collected over sixty years, filed and indexed in a system only Dick can understand but which enables him to turn up the answer to the most obscure query in something like half an hour. Since he was a boy in the early days of this century he has cut out and filed away every reference to every milestone in the career of every footballer and cricketer who ever lived. It is a unique collection. Sports editors of national and Sunday newspapers still send to Dick readers' questions which their own reference libraries cannot answer. Before the war, the two major football pools firms, Littlewood's and Vernon's, asked him to supply a service to the readers of the magazines which they published and sent out along with their weekly coupons, and even Dick was a bit startled at the volume of correspondence which piled up. He was beaten just once – by a man who wrote: 'Manchester United and Liverpool met at Old Trafford on Good Friday, 1910 – who played in red that day?'

Dick is a serious, and at times obsessive, collector of data, but there are other journalists who pride themselves upon their knowledge of such matters, even if they do not store up masses of yellowing cuttings in the spare bedroom. And here the wicked Williamson sense of humour has been known to get an airing. Hence – question directed to an extremely serious student of soccer: 'Who played for Burnley on Boxing Day morning and for Blackburn Rovers in the afternoon?' For something like two hours the tortured victim offered various suggestions, interspersed with appeals for supplementary information. 'Before or after the war?' 'Was he a forward or a back?' Finally: 'All right. You've got me this time, Williamson. Who was it?' A smile of utter joy accompanied the answer: 'The Oswaldtwistle Prize Band.' That exchange took place more than twenty years ago and the victim is still scarred by the memory.

Dick Williamson joined the *Telegraph and Argus*, Bradford's evening newspaper, in 'the 1920s' (he is sensitively secretive about his age) as a copy boy and general dogsbody on the advice, and with the help of, the schoolmaster he hated so much in his earliest years. He had a spell in the proof-reading department and then, as 'a lad who was daft on football and cricket', he was taken under the wing of the sports editor. When Dick was twenty-four, a man called Charlie Craven, who reported Yorkshire cricket and Bradford City football for the *Telegraph and Argus*, left the paper and Dick Williamson succeeded him in both roles. That was in the year of the General Strike, 1926, and apart from his wartime service in the Royal Navy he had an unbroken run in both sports until his retirement at the end of the 1966 cricket season – forty years of delight and anguish, of joy and frustration, forty years of press-box laughter and explosions of fury, forty years of rejoicing at the great deeds of Yorkshire cricketers and the more modest achievements of Bradford City footballers, forty years of raging anger at the human frailties of newspaper copytakers less familiar than himself with the spelling of household names.

Transcending even his intolerance of less-than-perfect copytypists is his seething impatience with Post Office telephone operators. Impromptu cabaret acts are staged whenever two or three members of the Cricket Writers' Club are gathered together, with a Williamson tirade as the leitmotif. They are never conducted *sotto voce* and one recent contest in Middlesbrough, which lasted for fifteen minutes, brought a round of applause from spectators within a hundred yards of the press box. The Yorkshire scorer, Ted Lester, mused afterwards: 'We could only hear one end of the conversation, of course, but a recording of that would have given the BBC the funniest quarter-of-an-hour programme in the history of broadcasting.'

When he retired from the staff of the *Telegraph and Argus*, Dick promptly undertook the reporting of Yorkshire cricket for the Exchange Telegraph Agency and later added the Sheffield morning and evening papers to his portfolio. The rasping tones, the gales of laughter, the vicious snarls, all remained part of the sound effects of Yorkshire cricket. The strongest telephone operator quailed as the well-known and equally well-loathed tones announced, 'Transferred charge call to Sheffield ... Come along, miss, come along, I haven't all day, this is a very important call. God give me strength, this is the twentieth century, miss, we've put men on the moon. For the love of

God, can't you get a move on? God give me strength, is this possible?'

The present state of Yorkshire cricket does nothing to bring balm to his soul because Dick Williamson has reported it through the great years of the county's history. It is probably no coincidence that many of his memories centre on George Macaulay, whose volatile temperament and caustic wit must have called out to a kindred spirit. 'I remember him bowling against Sussex at Bradford when they needed about 50 to win. Yorkshire were resigned to defeat and not too unhappy because an early finish, just after lunch, would enable them to catch a 3.30 train instead of making a dreary journey through the night. 'But Mac wasn't concerned with trains; he was interested in bowling and never in all my life before or since have I seen anything to equal his bowling after lunch. It was as if some supernatural power possessed him, as if the Devil himself had taken over. He took 5 for 8, Sussex were beaten by 20 runs, we missed the train and Mac threw himself down on a bench in the dressing-room and was "out" for ten minutes. He was totally emotionally drained by the sheer venom of his own performance. Never have I seen anything like it.'

And again, 'After a game at Lord's, Yorkshire had to travel to Swansea and there was a long delay at Gloucester while the team's coach was uncoupled and attached to another train.

'George was taken short but did his best to obey the instruction about "not while the train is standing in the station". Finally, the delay went on so long that he could wait no longer. This had unfortunate consequences for two railwaymen working underneath on the coupling of the coach. Angrily, one of them climbed onto the platform, stormed into the Yorkshire compartment waving a soiled hand, and demanded to know who was responsible. The ebullient Macaulay pushed forward, announcing without undue modesty that *he* was. "The stationmaster won't have this," protested the aggrieved party. "Well, share it out amongst t'porters then," snarled Macaulay.'

The immortal Wilfred Rhodes still had four years of his career to complete when Dick Williamson became a cricket writer and the Herbert Sutcliffe–Percy Holmes opening partnership had another seven years to run. The photographic memory, which backs up the unique record system to make betting against Williamson a prize mug's game, swung into action: 'First game – Leicestershire at Headingley – Holmes, Sutcliffe, Oldroyd, Kilner, Leyland, Macaulay, Rhodes, Waddington, Dolphin, with Major Lupton as skipper.' Glory be ... he missed one out! Or perhaps Yorkshire only needed ten men to beat Leicestershire in 1926.

Some things, at least, never change in the Yorkshire dressing-room.

'I remember coming back from Sheffield with Wilf Barber who had not yet got his cap and who was in such a state of fear of Wilfred Rhodes that he used to shake in the field at the prospect of a catch coming to him and the wrath that would follow if he dropped it. It was a fear common to younger players who got an occasional chance in the first team, and it so affected Barber that his wife begged him to go back to his job, and to Saturday afternoon cricket, because his life was becoming a misery. But the Old Man retired in 1930 and, fortunately for Yorkshire, the young Barber stuck it out to play for Yorkshire up to the immediate postwar years.'

Rhodes, in contrast to his great contemporary, George Hirst, was a hard man – a magnificent bowler but taciturn as an individual – and the lasting Williamson memory of him takes him to a long time after the great man had retired. 'I was on holiday in Bournemouth and, along with an old friend, Walshaw Glover, we went to Canford Cliff to where Wilfred, now long since blind, lived with his daughter and son-in-law.

'His daughter answered the door, called her father and I asked him, "Aren't you going to ask us in, then?" Thirty-one years after his retirement from cricket, eighty-three years old and blind, the thin, cracked voice exclaimed, "It's Dick Williamson, isn't it?" And I shall never forget the three hours we spent going over his career and the scathing things he had to say about coaching. One remark in particular I remember: "Was there any of us in my day, *any* of us, who needed coaching in any aspect of the game? Of course there wasn't, because if we hadn't been good enough to play for Yorkshire in the first place no amount of coaching would have got us into the side." '

The Williamson admiration for Herbert Sutcliffe is manifest from his opening words: 'You can't say anything wrong about Herbert Sutcliffe. He could not and would not suffer fools gladly and he detested people who presumed upon slight acquaintance. He would, I think, have succeeded in any other profession he might have taken up. He never wasted a minute of his life. And playing memories ... so many of them. That incredible innings at Bradford against Gloucestershire when he out-Hammonded Hammond. Wally got an incredible 100 and Herbert went out and got one in half an hour's less time. That was his hundredth century – an incredible match all down the line. He and his partner, Percy Holmes, were complete opposites' (a reflective Williamson chuckle).

In 1925, Holmes scored 315 not out against Middlesex at Lord's and afterwards told Dick Williamson this story: 'I had been out on a p.u. the night before and I got to the ground praying, "Oh Lord, let the

Major lose the toss and let's have a nice, cool day in the field where my head can clear." ' But Major Lupton *won* the toss and Holmes recalled, 'I never made such a start to any innings in my life. Jack Durston bowled the first over and I was morally out five times. I made contact with one ball and others missed the off stump by a cat's whisker. I did everything wrong that it was possible to do wrong and I didn't get out – it seemed I *couldn't* get out. And after about a quarter of an hour the feeling began to creep over me that this was my day. I could take any possible risk and get away with it. Nothing can prevent me getting a hundred.' He got three of them. A completely honest man, recalls Williamson, offering as supplementary evidence the confession of Holmes that in playing Tich Freeman for fourteen or fifteen years he was completely unable to spot Freeman's wrong 'un.

Dick Williamson's cricketing memories sound something like the reading of a *Debrett's* of the game and they bring him immense pleasure. If they induce a certain lack of patience with less capable but more pretentious practitioners of the modern era, it is an impatience shared by many. For, with a handful of exceptions, the game is not what it used to be in terms of individual ability, or character, or personality.

One section of the Williamson reference library might well be labelled: 'For amusement only'. This consists of cuttings exclusively from the prewar days of the *Hull Daily Mail*. Now Hull receives only rare visitations by first-class cricket sides and the writing on cricket in the paper in the 1930s was not entirely expert. Dick was typing with head down (and one finger employed for this operation, as it has been over the years) and missed a scoring stroke by Sutcliffe. He asked Charlie Craven about the shot he had missed and Craven replied, 'A three.' With dead-pan irony, Dick inquired, 'Was it all-run?' and was gravely assured that it was. That evening, as Dick and Charlie dined together in their hotel, Craven suddenly burst into peals of laughter and, unable to explain why, handed over that evening's *Hull Daily Mail*. There, Sutcliffe's 'all-run' three had been duly recorded for cricketing posterity. A conference took place over that dinner and the corporate decision of Messrs Williamson and Craven was that if a genuine inquiry was put to them by the local cricket correspondent, they would answer it truthfully. But if the *Hull Daily Mail*'s representative preferred to keep his ears pricked for technical or literary assistance, then he would be rewarded in full measure.

The story of the all-run three duly went the rounds and before the next season's game at Hull, Yorkshire played a match in Sheffield. Williamson (observed in close consultation with his fellow-conspirator) was asked, 'What evil plot are you hatching for that poor sod in Hull?' 'Well, what would you like?' was the reply. 'I think I would die happy if I could see in print "a hook past point" but he'll never fall for that.' 'Like to bet?' And a bet was duly struck.

The following day, Yorkshire played Sussex at Hull. Dick bided his time until Jim Langridge was batting against Hedley Verity and a stroke was played past point. Turning to Mr Craven, Mr Williamson offered the clearly audible view that that was the best shot of the day. More than that, it was the best hook past point that he had seen all season. His enthusiasm was unbridled – and infectious. Langridge (Jas)'s hook past point was described with loving detail in that evening's *Hull Daily Mail* and Mr Charles Tadman (the punter in Sheffield) may be assumed to have died happy. More was to follow in those few remaining prewar years, notably Nobby Clark (of Northamptonshire, who for 4 overs was just about the fastest bowler in the world) being credited with bowling a couple of googlies in the first over of a match.

I've seen those cuttings, the yellow of the nearly fifty-year-old newsprint now turning to brown. It would be wrong to say they are the pride of the Williamson collection but they are certainly the ones in greatest demand for viewing.

So, beware, any novice cricket writer venturing into a Yorkshire press box for the first time. Have a care, too, any cricket fan who encounters a sprightly, breezy character with a brown trilby hat at a jaunty angle, who appears to be musing quietly to himself, especially if the monologue goes something like this: 'Impossible. Interesting though ... but obviously impossible. How can anyone venture the impossible like forecasting the score of every batsman in the four innings of a first-class match. No, the odds against it must be astronomical. Astronomical ... and yet – I wonder?' Do not be tempted, because you'll lose. No – on second thoughts, *yield* to temptation and have a bet. It will cost you a bob or two but it will be worth it to learn that particular secret. And to get an insight into the mind of a man who worked out that particular way of making a modest crown or two while simply looking at the scorecard of a prewar Test match – a man whose unique collection of sporting records can conjure up the most incredible series of quiz questions ever devised.

Rumours are creeping around that Dick intends to cut down his journalistic commitments; stories circulate that he is progressively less inclined to suffer fools gladly; it is said that his merry quip and jest (and impossible queries) are heard less frequently these days in the Yorkshire press box. Dick has his special cronies and his pet hates, and a man who has seen the greatness – in playing and writing – that he has seen and who mourns its passing is entitled to his prejudices and his foibles. His pen can drip vitriol and his rhetoric can strip the paint from a door at fifty feet. He has no time for pomposity and less for pretentiousness. He is as rugged and uncompromising as Ilkley Moor in a winter sleetstorm. But if he met anyone in trouble, Dick Williamson would give him the shirt off his back.

Michael Dickinson

At thirty-three, Michael Dickinson had the most successful season of any National Hunt racing trainer in the history of the Turf. He has more than fifty horses in his stables at the foot of Harewood Bank, where the River Wharfe flows alongside his land. He is ambitious, determined, down to earth and yet essentially modest. 'What makes a good trainer? Good horses.' He also has a more than passing interest in cricket, as I discovered when I went to talk horses with him at his stables in August 1983.

F.S.T. When did you decide you wanted to be a trainer?

M.D. When I realized I wasn't going to be a very good jockey and that I wasn't going to be able to ride for ever. I was twenty-two then and I had been on horses and ponies since I was four. My father, Tony Dickinson, trained hunters and point-to-pointers at Gisburn (near the Lancashire border) and, really, I seemed to have been in the saddle since I could first remember. When my father took out a permit to train race horses for my mother and himself, he sent me to Frenchie Nicholson at Cheltenham, who was the best man for turning out young jockeys in the whole country. At seventeen, I rode four winners for my father, but I wasn't going to be in the really top flight and steeplechase jockeys can't go on much after they are thirty, so it was only going to be a short career.

F.S.T. So when did you set up on your own?

M.D. I didn't set up. My parents set me up and I have been here at Harewood for three years.

F.S.T. Now, before we go on to look at the development – the astonishing development in just three years – can we set out the details of that remarkable 1982–83 season?

M.D. We won £350,000 in prize money (winners only) which was a record, breaking our own record which was set up the previous season.

F.S.T.   You say, 'We ...' and 'our' record?

M.D.   Certainly. No one does this sort of thing on his own. It's a team effort by everyone in the stable but most of all by the horses.

F.S.T.   Right, sorry. Carry on, Michael.

M.D.   We won 120 races, breaking the eleven-year-old record of Arthur Stephenson, which was 114. We beat the previous world record for the number of winners in a day – we had twelve on Boxing Day, highlighted by Wayward Lad winning the King George; we had three winners at the Cheltenham Festival, including the 'famous five' – the first five home in the Cheltenham Gold Cup.

F.S.T.   And the famous five ... they were?

M.D.   Winner, Bregawn; second, Captain John; third Wayward Lad; fourth, Silver Buck; fifth, Ashley House.

F.S.T.   Did you expect that to happen – I mean, saddling the first five in a classic steeplechase really is something rather special, isn't it?

M.D.   Yes, it is something special and, no, I didn't expect it to happen.

F.S.T.   So how did you feel?

M.D.   Relieved, more than anything else. We hoped desperately to win the race but certainly not to get all five.

F.S.T.   Relieved? How was that?

M.D.   We had had quite a few training problems with the horses because steeplechasers are very injury-prone – as are top sportsmen. And we had had quite a few problems leading up to the Gold Cup. It was very difficult to get them all to Cheltenham fit and well. Two or three of them had had very interrupted preparations and I was extremely worried that perhaps they should not have been running because they weren't completely fit.

F.S.T.   When you started training here, how many horses did you have?

M.D.   Fifty.

F.S.T.   Really, fifty to start with?

M.D.   Well, my father started training at Gisburn with six horses and the next day we had ten, then we had twenty, then twenty-five, and we had thirty-six when we moved to Harewood, and soon we had fifty horses. Father trained for one year at Harewood with fifty horses, then he retired and handed over to me. So I was very lucky that I stepped into a super yard, already full of good owners and good horses. So, fortunately for me, I started threequarters of the way up the ladder. And, again fortunately, I have managed to keep

Silver Buck leads Night Nurse over the last jump at Kempton Park (King George VI Chase, 1980)

> going. If I hadn't, there would have been plenty of people on the touchline to say, 'Oh, he isn't as good as his dad.'

F.S.T.   Isn't that an eternal problem in sport? But at the same time, think how good it is when someone says, 'Thy lad's a lot better than thee.' Good for the parent, that is.

M.D.   Yes, I suppose that's right. But it was a worry. And it was a great relief to me when Silver Buck won the King George VI Steeplechase at Kempton Park, which was the first big race that I had won in my first season. That, I suppose, gave me more pleasure than any other big race winner because it was my first. I said to myself, 'Well, I've won a King George now so, whatever else I do, they can't say I was a *complete* failure.'

F.S.T.   What makes a good trainer?

M.D.   Good horses. Very definitely, good horses.

F.S.T.   Well, that makes a start, but there's more to it than that.

M.D.   Well, I think the horses do most of it, really. No one, however good he is, can win with bad horses. Definitely not. And it's the same with jockeys, too. When you went out to bowl it was 100 per cent your effort, wasn't it? When I go out on a racecourse, it's the horses that are doing all the work. When a boxer's in the ring, he's there by himself. The trainer may have done everything possible to get him into the right shape and the right frame of mind, but from there on it's the boxer who has to do it. On the racecourse, the horse is doing all the work.

F.S.T.   You mentioned Silver Buck as your first winner and that brings us a bit closer together because when the horse first came over from Ireland he was owned by Jack Mewies, my solicitor.

M.D.   He's our solicitor too.

F.S.T.   He's everybody's solicitor! Keen on his racing and keen on his cricket.

M.D.   He bought the horse and then raced him for a season and then sold him to Mrs Christine Feather ...

F.S.T.   ... who is the daughter of a former Yorkshire cricketer [J.R.S. Raper] and the wife of a former Yorkshire Second XI captain [R.L. Feather]. And Silver Buck won the Cheltenham Gold Cup for Chris. Is Cheltenham your favourite racecourse?

M.D.   I haven't really a specific favourite. I like them all. For instance, there's all the difference in the world between Cheltenham and Cartmel but I love them both. Cartmel, on the fringe of the Lake District and the northern shores of Morecambe Bay, has a most beautiful setting but isn't really much like a racecourse at all and the horses that run there are not very good, but you get 20,000 people at their meetings and that speaks for itself.

F.S.T.   Isn't that where you had a fall which finished your career as a jockey?

M.D.   I was finished before that. That was just an excuse! But I love both those courses in different ways. I love Wetherby because it's local.

F.S.T.   *I* like Wetherby – a lovely family course. You can stand up on the bank and see all the way round.

M.D.   And the members can drive in and watch the racing from that grass bank from the backs of their cars and have their cocktail parties out of the boot. It's a family course and you can have the whole picnic lunch at the car and not miss any of the racing.

F.S.T.   But there's something about Cheltenham, isn't there? I may be a bit prejudiced but I like it because I have seen three great horses run there – Mill House, Arkle and Silver Buck. You may disagree

– you're the professional. But I have always felt there was something special about Cheltenham. There's always a great influx of the Irish and a lot of Irish priests, and they all bet!

M.D.   Yes, a lot of Irishmen take the whole Cheltenham week for their holiday and it's the highlight of their year. The great feature of Cheltenham, for me, is the atmosphere. It's remarkable. Much as I love Royal Ascot and other great sporting occasions, Cheltenham takes some beating.

F.S.T.   Where do you go from here, Michael? You've trained more winners in a season than anybody else. Do you ever worry about being able to keep up this wonderful standard? Or have you enough confidence in yourself and your dad to be sure that this wonderful tradition carries on?

M.D.   My ambition always has been to win the Grand National. That's one of my next major targets. The other thing is, I am sure we can do better. We had a lot of luck last year. Things went right for us. I would like to rely more on skill than the luck we enjoyed. We are looking for a bigger farm in Yorkshire. We have got 100 acres at the moment and we would love to have about 300 acres. It would take us about ten years to get it just as we want it but I am sure, then, we can make a better job of training the horses.

F.S.T.   An even better job?

M.D.   Definitely. An even better job. Definitely.

F.S.T.   Better than bringing home the first five in the Cheltenham Gold Cup?

M.D.   Oh, yes. Some of that was more luck than skill and that was only one race. We have to take the season as a whole.

F.S.T.   Nevertheless, after your record season at home you have been out to the United States, haven't you?

M.D.   Yes, to California, to Charlie Whittingham, who is the leading trainer in the States. He's a very good trainer and a very nice chap.

F.S.T.   Did you think you had something to learn still?

M.D.   Very definitely I have something to learn. I'm thirty-three. Of course I have something to learn. We are always learning all the time. When he heard about it, Fred Winter said, 'I don't mind him getting the first five in the Gold Cup but when he says he's going to California to learn how to train, that's a bit much!' But seriously, I feel I have an awful lot to learn and my visit to California helped.

F.S.T.   I love watching racing. I am not a betting man, never have been, never will be. My father once said to me, 'The best way to back a horse is into a pair of shafts.' But I do love watching it and I love horses. But I hate to see anyone get hurt, a horse or its rider.

M.D.   We're lucky in Yorkshire in that we've got a really good jump-ing track in Wetherby and arguably the best flat-racing track at York, and I go to all the flat meetings at York. I never take holidays and the stable joke is that I have my holidays at York Races. Never having any runners, it's a holiday for me.

F.S.T.   You don't train on the flat. There must be a reason for that.

M.D.   Basically it's because I try to do one job and try to do it well. There aren't many people who train both and do a good job. For instance, Dick Hern and Henry Cecil don't have any hurdlers. They just concentrate on the flat. Fred Winter and Fulke Walwyn just train jumpers and not on the flat.

F.S.T.   You have rather a bawdy sense of humour, haven't you?

M.D.   I don't think so, not really.

F.S.T.   What about your encounter with Prince Charles at Chelten-ham?

M.D.   Who told you about that? Well, yes. There had been about two days' solid rain and it looked as though we weren't going to be able to race but the drainage was so good that racing did take place. After the Gold Cup Prince Charles said, 'Well done,' and I said, 'Well, it isn't really "Well done" to me; it's "Well done" to Captain Gosling's [Clerk of the Course] drains.'

F.S.T.   And how did the Prince of Wales react?

M.D.   I think he was a bit baffled.

F.S.T.   Sorry to keep coming back to Silver Buck, but he's a sort of family friend as far as I am concerned and it's a bit of a thrill to me to be patting him on the nose here and feeding him mints. He's had a lot of great races with Night Nurse, hasn't he?

M.D.   The best race they ever had was in the Lambert and Butler Final at Haydock Park when they took each other on for the last mile and a half, over every fence, upsides. It was a terrific race. They battled solidly with each other for a mile and a half and there was never more than a length in it, either way. You know how towards the end of a race the crowd start to shout? Well, at Haydock they were shouting themselves hoarse a mile and a half from home.

F.S.T.   What was happening to you at the time? Did you know Silver Buck was going to win?

M.D.   No, I didn't, not until he was passed the lollipop.

F.S.T.   How do you feel about the Grand National?

M.D.   Oh, I love the race. I rode in it twice. It's a super race. There aren't many horses that get hurt in it, whatever you say, and not many jockeys get hurt, either, because the speed is slower than the average race.

Michael Dickinson gets a few bowling tips from F.S.T.

F.S.T. gets a few training tips from Michael Dickinson with Silver Buck looking on

F.S.T.   Did you get round each time?

M.D.   No, I fell both times, but I got round in two Tophams, over the same fences. The average sort of horse gets round with no problems. It's just that some of the horses in the National are not that good before they set off. One horse ran one year, Barony Fort, and it had been beaten in a point-to-point the week before. And some of 'em wouldn't get four and a half miles in a horsebox, let's face it, let alone on their own four feet. There's nothing wrong with the National. They've been doing it for a hundred years and in that time lots of horses and lots of riders have got round over those fences so they can't be so bad. It's just that lots of horses and lots of riders have no chance before they set off. It's nearly always won by a pretty good horse.

F.S.T.   We first met at my house, didn't we?

M.D.   Yes, it was at a birthday party for someone.

F.S.T.   Yes, for me. We had some outside caterers in and I think you were friendly with the young lady from the catering firm, weren't you?

M.D.   Yes, that's right.

F.S.T.   At any rate, I found you in the kitchen, washing up, so you must have been a bit keen on her! Then, as I got to know you better, I learned that if ever you go on holiday – and it makes a bit of history if you do – you take an overnight bag with a couple of shirts and spare pair of jeans, and a copy of *Timeform*.

M.D.   So I might just as well go to York Races as anywhere. I don't like holidays, really. I'm very happy in my job. If I was in an office or a factory, I would need to get away, but we go to France twice a year, we go to Ireland about four or five times a year, so I do a bit of travelling.

F.S.T.   That's buying horses?

M.D.   Yes, it's business, but it's pleasant business and it involves me in a change of scenery.

F.S.T.   How d'you know when you are going to get a good horse ... paying out thousands of guineas for yearlings?

M.D.   You don't know. You go on conformation and breeding.

F.S.T.   Conformation?

M.D.   The look of a horse and the movement. It's a bit of a gamble. But let's say that if I were to go out and buy ten well-bred, good-looking horses I would have more chance of getting good ones than you, if you bought ten bad-looking and badly bred horses.

F.S.T.   Or if I bought *any* horses ...

M.D.   No, but I mean all my ten wouldn't be good ones and all your ten wouldn't be bad ones. But let's talk about cricket. You're the expert there.

F.S.T.   How did you come to get the bug?

M.D.   I played at school, but very badly, and then nothing happened until the Headingley Test in 1981 when Ian Botham played that marvellous innings against Australia. We (the lads here at the stable and myself) watched a bit on television and I think it was the odds of 500 to 1 against England on the Saturday night which attracted our attention. Odds like that against *anything* have got to be interesting, so we watched on the Monday and Botham got 149 and then Bob Willis bowled out Australia for next to nothing. And we thought, 'It's not such a boring game after all.' We made a set of stumps out of three broomhandles and they are carried in the boot of my car, with a bat and a ball. We formed two teams here at the stables: the Lions, which I captain, and the Tigers, skippered by one of the jockeys, Chris Pimlott, and when word got round we were challenged by the local village institute at Huby-and-Weeton. They turned out their Second XI and we beat them. They couldn't quite take that, so they challenged us again with the First XI and we beat them, too. Mind you, we put in a couple of ringers from the MCC Young Cricketers at Lord's who were rather close relations of one of my owners. But I think we'd have won, even without them! But I'm not quite happy about my bowling at the moment and I was hoping for a lesson from you, Fred.

F.S.T.   In a minute, young man; all in good time. What about your own particular heroes?

M.D.   Well, you were my boyhood hero – Fiery Fred. I've been disappointed since then, mind you, since meeting you.

F.S.T.   That'll do. What about present-day heroes?

M.D.   Vincent O'Brien, the best trainer.

F.S.T.   And who would you rate as the best jockey?

M.D.   Lester Piggott on the flat and John Francome jumping. John is probably the best jump jockey there has ever been. It's difficult to compare people of different generations but a lot of people who know better than me rate him the best ever.

F.S.T.   Do you have favourites amongst your horses?

M.D.   No, I like them all. Well, nearly all.

F.S.T.   You seem to have a genuine affection for them.

M.D.   Oh, yes, definitely. You've got to have. You've got to feel for the horses. You can't treat them as machines.

F.S.T.   We've brought a supply of Trebor Mints and Polo Mints ...

M.D.   ... to go round the horses. Good. I love doing that because it's one of the few ways I can say thank you to the horse for all its hard work. When a runner wins he gets a gold medal; if a tennis player plays hard he gets well paid, doesn't he, or a golfer. But when a horse wins, he just gets a pat on the neck and he still gets the same food whether he wins or loses. So they are doing it for love, for pure enjoyment. I don't know if I would do the same if I were in their position, so one of the few things I can do, apart from looking after them well, is to go round and give them a mint or two and give them a pat on the neck and say thank you. I can't do much else. I can't really give them a holiday in Majorca like a winning football team, can I?

F.S.T.   Are they competitive by nature? I mean, if you put them out in a field to run about, would one want to come first?

M.D.   To a certain extent but not with the stress they are put under in a race. If we were to put them out in a field, they would gallop round until they were tired and then put their heads down and eat grass. But when they have galloped for two and a half miles over, say, eighteen fences and we have to say to them, 'Come on, you're tired but you've got to go on for another half mile,' well then, you've got to take your cap off to them because they really battle and they are exhausted. Well, that's pretty good, isn't it?

F.S.T.   D'you think they know when they've won?

M.D.   No ... I wouldn't really say they know when they've won. But they do know when they've had a hard race, because it hurts.

F.S.T.   You've mentioned a sense of enjoyment. Is that a conscious thing? Do you know when a horse has enjoyed itself?

M.D.   Oh, yes, they enjoy it until they get very tired. That's why I love to put them in a little race which they can win easily and on the bridle. And that's great. But I hate seeing them having a hard race, whether they come first or last.

F.S.T.   You hate to think it's strenuous, an effort for them? D'you feel, perhaps, they are saying to themselves, 'What the hell am I doing out here running my bollocks off?'

M.D.   Yes, and this is where you have got to be so careful because time and time again it's been shown that when a horse has had a hard race, next time he'll run badly. It's commonsense. Let's say you went into a pub and got beaten up, which, in a way, is what horses do because their jockeys whack 'em. Next time you went past that pub, you'd shake and shiver, wouldn't you? If you went round a sharp bend in your car and ran off the road, you'd remember it. Right. Horses haven't got a lot of brains but they've good memories. If they've been in a race and got whacked and felt a lot of pain, they'll start to sweat and shiver. There will be very little sense of enjoyment.

F.S.T.   Amazing! There's a great sense of affection between man and beast.

M.D.   There's got to be. If we start abusing the horses they're going to say, 'No thanks.' We have got to keep them so they *enjoy* racing. All right, I love the horses so I'd do it anyway. But if I did it any other way I wouldn't train so many winners. I always impress upon my jockeys not to be too hard on the horses. When I finished riding I sold my whip, after four years, at the Nearly New shop.

F.S.T.   Would you really rollock one of your jockeys if he laid into a horse?

M.D.   Too true. But I'm glad to say they'd never do that because they know how I feel.

F.S.T.   Have you any interests outside racing?

M.D.   I like to work through the day and play tennis or cricket in the evening.

F.S.T.   And you're not married ... you haven't had time for that, yet?

M.D.   No one will have me. I'm trying hard, but there are no takers. But I'm more interested in you, Fred (not in terms of getting married, of course!). How about my bowling lesson?

F.S.T.   Hold on a minute. I've nearly finished. You'll know Harvey Smith, of course?

M.D.   Oh, yes. You know what Harvey said: 'If you are good at sport in the south you get honoured; if you are good in the north, you get disqualified.'

F.S.T.   He's certainly got a point there. Do you find any sort of bias against northern people in your own racing fraternity?

M.D.   None at all.

F.S.T.   If you were not as successful as you are, do you think it might be a different story?

M.D.   Oh, definitely, yes. Quite a few people in the south think all northerners are rubbish and I like to think that you and Harvey and, I hope, myself have proved them wrong, haven't we?

F.S.T.   Just a little bit. Now, before we have a look at your bowling, what's your immediate ambition?

M.D.   To beat the Yorkshire television cricket team next week, so let's get on with the lesson.

Footnote: Yorkshire TV won the match – despite the lesson!

Briggs Mill, Clayton, nr Bradford

History

Bradford

Early in 1983 came an announcement which raised a few eyebrows in the world of tourism – the city of Bradford had achieved a greater percentage increase in tourist visitors than anywhere else in the country. Bradford? Tourists? Somehow the two just don't go together. It's easy enough to see why York attracts visitors, and it wouldn't cause any sharp intake of breath to learn that many more had decided to visit a spa town like Harrogate, the traditional coastal holiday centres of Scarborough and Bridlington, or the quaint or more homely resorts such as Whitby, Redcar, Saltburn, Withernsea and Hornsea. But Bradford, deep in the heart of the industrial West Riding? It just didn't make sense if you considered simply the traditional aspects of tourist attractions. Bradford has modernized its centre, streamlining some of its traffic problems and cleaning up its shopping and administrative areas, but so have many other major cities around the country. It is twentieth century in its general appearance but essentially nineteenth century in character because modern Bradford was built on wool. And then you start to get a clue to this newfound fame. There is industrial archaeology in abundance in Bradford and within a ten-mile radius. It is very rightly proud of its pioneering work in the field of free education; it has returned many Liberal reformers to Parliament and the more enlightened of its Victorian industrialists were great philanthropists. Someone has put in a lot of time to build up Bradford as a tourist centre in a campaign which perhaps was given a spur when local government reorganization took the Brontës' Haworth into the Bradford Metropolitan area.

But the more you dig into the story of Bradford, the more you realize that it deserves this new status as a tourist attraction. The façade of a marvellous nineteenth-century development has created a whole city history in itself, but for around two thousand years the area has been peopled by tribesmen and townsmen belligerently opposed to outsiders. It was pretty certainly a tribal centre of the Brigantes before the disciplined organization of the Legions finally quelled the last enthusiastic aggression of the natives. It was most assuredly a rallying point for organized resistance to the Normans to such a degree that Duke William swore a great oath that he would not leave a soul alive in the northeastern area of the England he had conquered. And, by and large, he kept his vow. One Norman chronicler recorded that, in what was to become Yorkshire, no fewer than 100,000 people perished and the survivors – there can have been few of them out of an eleventh-century population – lived on rats, mice and 'other vermin'. Ilbert de Lacy, one of the knights who had fought with William, was granted 150 manors in West Yorkshire for his services but that cannot have been such generous payment as its sounds after the army had taken toll of the area for its resistance to conquest. The Domesday survey said tersely of Bradford: 'Ilbert has it and it is waste.' Yet it clearly took more than a touch of genocide to suppress the Yorkshire spirit, even nine hundred years ago, for the population began once again to increase; land came under the crude plough and various forms of trade and handicraft began to develop. By 1277, with the de Lacys still in feudal control and now Earls of Lincoln, a thirteenth-century census revealed that 'Henry de Lacy hath many liberties in the town of Bradeford: to wit a gallows, assize of bread and beer, a market place and a free court from ancient times.'

The free court imposed fines for such offences as 'unruly temper', card playing at night and assault (a 10s fine for an assault in which blood was shed, 3s 4d for an assault with no spilled blood – they were pretty hefty fines considering the value of money in those days). The assize of bread and beer was a sort of weights and measures inspectorate, adjudicating on whether quantities and ingredients were correct.

This was the sort of fascinating data unearthed by the mid-Victorian writer John James and, such was the thirst for knowledge as education, in one form or another, started to come within reach of the humblest worker that it was followed only a quarter of a century later by a book from William Scruton, a man not overconcerned with false modesty. He began his extremely detailed work: 'I have no apology to make in submitting this work to my numerous subscribers and the public. That there is abundant scope for it, and that the proper time for its appearance has arrived, I am fully assured. That it will meet with a favourable reception I have very little doubt.' Well, that was a confident enough statement of policy but, like a good Yorkie, Mr

Scruton decided to make sure of distinguished patronage by 'most respectfully dedicating' his work to the Right Honourable, the Viscount Cranbrook, GCSI, Lord President of the Privy Council, who was a native of Bradford.

But for all this obsequiousness and, as we have seen, a touch of pomposity, Scruton was no mean historian, like John James before him. Together, they paint a colourful and graphic picture of the Brigantean tribal village which was to become the centre of one of the world's greatest industrial conurbations, and in particular the sheer pace at which change occurred in the later stages of the Industrial Revolution.

'More than twenty years have elapsed,' said Scruton, 'since the publication of Mr James' *History of Bradford* with *Additions and Continuations* and during that period so great a transformation has taken place, and the old has so completely given way to the new that anyone revisiting Bradford after a quarter of a century or so would fail to recognize it and would require the magic aid of Alladin's [sic] Lamp or Fortunatus' Cap in wandering through its labyrinth of newly formed streets and thoroughfares. Few indeed are the relics of Old Bradford that remain to revive the lingering memories of its old inhabitants or to awaken the curiosity of its young and rising generation.'

Bradford was staunchly Lancastrian in the Wars of the Roses, which might seem strange to some ears but not when it is remembered that the civil strife of the fifteenth century was not so much about individual allegiance to one's home territory as service to one's overlord, and Bradford, at that time, was part of the lands of the Duchy of Lancaster. In the Civil War of the 1640s the town was Parliamentarian and suffered greatly for its convictions. Think of the Civil War in schoolday terms and battles come to mind like Edgehill and Marston Moor and Naseby, but Bradford was, in fact, the scene of one of the first engagements and was twice under siege. It was a gallant Captain John Hodgson with a well-armed body of Halifax men who drove off the troops sent by King Charles to occupy the town almost as soon as his breach with Parliament had been opened. The Royalists retreated to Leeds and as Sir Thomas ('Fiery Tom') Fairfax rode in from Selby to take command of the Parliamentarians, Hodgson and his men were reinforced by hundreds of Puritan clothworkers armed with clubs and scythes tied to long poles.

A second siege followed quickly, as the Royalists, led by the Earl of Newcastle, gave Bradford a tremendous hammering with their vastly superior artillery until Fairfax was reduced to just one barrel of gunpowder (with, it is said, no tinder to ignite it!). Now comes one of those strange stories which seem so crazy if you try to relate them to modern warfare where usually a place is firmly in the hands of one side or another. Fairfax was faced with a choice of surrendering or fighting his way out through the besiegers. He chose the latter course and reached safety in Leeds, whence his enemy had fled so recently. And here you also get one of the stories which have for so long established the Royalists as the 'goodies' of the Civil War and the Roundheads as the 'baddies' – at least to the idealists unconcerned with the rights or wrongs of the causes and principles involved. While Fiery Tom was hacking his way to safety, his lady wife was taken prisoner in Bradford High Street. How had the great Parliamentarian general come to leave her behind? Did he, while detesting the Papist leanings of the Royalists, still respect their reputation for chivalry and knightly attitudes towards the fair sex? If so, how right he was, because the Earl of Newcastle sent her off to join her husband *in his own carriage*. If things like that could happen, it makes you wonder what the hell they were all fighting about.

Bradford Grammar School has long been one of the outstanding educational establishments in the county with a great sporting, as well as academic, tradition. There is evidence of the existence of a free grammar school in the town in the mid-sixteenth century through the records of a Duchy Court held in the reign of Edward VI, showing it to have an endowment of three (modern) acres of land worth 2s 5d in rent. In the next hundred years the school obviously received other and greater endowments because a formidable list was recorded by a panel of charity commissioners in 1655. It was not until eight years later, however, that letters patent were issued to 'the Free Grammar School of King Charles the Second at Bradford, for teaching, instructing and better bringing up children and youth in grammar and other good learning and literature to consist of one master or teacher and one usher or under teacher'. There were to be thirteen governors, of whom the vicar of Bradford was one, to be drawn from 'the most discreet, honest and religious persons in the neighbourhood'.

So was formal education established in Bradford, but obviously the grammar school could benefit only a fraction of the population of a town which was growing steadily, if slowly, after the Civil War had ravaged it so seriously. Ten years after the execution of Charles I, the number of baptisms and marriages in Bradford was half that of 1639, immediately before the war began. If the town could claim to have been on the winning side, it had certainly paid for it in the number of deaths amongst its male population. For the next century and a half, learning was restricted to a privileged few and even when Joseph

Priestley set up a Philosophical Society in the late eighteenth century, it was disbanded after a few years. In 1823, they tried again, this time led by one Samuel Hailstone Esq., with a rather broader-based Literary and Philosophical Society in which forty-two people subscribed £50 each to build a hall and set up a 'library, apparatus, etc.'. Once again it was going to be something of an elitist society but it was sabotaged by the vicar who preached a sermon in which he enlarged upon the irreligious tendencies of a philosophizing spirit! Several of the subscribers, reports John James, 'took fright and withdrew their subscriptions. Thus was a society, so auspiciously formed, broken up.'

But there were still some pretty persistent chaps around in Bradford, even in those days, and in the winter of 1838–39 a course of lectures on several aspects of natural philosophy was delivered by a local man, William Sharp, who was a Fellow of the Royal Society. At the end of the course, Mr Sharp invited his students to form – wait for it – yes, a Philosophical Society in the town and it came into being on 12 April 1839. The society's second rule called for 'the formation of a local museum, or a collection of the natural productions of the district within 15 miles of Bradford'.

The idea was that if this lead was followed by all the towns in the country the value to science generally would be enormous. Bradford had set a challenging lead and Mr Sharp, his exciting new educational development well and truly launched, followed up by bombarding the British Association for the Advancement of Science and the Royal Society with propaganda for his local museum. It was taken up by several of the top scientific minds in the country; the idea had got under way.

At the same time, the Bradford Philosophical Society was pressing on with enthusiasm. Nearly two hundred members were enrolled in the first year and here the founders showed a bit of good Yorkshire cunning. They invited fourteen of the country's top scientific thinkers to become honorary members. Flattered, most of them accepted. It cost the society nothing at all, but the honorary members felt it was only right to send a book to the library, an exhibit for the museum. And when you consider that amongst the first honorary members were Hershel, Buckland, Sedgwick, Brewster, Faraday, Roget, Lyell, Phillips and Whewell, a fair amount of intellectual loot must have flowed into the coffers.

Side by side with this rather up-market form of education was growing the Mechanics' Institute which, by definition, was aimed at that section of the populace to whom contributing £50 towards the construction of a hall would be unthinkable. The aims of the institute were: 1) The provision of an extensive and well-selected library for the use of all members and subscribers. 2) The supply of popular and attractive instruction, through the medium of public lectures. 3) The formation of classes under well-qualified masters in which every facility should be afforded for pursuing the various branches of useful knowledge with pleasure and success. It was set up in 1832 and in the first year had 352 members, 800 volumes in its library and issued them to 4642 borrowers; by 1838, there were 541 members, 2249 books and they were issued on 19,000 occasions. So by the time the young Princess Victoria had become Queen of England there was a growing literacy amongst the population, but the numbers were still painfully small in relation to the now rapidly growing factory towns. How could working-class children get any form of basic education?

The Sunday schools, which had come in the wake of John Wesley, preceded the day schools by many years. A National School had been opened in 1831 and was 'kept' in a Sunday school belonging not, in this instance, to a Wesleyan chapel, but to Christ Church. Fifteen years earlier, the Quakers had opened a British and Infants School off Leeds Road. It cost the enormous sum for those days of £2300, all of which was raised by subscriptions from the Society of Friends, but was open to children of all denominations. As with the National School, there was a charge of 2d a week for each pupil and an extra penny for those who learned to write! Now here at once we see the vicious circle which so retarded the improvement of general education through the early and mid-Victorian years. Child labour was extensively used because it was cheap. Parents needed the miserable pittance of the kids to supplement their own small wages (if, indeed, they had jobs); therefore to send the youngsters to school, even part time, was to lose that pittance, or part of it. To have to *pay* 2d or 3d as well was enough to deter all but the most farseeing and deeply caring parent. And so, while the first crude elements of formal education for the masses attracted only a tiny percentage of working-class children, Sunday schools must have bulged at the seams with their huge intakes on the Day of Rest. Here the children could at least have some sort of window on the world outside the gloomy factories, the narrow streets, the tiny cottages which were the whole of *their* world for six days a week. In the mid-nineteenth century there were 985 names on the register of the Parish Church Sunday School, 700 at Christ Church, 437 at St James's, 280 at the Roman Catholic church, 426 at the Independent chapel in Horton Lane, 417 at the Salem chapel, 400 with the Baptists in Westgate, 380 at Sion chapel and so on – thousands upon thousands of children in their Sunday best turning up for teaching of a religious nature. And

there was no shortage of teachers, either – seventy at Sion, seventy-seven at St James's, seventy at Salem and no fewer than 138 for the Baptists in Westgate. That's a teacher–pupil ratio of one to three!

At this time there were around seventy worsted spinning mills in the greater Bradford area, housing roughly 2000 frames, each of which spun between 700 and 850 hanks of yarn a day – each hank measured 560 yards. In 1830, a total of 43,736,386 lb of wool was devoured by machinery which was becoming more efficient every day. And child labour was an essential part of this industrial activity so that, as more day schools began to open, the cheapest section of the labour force was in danger of being lured away. The mill owners had a problem. Some, like Titus Salt, had a paternal, benevolent approach to their workers; others were cast in the Dickensian mould – greedy, grasping, ready to exploit. 'Half-timers' provided something of an answer – children who spent half their time in school, half working in the woollen mills. It was not an ideal solution, but at least by the beginning of the 1870s almost every child had a chance of some rudimentary education.

The village of Clayton, which in those days was a half-industrial, half-agricultural community on a hillside to the west of urban Bradford, has long since been engulfed by the spread of housing but still retains something of the nature of a village community. Indeed, its inhabitants talk naturally of 'the village' and it retains a strong sense of identity. The name of Ben Ashton, first headmaster of the school which opened there following the 1870 Education Act, is mentioned with the sort of respect accorded a village headman in earlier days. He taught the great-grandparents of people still living in 'the village' and his meticulously kept school journals make fascinating reading.

March 25th, 1872: Clayton British School was opened this morning at 9 o'clock. During the day 126 scholars were admitted.

March 28th: This week I have selected two boys out of the first class to teach the Infants. We broke up today for Easter (a five-day break).

April 3rd: Admitted five new scholars.

April 8th: Admitted 22 new scholars.

April 12th: Writing of the fourth class is improving.

April 16th: I warned the children about coming late.

July 11th: I cautioned a half-timer about absenting herself without leave.

October 12th: The upper part of the school have, during the past week, taken their dictation on paper instead of slates. Some of them have, so far, written it very neatly.

And by the end of the first year of the school's existence the education inspector reported: 'The work is, as far as it goes, of a satisfactory character. Separate accommodation, however, is required for the infants.' This was duly reported to the managers, with a request for the provision of more accommodation, and signed by the entire staff – Benjamin Ashton, first-class certificated teacher; Bessie Day, assistant; Herbert Barker, pupil teacher. By May, an infants' room had been set up and the school advertised for a certificated infants mistress who arrived on 9 June. And then we get a glimpse of a darker side of life in this world of part-time education as, on 20 November, Mr Ashton reports: 'A deplorable event happened last week. A boy named Henry Illingworth (a half-timer at Messrs Benn's mill) was kicked by an overlooker and died a few days after.' (An inquest was held, the overlooker committed for trial on a manslaughter charge and got twelve months' hard labour.)

Through the years, truancy and late arrival plagued the headmaster so that by 6 October 1877 he recorded testily: 'The boy H. Seager persists in being absent from school without the consent of his parents.

The lateness of a considerable proportion of our scholars appears to be incurable. Some boys are *never* on time, morning or afternoon.'

June 29th, 1878: During the past week the heat has been intense. The children have been very languid and inactive.

That must have been a pretty fair heat wave because a fortnight later, Mr Ashton was still reporting on it.

July 13th: Very hot weather ... great lassitude prevails. Edmund Ward – 31 attendances; Frederick Peel, 22; Joseph Illingworth, 23 (all over a nine weeks' period).

At the end of the school year, 1879, E. E. Rawnsley (Miss) qualified after five years as a pupil teacher.

August 25th, 1879: As a public clock has now been obtained for the village it is to be hoped that our late scholars will in future be more punctual.

Tragedy struck the school in the winter of 1882.

November 11th: Much sickness. Two children died.
December 2nd: Another four died. Scarletina.
December 9th–16th: Heaviest snowstorm for many years.

And so the years rolled on, with changes in staff which were not always for the good, judging by the report of Her Majesty's Inspector on 8 January 1886:

Third standard. Reading was inaccurate, dull and hesitating and was also marked by indistinct utterance and bad pronunciation. The handwriting is bad and betokens an absence of systematic instruction. Spelling is by far the weakest subject. In the second and fifth standards it was almost an entire failure and it was also very faulty in the fourth and sixth standards. The composition was very poor. The scholars are not prepared by oral arithmetic for the new Rules and in the higher standards they have accordingly no idea of the meaning of fractions. In the second standard, three-fourths of the children failed to take down their sums correctly. In grammar, the second standard failed entirely and the other classes were so backward and unintelligent that no grant can be recommended in the Class Subject. The garments were badly made and no grant can be recommended for needlework. These bad results are due in great measure to very lax discipline and to a great deficiency in the teaching staff.

On 9 December 1893 it was reported that 'workhouse children were admitted on Monday last' and two years later we learn something which makes you wonder how the workhouse children could bear to leave the portals of Mr Bumble. 'Fifty children', reads the school record, 'are being taught in a classroom measuring 21 ft by 10 ft and

49 in a room 16½ ft by 14½ ft. In the smaller room the air is so bad as to be positively injurious to health of both teachers and scholars. In the main room, ventilation is defective. Only one of the ventilators will act and this is closed.' Phew!

Mercifully, in September 1898, the school took possession of the new board school and, I'm sure, with as much relief as pride, 'marched in procession round the cricket field and entered the new school'. Their troubles were not ended, however. In January 1900, the school was closed for three weeks because of measles and six months later: 'Moved from classroom into Assembly because of rain coming through ceiling.' June 2nd, 1902, brought a half-day holiday to mark the end of the South African War. And as we approach the Great War, the school's story begins to take on a bit of the character of Noël Coward's *Cavalcade*. The headmaster in these days is Mr Arthur Senior.

May 12th, 1915: Received notice to report for duty with 5th Battalion, West Yorkshire Regiment. Mr Catherall takes over as acting headmaster.
August 31st, 1916: Lt Senior visited school and took afternoon prayers.
March 28th, 1917: Lt Senior called at school this morning.
May 18th, 1917: First batch of potatoes planted.
January 14th, 1918: Captain Senior visited school this morning.
May 29th, 1918: King and Queen visited Bradford. Attendance affected.
October 10th, 1918: No woodwork classes today. Teacher had to report for military duty.
January 16th, 1919: Captain Senior recommences duty after three years eight months *leave of absence* on military duties.

But now let's skip through eighteen years to 14 July 1937, when the head logged this little bit of social history:

I have had occasion to report to The Office the case of Joe Hollingsworth. This boy is 14 years of age but not qualified to leave school until the end of term. His attendance has been most irregular and after a day's absence on an excuse of illness I have met him on my way home from school taking out meat for a butcher. On Monday of this week he was taking out meat during school hours. I reported the matter to the Education Office and this morning an official from the office warned the boy's mother and also the butcher concerned. On my way to school this afternoon I was stopped by the father who was most threatening and abusive.

It seems things hadn't changed very much over the years.

Captain Cook

The second oldest tale in cricket takes the form of a conundrum: 'Who is the only Yorkshire captain to go to Australia and never play in a Test match?' Answer: 'Captain Cook.' Yes, it's an old one, its antiquity exceeded only by the story of the southerner who, for some reason which escapes everyone north of the Trent, went to a Roses match and, after applauding the play of men on both sides, was told by the Yorkshireman on his right and the Lancastrian on his left to mind his own bloody business because that game had nowt to do with him. But, Test-appearance conundrums apart, the story of Captain Cook is fascinating because his career, which is a major part of English history, had the most unlikely beginning.

James Cook was born on 27 October 1728, in a two-roomed thatched cottage in Marton, a hamlet just south of the dreary mudflats alongside the River Tees where the great industrial complex of Middlesbrough and Tees-side later grew. A week later, at St Cuthbert's Church, 'James, ye son of James Cook, day labourer [was] baptised,' according to the register. That, at least, is a matter of record but it is uncertain whether he was one of seven or eight children born to the unlettered labourer of Scottish descent and the former Grace Pace, a local girl. Their neighbours, the Walker family, were rather better off than the Cooks, and it is, perhaps, to them that we owe the deepest debt of gratitude because, while doing odd jobs for Mr Walker, young James learned to read and write from *Mrs* Walker, making him substantially more accomplished than most youngsters of his social standing. Consequently, when the elder James Cook moved five miles down the road, towards the Cleveland Hills and to a better job as hind to Thomas Skottowe, of Airyholme Farm, Great Ayton, young James – not yet eight – impressed Squire Skottowe with his quick wits and his ability with 'his letters'. And it was the farmer who sent young Cook,

The apprentice haberdasher learned his trade in Staithes

when he was twelve, to be apprenticed to a grocer and haberdasher in the fishing village of Staithes, one of the many attractive coastal villages which still exist, despite greedy erosion, at the foot of the great cliffs of northeast Yorkshire. But we run ahead of ourselves. To appreciate fully the miracle of Cook the navigator and explorer it is essential that we look more closely at his background.

It is unlikely that young James had ever seen the sea when he moved from Marton to Great Ayton and it could well be that his first glimpse of the North Sea was from the dramatic summit of Roseberry Topping,

the signal beacon hill which rises sharply behind Great Ayton as one of the northern outposts of the Clevelands. It may sound something like a whipped-cream confection in one of those TV advertisements, but Roseberry Topping has its place in history. It was here that warning was given of the approach of the Norsemen and the danger signals shone out from one beacon top to the next, deep into the heart of the countryside. And it was from here, if the prevailing mist was not clinging to the steep, upper slopes, that James Cook could look out to sea, far to the northeast. Who knows whether he dreamed then of exploring the southern seas, charting new coastlines, discovering new outposts of Empire. It seems impossible that such thoughts could ever spring to the mind of a boy who lived with so many brothers and sisters – many destined to die young – in a cottage of modest dimensions. And yet young James stood out in the Cook brood. He was not sickly like most of the others; he was quick to learn; and, building upon the rudiments taught him by Mrs Walker back in Marton, he made further progress at the Michael Postgate School in Great Ayton. The rest of his time was spent helping on the farm so that, by his early teens, James Cook was very much a country boy. He was, however, a well-educated teenager by eighteenth-century standards – certainly for the son of a farmworker – when Squire Skottowe sent him off to apprenticeship with William Saunderson, grocer and haberdasher.

Staithes must have seemed a rather wonderful place to James Cook – a place of locally built fishing cobles (pronounced 'cobbles'), of smugglers, of towering cliffs fighting an incessant, losing battle against irresistible tides, of damp, clinging sea mists. There would be around a hundred fishing cobles based on Staithes in Cook's day and their sturdy, clinker-built hulls impressed the young Cook by their stout resistance to the cruel seas. He watched them being built in Staithes and he remembered them … And it was here that he met another family called Walker who, in turn, were to have a powerful influence upon his life.

His apprenticeship to William Saunderson completed, Cook ventured another fifteen miles or so farther from the family nest, to Whitby. If the fishing port of Staithes had seemed huge and romantic to him, Whitby must have looked like the centre of the universe. Again, great cliffs loomed high above the harbour, but whereas at Staithes they seem to be locked in eternal, senseless and futile combat with the ocean, at Whitby they somehow give an impression of solid protection, clasping the anchored shipping in affectionate embrace. In 1746, Whitby was one of England's leading seaports, with great, ocean-going sailing ships in the harbour as well as the fishing fleet.

And it was here that the forerunners of Masefield's dirty British coasters were built – no 'salt-caked smoke stacks', but 300–500-ton sailing ships which carried cargoes of Tyne coal down the east coast to London. And the Walkers of Whitby, a Quaker family, were the owners of a fleet of these colliers in which James Cook now began an apprenticeship of a very different kind from the haberdasher's of Staithes. His first voyage was in a ship of 450 tons called the *Freelove* and when, years later, he laid down to their Lordships of the Admiralty his specifications for the type of ship he wanted for his voyages of explor-

ation, Cook plainly had the east-coast collier in mind. He wanted 'a ship not of great draught of water, yet of sufficient burden and capacity to carry a proper quantity of provisions and necessaries for her complement of men, and for the term requisite to perform the voyage. She must also be of a construction that will bear to take the ground and of a size which, in case of necessity, may be safely and conveniently laid on shore to repair any accidental damage or defect.' Something between a fishing coble and a collier, perhaps? Certainly Cook could not find all the characteristics he thought desirable amongst 'ships-of-war of 40 guns, frigates, East India Company ships, three-decked West India ships'.

By the time he was twenty-six, Cook was ready for command of one of the Walker ships. Instead, he decided to join the Royal Navy. England was at war with France and while the crews were largely made up of reluctantly 'pressed' men, promotion prospects were good for enthusiastic and skilful officers. Cook was both enthusiastic and skilled and during the Seven Years' War between England and France he had ample opportunity to improve his skills in the 64-gun *Pembroke* when she convoyed the troops of General Wolfe to Canada. Cook was in charge of navigation and was encouraged by the *Pembroke*'s captain to further his studies in mathematics, astronomy and hydrographic survey. All these – plus his experience in sailing colliers up and down the east coast of England – were now put to use in charting a difficult stretch of the St Lawrence River which was especially hazardous to vessels trying to move upriver to Quebec. Cook's skills undoubtedly helped Wolfe to land his men in position to scale the Heights of Abraham and to capture Quebec in 1759.

Three years later Cook married the twenty-one-year-old Elizabeth Batts at Barking, but that young lady was destined to see very little of her husband. Within months he was away surveying the Newfoundland coast and during the course of this voyage his knowledge of astronomy was enriched by observing and recording an eclipse of the sun. This was recalled by the Lords of the Admiralty when, six years later, they were asked to provide a ship to take members of the Royal Society to Tahiti to observe the transit of Venus across the sun. James Cook was given the rank of lieutenant and command of the *Endeavour* over the heads of many more senior officers. Three years were allowed for the voyage, which was perhaps as well since *Endeavour* could manage, flat out, about 7 or 8 knots. She displaced 366 tons, had a length of 106 feet and a beam of 29 feet.

In this little cockleshell, Cook, with his crew and a group of scientists, set out round the Horn for the largely unexplored and completely uncharted waters of the South Pacific. Once the scientific work had been completed in Tahiti, Cook then broke open his sealed orders from the Admiralty and found himself commissioned to establish the existence (or not) of 'a continent or land of great extent' in the southern oceans. Cook discovered no land filled with gold and spices, as European folklore suggested, but he did find New Zealand, the land of the long white cloud, which had been mistakenly identified as part of Australia a century earlier by the Dutchman, Abel Tasman. Meticulously, Cook charted the coastline to show that, quite apart from being separated from Australia by 1000 miles of sea, New Zealand consisted of two quite distinct islands separated by – what else? – the Cook Strait. And he logged his opinion that the islands were admirably suited for settlement 'should this ever be thought an object worthy of the attention of Englishmen'. Well, that proved prophetic enough, not only for Englishmen but for Scotsmen as well, especially in South Island.

Cook charted the eastern coastline of Australia, returned to England in July 1771, and the following year was off on his travels again. Poor Elizabeth! This time Cook was commanded to 'complete the discovery of the southern hemisphere' – a pretty tall order, but at least he had the help of improved equipment, including a chronometer devised by another Yorkshireman, John Harrison. And this time he had two ships, *Resolution* and *Adventure*, which probed beyond the Antarctic Circle, landed domestic animals on New Zealand and planted a number of vegetables, and, most important at all, found a way to combat scurvy by feeding his crew a diet of lemons amongst their rations. Cook's third voyage, in 1776, took him amongst the pack ice of the North Pacific into the Bering Strait, then back to Hawaii where he died, speared in the back, on St Valentine's Day, 1779.

During his charting of the Australian coast in 1770, the first landfall was a headland which was given the name Point Hicks, because the sighting was first reported by the officer of the watch, Lieutenant Hicks, and Cook gave the country the name of New South Wales. Looking for a safe anchorage, Cook sailed past Point Hicks into the sheltered water of what now became Botany Bay, which for many years afterwards had a dreadful ring to the ears of prisoners in England sentenced to transportation. Sydney, with its quite marvellous and beautiful natural harbour, is just around the corner and present-day Australians always make me laugh by suggesting – with genuine sadness – that if only Cook had sailed just that bit farther he would have discovered one of the greatest natural ports on earth. It's true, of course, but Botany Bay was perfectly adequate for the shallow-draught *Endeavour* and even the farsighted James Cook could not be expected to anticipate that one of the greatest, most vibrant and bustling cities of the southern hemisphere would rise, over the next two centuries, at the head of the tremendous anchorage a few miles to the north.

Sydney is one of my favourite cities. It is so aggressively Australian that from the first moment I toured there, in 1958, something in me responded instantly. I was as young and brash a cricketer as Australia was a nation and we immediately established a love–hate relationship. The hate part of it was confined to the cricket field, I'm glad to say, and once we were off it, some wonderful friendships were established. Great bowlers like Ray Lindwall, Keith Miller and Alan Davidson are amongst my closest friends today and I look forward to every trip to Australia with the eagerness of a schoolkid awaiting his first trip to the seaside. It's a wonderful country – young in outlook, vigorous, vibrant, challenging. And I am delighted to think that it was a Yorkshireman who brought it into the Commonwealth's family of nations.

Ribblesdale & the Settle–Carlisle Railway

There is a natural tendency to think of the Ribble as a Lancashire river since it arrives in some style at Preston and meets the Irish Sea through a wide estuary where there was once a flourishing, if minor, port. Yet the truth is that it rises very close to the Wharfe and at least half its journey to the sea is, from north to south, in Yorkshire. North Ribblesdale, between Ingleborough and Pen-y-ghent, and Chapel-le-Dale, between Whernside and Ingleborough, are valleys of some importance to our Yorkshire story because they form a vast, natural outdoor-pursuits centre for town dwellers of the industrial West Riding and, indeed, from areas far beyond. This is the land of the climber, the fellwalker and, above all, the potholer. There is a whole kingdom still to be explored under the great triangular landmass of the Three Peaks even though miles of caves have already been discovered, explored and mapped. Speleology is not a science to attract the claustrophobic but, for the adventurous souls who do not mind close, dark and often wet, confinement, it holds an endless fascination. When you think about it, there are not many parts of the earth which have *not* been explored by man, and although we have been a quarter of a million miles into space, there are still caves and caverns and lakes just two or three hundred feet beneath the surface of these Craven peaks still awaiting their first visit by man. I find it an utterly captivating thought.

Ribblesdale, in its upper reaches, is relatively inviting, with its grey villages clustered around areas of greenery and pleasant pubs to refresh the traveller. Chapel-le-Dale, by contrast, is stark and forbidding. Here, with an average rainfall of around 70 inches (it has been known to top the 100 inches mark in some years), the wind keens through gaps in the hills to the southwest at 70 knots on occasions. Small wonder then that vegetation is largely restricted to bracken and ling and the ground is a mess of peat bogs. The few farms cling to the bare

fellsides; even the phlegmatic sheep seem to wonder what they are
doing there as the wind howls and the rain sheets across the valley,
turning trickling streams in a matter of minutes into roaring torrents
tumbling angrily down the slopes. Some disappear underground to
chase through the honeycomb of limestone passages, trapping the novice potholer. Others swell the main waters of the two rivers which
emerge from opposite sides of Whernside, Yorkshire's highest peak at
2415 feet. The Doe runs the shorter course, from the east of Whernside;
Kingsdale Beck sweeps from the west and the two meet in Ingleton,
'the land of woodland and waterfall' to form the Greeta. From a point
a couple of miles above the town, the rivers plunge over a series of
limestone shelves in miniature valleys flanked by trees to provide a
network of glorious woodland walks. Colonies of dippers splash merrily in the upper reaches; families of red squirrels once frolicked
amongst the trees, but I fear they may now, like so many of their kind,
have been driven to more cloistered territories. Ingleton is a haven for
the day tripper and the caravan fraternity and it is easy to see why.

In the parallel valley to the east, the Ribble flows serenely through
Settle, that lovely old halfway house of a town between the industrial
West Riding and the Lakes, or the Lancashire coast. The great lime-

stone mass of Castleberg towers so sheerly over the market place that at times it seems to be hovering suspended in the air, and on market day the stalls of farm produce stand side by side with those of Indian traders from Bradford, selling 'seconds' from the textile mills of two counties. Now the Ribble moves out onto the more fertile plains of Bowland before it crosses the border into Lancashire and is lost to us.

But let us go back to the bogs and the fells of Ribblehead, where, around 120 years ago, the old Midland Railway Company conceived the idea of building a line over country so difficult that its ultimate construction ranks as one of the most ambitious concepts of engineering ever carried out. Certainly the hold this line exercises on the minds of railway enthusiasts is stronger than any other in the British system. And when, in 1981, engineering prudence and caution prompted a suggestion that the line should be closed, there was an immediate and impassioned outcry, led by John Watson, MP for the area, who probably summed up the feelings of the romantics when he declared: 'The Settle–Carlisle reflects some of the most heroic achievements of Britain's railway age. Many men and women died to build the line. It properly occupies a position of immense importance in our history.' All that is undoubtedly true, but it has to be weighed against warnings that the great Ribblehead viaduct, spanning one of the most difficult and bleakest parts of the route, is deteriorating. The cost of replacing it runs into millions of pounds.

It was the cut-throat competition of the railway companies in Victorian Britain which led to the construction of the line in the first place. As W. R. Mitchell and David Joy recount, in their admirable *Settle to Carlisle*, the Midland Company could transport passengers and freight as far as Ingleton but anyone or anything requiring to travel further north had then to transfer to trains of the London and North-Western Company – a serious competitor! So if the passenger coaches or freight cars travelling on from that point were overburdened, who would be left at the wayside to wait for the next train but those whose bookings originated with the rival Midland Company? That was not exactly the most pleasant fate for a passenger in the 1860s. Apart from barges, there were no alternative forms of transport – no cars, no buses, no aircraft. Everything has progressed so quickly in the twentieth century that it's a little difficult for us to realize that just over a hundred years ago you might find yourself utterly stranded in the middle of the Yorkshire Dales. So there was little alternative for the Midland Railway Company but to build its own line.

It almost certainly could not be done today; it couldn't have been all that easy at a time when Karl Marx was publishing his treatise on

Kapital, John Stuart Mill his *Subjection of Women* and the Suez Canal was just being opened. The cost of building the 72 miles of railway from Settle to Carlisle was £3,500,000 – a mind-boggling sum at that time and utterly unthinkable in today's terms. And from an engineering point of view the project was just as formidable. If you remember that locomotives were limited in their pulling power 110 years ago, then consider that the line had to climb to one of the highest parts of the Pennines and go right through the range at 1169 feet above sea level, you begin to see that one of the first problems was achieving an acceptable gradient. Only when that had been worked out could the engineers think about tunnelling and drilling through immensely hard rock. After that came comparatively minor matters like housing a workforce of thousands far from any town or village; getting supplies and materials to them by horsedrawn transport; filling in the bogs to provide a sound base for bridges and viaducts; and working with equipment which must seem to us, in the 1980s, to have been primitive. And all this had to be done in whatever weather one of the most inhospitable parts of Britain decided to serve up.

The Settle to Carlisle railway, then, is an engineering marvel. It has no sharp bends, the result of a brilliantly ambitious concept of driving it in an almost straight line to link the valleys of the Ribble and the Eden, even though that meant cutting through a wilderness of almost impossible country between the two. There are fourteen tunnels, the longest of them, Blea Moor, 2629 yards long, and twenty major viaducts, of which the masterpiece is Ribblehead, 1328 feet long and supported by twenty-four arches. As this is the only construction larger than an isolated farmhouse in this wild and lonely part of the dale, a first glimpse of it is often startling. It seems, initially, totally incongruous, especially when it sometimes appears out of swirling mist or low cloud. But then, if you stand and look at it for a long time (as I like to do), letting the imagination run free for a while, gradually its severe lines begin to blend into the whole austere scene.

Here, in the squelching treachery of Batty Moss, it can be a rewarding exercise to give full rein to the imagination and picture this forbidding land in 1870, the hutted homes of a thousand masons and engineers and navvies, with their imported 'wives', their drunken sprees, their Sunday services conducted by travelling preachers, their fights, their deaths. This was England's Klondyke, without the rich rewards. The masons got 6s 3d for a nine-hour day (31p in modern terms), which would have made them well-to-do workmen of their day, but they must have earned every penny of it, as did the miners working, incongruously, *above* the masons to drive their tunnel through the dripping dampness of Blea Moor. Every one of those 2629 yards cost £45 to blast away, making use of the recent discovery of the Swedish chemist, Alfred Nobel. His dynamite cost £200 a ton, largely because it had to be transported from Newcastle to Carlisle by road before starting another 50-mile trip into the Pennines. The first surveys were carried out in 1869; not until May 1876 was the line open for regular passenger traffic.

Ribblehead's station then provided a new focus for the slight social life of the dale. The vicar of Ingleton drove in pony and trap to conduct services in the passengers' waiting room and a harmonium was brought in to accompany the hymn singing. Years later it became a weather station for the Air Ministry.

At the other end of Blea Moor tunnel the little valley of Dentdale shoots away to the west to what must be one of the remotest townships in England, even today. Dent has a fascination all its own, perhaps because of its remoteness, but it achieved an odd fame during the First World War because of the abundance of knitted woollen comforters produced by its womenfolk for the men in the cold and muddy trenches of Flanders. So it's perhaps right that Dent should have been given a unique station, far from the town itself and, at 1100 feet, the highest on English railways. The station clings dizzily to the hillside, reached by a road that climbs, from the valley bottom, 450 feet in about half a mile. I don't really see it as the ideal start to a holiday, lugging a suitcase three miles up the valley before climbing that last hill to the train. On the other hand, I've stayed at the George and Dragon in Dent and enjoyed a perfect breakfast of trout freshly caught by an angler holidaymaker.

The line grinds on, still climbing, burrowing through Rise Hill to the highest point of the line at Aisgill Summit, and now it has to cross the desolation of Mallerstang Common, the very roof of this part of the Pennines, before starting the gradual descent into the broad and lovely valley of the River Eden and on to Carlisle.

The Midland Railway made its point; it got its mainline passenger and freight route into Scotland. The cost, in every way, was staggering but the legacy was a piece of engineering and communications history. A whole generation has grown up taking Britain's railway system for granted as something sleek and streamlined – and diesel-electric powered. But when British Rail today puts on one of its nostalgic 'steam specials' and one of the wonderful engines hauls its train gingerly across the venerable Ribblehead viaduct, you will see hundreds of romantics with their cameras, capturing the scene on film. They know that each occasion may now be their last opportunity to do so.

'The Good Old Days'

In 1953, the newly established northern outpost of BBC Television submitted to London a one-off programme on the history of the music hall. The superb City Varieties theatre in Leeds was the ideal setting for the documentary which traced traditional music-hall entertainment from the Victorian era up to 1953. One box in the theatre was set aside for shots of the audience and as the different eras were portrayed on stage, the eight occupants had to leap out of the box after each act for a quick change of costume. It was an historic moment for one or two stage personalities – Joan Turner and Stan Stennett, for instance – as well as for the theatre, for television, and for those people in the box. The narrator, named for the occasion 'The Spirit of the Theatre', was Derek Guyler, already a much loved radio personality in the 'ITMA' series, and the traditional chairman of the show was Don Gemmell, from the Players' Theatre in London, where the idea for the documentary had first occurred to its producer, Barney Colehan.

The programme was enthusiastically received at television head-quarters in London and back came an inquiry to Barney Colehan: 'Can you do some more?' 'Well,' said Barney, 'we can't really do the history of the music hall again, but we'll take the best of the idea and develop it.' And the best of the idea was the participation of an audience not only willing, but wildly enthusiastic, to don Edwardian dress, to grow (or glue) sidewhiskers of the most luxuriant quality and generally to enter into the spirit of a music-hall performance as it originally developed. The first 'Good Old Days' was recorded at Leeds City Varieties in July 1953 and, like Topsy, it growed and growed. The growth, in fact, was more at the rate of Jack's Beanstalk than little Topsy's.

Thirty years later, when the BBC decided to take the show off, there was a waiting list of 25,000 people clamouring for a chance to put on hooped skirts, starched shirtfronts, tails or dazzling military dress uniforms, to boo and hiss, to join in choruses, to acclaim or deplore the articulate artistic alliteration of Leonard Sachs, its chairman for all but the first four programmes. It would have taken nearly ten years for the last people on that waiting list to reach the head of the queue for a seat in the stalls or circle of the City Varieties at 'The Good Old Days'.

The beginnings were modest. In 1953 there was no 'run-out' at the front of the stage where the chorus line could kick their collective legs, or the balladeers serenade the audience, and no separate box for the chairman, who simply had a seat on stage. The playbill for the first show on Monday, 20 July 1953, reads like this: Billy Wareham (acrobat), Florrie Ford (played by Marjorie Manners, one of the great principal boys of pantomime), Eric Williams (magician), Joe King (comedian), Jack Pleasants (played by Geoffrey Hibbert, doing 'Twenty-One Today'), Pop, White and Stagger (comedians), Vesta Tilley (played by Joan Sterndale-Bennett) and the Can Can Girls. Alyn Ainsworth was the musical director; television direction was by Derek Burrell-Davis and the producer was Barney Colehan.

As the show grew in popularity with both theatregoing and television public, so the big-name artistes of the theatre began to show more interest. Within a few years Morecambe and Wise, Bruce Forsyth, Des O'Connor were all happy to appear on 'The Good Old Days'. The audience became ever more enthusiastic and a queue for seats began to form. Then, colour television arrived to add a completely new dimension to the scene and there was a positive explosion in the demand for seats. They became more precious than Cup Final tickets and theatrical costumiers who might well have been ready to close their businesses in the sixties and seventies suddenly found a new demand for frills and feathers and furbelows. The theatre itself, a glory of scarlet and gold Edwardiana, became another star of the same show.

'The Good Old Days' had by now reached the stage when the audience were better dressed than the artistes; the decor of the theatre was more elaborate than the sets. So producer Colehan had to prise a bit more money out of the BBC to dress up his show and to buy really big names to open and close it. It began as a vehicle for the *real* music-hall performers like Rob Wilton, G. H. Elliott, Randolph Sutton; after twenty years it had entered the age of the television star – still with a nostalgic appeal of its own but now, in the more sophisticated era of the small screen, having to compete on its merits as a television programme. Yet over the years the style of 'The Good Old Days' never basically changed. It got better in terms of content, dress and sets (and audience participation). It saw the age of the satire programme ('That Was the

Week That Was') come and go; it survived competition from the big-budget spectaculars like 'The Shirley Bassey Show' and 'The Morecambe and Wise Show'; it saw one situation comedy series after another wax and wane. But 'The Good Old Days' for thirty years retained its appeal to the public by simply putting on a music-hall performance.

The programme has gone out live and as a recording; it has gone out on every night of the week, at one time or another, from Monday to Sunday; it has been screened as early as 7 p.m. and as late as 11.30 p.m., and yet it has always found a television audience. The programme has been sold to Norway, Denmark, Sweden, Holland, Belgium. It gained a big audience in Australia and letters started to arrive from the other side of the world asking if seats could be booked for a time when Australians were on holiday visits to this country. One chap

The final chorus of 'The
Good Old Days'

Edwardian dress for the City Varieties Theatre

came to a show at the beginning of 1983 and started chatting to a girl called Jackie Toye, who used to be a chorus girl but on this occasion had a spot of her own. He said, 'I know you. I've seen you before.' 'Where?' asked the girl, a bit surprised. 'Watching the programme in Australia,' he replied. 'You were in the chorus then, but I recognize you.' The big stars had come to love it not only because it was the last major bastion of music-hall entertainment but because it was difficult – virtually impossible – to 'die' in front of such an overwhelmingly friendly audience.

Dear old Arthur Askey perhaps summed it up best of all. 'If you can't succeed on "The Good Old Days",' he said, 'you can pack it up because the audience have been waiting years to come, and when they get there, they nearly eat you.' According to Barney Colehan, the success of the world's longest running television show was based on a mixture of ingredients – the nostalgia, the joy of hearing and joining in the singing of favourite old songs, the delight of dressing up in colourful and flamboyant costume, the communicated pleasure of the artistes and the perfection of the theatre itself. Leeds City Varieties developed from what was really ,a large bar where people went for a social drink and the entertainment was a secondary attraction. It developed with the addition of stages and, in the case of the City Varieties, a custom-built theatre – but the original bar still remains.

Ten years earlier, Barney's secretary, Dorothy Bickerdike, closed the waiting list for the audience. Her filing system matched the mass appeal of the programme, listing the people who had been part of the show and those who were still hoping to make it. Those called up for the final 'Good Old Days' in 1983 had been on the waiting list for between eight and ten years! Dorothy, over the years, has sent out tens of thousands of letters advising would-be members of the audience that their turn would come in *x* years' time, then the glad tidings that their turn was now at hand, each letter accompanied by a leaflet with advice on authentic Edwardian dress. Recordings, in the later years, were made on Sunday evenings. 'I've often thought that a lot of people must have had a bit of a shock,' says Barney Colehan, 'walking round the centre of Leeds on a Sunday night and seeing a super-looking Jaguar stop and deposit four or five people onto the pavement in the colourful gear of eighty years ago.'

And Barney Colehan, the television innovator, has now been virtually immortalized by having the original City Varieties bar named after him: it's Barney's Bar today. And he deserves it because Barney is very much a part of Yorkshire's entertainment history. His name was known throughout the country even before 'The Good Old Days' took the stage. In fact, a phrase incorporating his name – and I mean *his* name, not just 'Barney' – was in use in just about every household in the country in the forties and fifties. Remember 'Give him the money, Barney'? The words were those of Wilfred Pickles, whose rich Halifax voice was heard on one radio programme after another at a time when television had not reached the north (or very many other parts of the country outside the London area, for that matter), but 'Barney' was none other than B. Colehan, producer of the homely, slightly vulgar, but greatly loved programme, 'Have a Go'.

Just as the audience for 'The Good Old Days' was to form an orderly queue in the future, so the towns and villages of Britain queued to be featured in 'Have a Go' in which Wilfred Pickles, accompanied by his wife Mabel and with Violet Carson (later to become Ena Sharples of Granada TV's 'Coronation Street') at the piano, interviewed local

THE BRITISH BROADCASTING CORPORATION

WOODHOUSE LANE   LEEDS LS2 9PX

"The Good Old Days"

Dear Sir/Madam,

Thank you very much indeed for agreeing to come along to the above programme in old time costume.

People who want to be in the theatre audience should dress and look like Edwardians. This can be achieved with a little ingenuity, as shown in the sketch on the right. Most important in the theatre is the costume above the waist, for only heads and shoulders of the audience will be televised.

What then is necessary ?

FOR A WOMAN : Hat shaped like a toque. Trim a modern pillbox type with a large flower at the back, or frothy veiling. Wrap or shoulder cape of fur, velvet or silk. Otherwise a slim-fitting coat with a high collar, worn with an old feather boa. Gibson Girl blouse, or an evening gown given an Edwardian neckline with an off-the-shoulder collar. Additional accessories could be a muff or a tiny artificial posy.

FOR A MAN : A wing-collar, with a cravat. Walrus moustache, hair parted in the middle and flattened down. High-buttoned waistcoat and a buttonhole.

"The Good Old Days" is now tele-recorded in colour. We shall, therefore, be most grateful if the members of our audiences will bear the following points in mind when deciding on their costumes :

PLEASE TRY TO AVOID WEARING WHITE DRESSES, HATS AND BLOUSES, THE GENTLEMEN ARE, OF COURSE, PERMITTED TO WEAR WHITE SHIRTS AS THESE ARE NOT TOO OBVIOUS.

LADIES — PLEASE DO NOT WEAR BLACK HATS OR DRESSES IF YOU CAN POSSIBLY HELP IT.

GENTLEMEN — NO BLACK SIDEBOARDS OR MOUSTACHES TO BE ADDED, PLEASE ; BROWN OR GREY ARE PREFERRED, UNLESS, OF COURSE, NATURE HAPPENS TO HAVE ENDOWED YOU WITH BLACK ONES !

(BARNEY COLEHAN).

characters, asked them a few simple questions and rewarded the answers with half a crown, five bob, ten bob. Pickles himself was, of course, a nationally known personality and his inevitable question to every unmarried interviewee aged between nine and ninety – 'Are you courting?' – went into the national vocabulary as well.

But producers are the unsung heroes of television and radio. They are the men and women who conceive the ideas for programmes (or work out the ideas of others), decide on the personnel they want, work out the budgets, set up the mechanics of the programme, supervise its transmission or recording, and stand or fall by the end product. To the public, I suppose, they are just names in the *Radio Times*, the *TV Times*, or at the end of the credits on the small screen, causing those viewers and listeners who notice the name to wonder, 'What does *he* do?' Well, the answer is quite simple: without him you wouldn't have been watching or listening to the programme that has just ended.

Such an anonymous creator was Barney Colehan. He was born in Calverley, five or six miles from Leeds, and started his working life as an apprentice to a chemist, but a love of music encouraged him to learn to play the piano, and the organ in his local church. He joined the Army as a private and the end of the Second World War found him a major, commanding a company of engineers in Germany. To this day he retains what is known as a military bearing, that is to say, he has kept his middle-aged figure in good trim, his back is as straight as a ramrod and he sports a magnificently curling moustache which is very much his trade mark. In Hamburg, while still in the Army, he felt he had a few ideas which might work on radio so he approached British Forces Broadcasting station there, then staffed by men like Geraint Evans, Cliff Michelmore, Jimmy Kingsbury, Robin Boyle. He was asked to present a programme called 'A Melody, a Memory', which I bet a few old soldiers will remember. They were invited to write to the radio station requesting a piece of music which evoked special memories for them. The programme was popular and a BBC career can be said to have begun right there for the apprentice-chemist-cum-Engineers'-major.

A BBC executive came over on the lookout for new recruits and Barney was invited to present himself at the studios in Woodhouse Lane, Leeds, with a view to joining the Corporation 'should a vacancy arise'. One did, and Barney Colehan joined the staff of the BBC and, amongst other programmes, produced 'Have a Go' for six years. As the television service started to develop he was invited to remuster, and, as a television producer, Barney remembered a series on which he had worked in radio called 'Top Town'. This brought together artistes representing the talent of one town or city to compete against others from another. Civic pride was very much involved and the series proved popular, so when Barney transferred to television, he resurrected the 'Top Town' idea. Soon, representatives of French television came across the Channel to look at the programme with the idea of developing it as a co-production with games and physical contests rather than artistic performances. The BBC, apparently, were not then quite ready for an international contest but they tried out the idea on the sands at Morecambe with competition from the neighbouring Lancashire resort of Blackpool. However, everyone seemed to have forgotten the rate at which the tide comes sweeping across Morecambe Bay. The first 'It's a Knockout' was almost literally swept away by the sea. But with two humorists like Ted Ray and Charlie Chester in charge of the presentation, the assembled throng managed to laugh away the problems and a successful show was in the can. 'It's a Knockout' went round the country, pitting one town against another, with David Vine as the presenter and Eddie Waring as referee, and finally it went into Europe. 'Jeux Sans Frontières' developed from 'It's a Knockout' and British civic pride was carried on a stream of ever more elaborate slapstick entertainment (requiring, nevertheless, a great deal of strength, fitness, timing, balance and practice) into France, Germany, Holland, Belgium, Switzerland, Spain, Portugal, Italy, Yugoslavia, the contestants playing their games across the frontiers of Europe.

So Barney Colehan emerged as one of the creative talents of television, operating for more than thirty-five years from his base in his home town of Leeds. The man whose ideas have provided spectacular but harmless, wholesome fun for millions of listeners and viewers, shrugs it away modestly. 'I've been lucky to have had the best years of television because I got into it when we were all innovators, inventors, experimenters. Nowadays, everyone is a specialist of some sort, but in my early days, like everyone else, I had to be prepared to turn my hand to anything . . . an excerpt from a theatre, a Rugby League match, I even did the first televised High Mass from Leeds Cathedral. It's a good life. At least it's never dull.'

So what of the BBC's decision to take off 'The Good Old Days' which has been so much a part of his life for thirty years?

'Well, people ask, "Don't you ever get fed up of doing the same old thing?" and I reply no because it's *not* the same old thing. The rules are the same, but there is a freshness every time I go to the theatre because it is a different set of people I am going to put together in this great jigsaw. I shall miss it very much indeed. I shall miss the people;

I shall think of all the artistes for whom we have been able to provide a break. "The Good Old Days" was never a "discovery" programme, but Ken Dodd made his first TV appearance in the show in 1956, with Hylda Baker in the same programme, and then there have been people like Lennie Bennett, Rod Hull and Emu, Hinge and Brackett, Frankie Vaughan, the King's Singers.

'What has gratified me has been the reaction to the news. Of course, there are the 25,000 people still waiting for a place in the audience but so many other people have said, "It's a national institution. They can't take it off." Artistes are conscious that there are so few places left where they can show their talents. It's all very sad, but in its way, pleasing. The worst thing that can happen is for the reaction to the end of a series to be: "And about time, too." Exactly the reverse has happened in this case and I am very, very glad about that. It means it has all been worthwhile.'

Lord Wilson

The Right Honourable Baron of Rievaulx, Knight of the Garter, Privy Councillor, OBE, Fellow of the Royal Society, Member of Parliament, was Prime Minister from 1964 to 1970 and from 1974 to 1976. In one of his more spectacular non-political pronouncements as Premier he described Frederick Sewards Trueman, then a Yorkshire and England fast bowler, as 'the greatest living Yorkshireman'. This conversation took place in his office at Westminster in June 1982.

Lord W.   I never watched much cricket, Fred, but I can recite you the Huddersfield Town teams of the 1920s and 1930s – great teams, great players. Once or twice I went to Headingley. You'll have been there, Fred . . .

F.S.T.   Aye, once or twice!

Lord W.   I seem to remember that in my last cricket season at school, my average was nought. But my best innings was nought not out. I don't think cricket was really my game.

F.S.T.   Did you ever know James Mason, the actor, because I seem to remember seeing a cricket medal with his name on it?

Lord W.   I don't know anything about that, but, yes, I did know James Mason. And when I became a junior minister (Parliamentary Secretary to the Minister of Works, about the lowest form of ministerial life, except the post of Assistant Postmaster General – that was a post I later abolished!) and then went to the Board of Trade, in 1947, as President, I had to save the British film industry. We had no dollars and I got permission to put some money into the home film industry. I went to see a premiere of an Alex Korda film – an absolutely ghastly film, it was – and he was having a very lush party in his very lush apartment. He said, 'What did you think of my film?' and I said, 'Well, it cost £700,000 to make and it won't make

£150,000 at the box office.' (I was wrong; it made £151,000!) He said, 'Ah, but wait until you see my *next* film.' I told him, 'But I *can't* wait, Alex. There's an awful lot of government money going into these films.' Korda simply went on, 'It's going to be filmed in the sewers of Vienna.' Great, I thought. I just can't wait for that! But the film, of course, was *The Third Man*, which was just about the greatest hit there had ever been.

I used to go to the pictures in Huddersfield as a boy. It was a big occasion to go to the pictures. It cost twopence ha'penny downstairs, fourpence upstairs and when I was feeling flush and sitting upstairs I joined in throwing stuff at the heads in the twopence ha'pennies (I was very badly dragged up, despite my Nonconformist origins.)

F.S.T.   When did you experience your first inclinations to be a politician?

Lord W.   I think when I had my photograph taken outside 10 Downing Street as a very young lad. I remember that in 1923, when I was seven, I had just had an operation for appendicitis and I had just come round in hospital in Huddersfield. It was polling day and my mother and father had come to see me in the motorbike and sidecar, WR 183, a Royal Enfield, and I said, 'You must get back in time to vote for Philip' (Philip Snowden, the first Labour Chancellor of the Exchequer). My father said, 'There's plenty of time – it's just up the valley.' However, they ran into thick fog and *didn't* get back in time to vote, but Snowden won, and Labour won (at least, with Liberal support), and from then on, right through my school career, my university days, my early political career, my ambition was to be Chancellor of the Exchequer. And I never was, I never was.

F.S.T.   Is that so, really? You wanted to be Chancellor rather than Prime Minister?

Lord W.   Well, through being interested in figures, so to speak, and remembering that ambition, none of my Chancellors did very much on their own!

F.S.T.   You were an Oxford don, weren't you?

Lord W.   At twenty-one. There was a shortage of economists. I had won the Gladstone History Prize the previous year. That was going to be published as a book. My subject was 'The State and the Railways, 1823–63' and after getting the prize I wrote it up into a full-length book. It was in page proof but that was the middle of the war and the publishers said, 'Oh, no one will be interested in railways after the war.' (How wrong they were!) Then, the day I went into No. 10, a stupid member of my staff sent the manuscript in its box off to a 'safe storage'. Well, No. 10 is the safest citadel in London but the papers weren't there. Some burglars got into the 'safe' place, ripped open the box looking for something more valuable, and it disappeared. But about six weeks ago [May 1982], in the next room to this where I have a lot of stuff stored, I pulled open a drawer and found the whole of the missing manuscript. How did we get on that subject?

F.S.T. I was marvelling at you being a don at twenty-one.

Lord W. Aye, well, Beveridge was coming to Oxford and wanted a research assistant. He said, 'Find me a lad but he'll have to finance himself.' Even the great Beveridge couldn't get money for research in those days. Well, I topped the school that year so I got a research fellowship, £300 a year. It was a lot of money in those days. My father had lost his job again and I was paying the rent as well, at home. After one term at University College, I went to New College where the only economist was getting a bit overburdened, and that was where all the Winchester boys were, the Wykehamists. After one lecture of mine, they knew more than I had ever known! But they were nice lads. Then Beveridge wanted a second economist at University College. There was G. D. H. Cole, but he was very busy and wasn't much up on the theory side, so I became a lecturer with my own rooms and everything.

F.S.T. From that academic background you became a Labour Prime Minister, and from my background I became an extreme right-winger in my political views. I don't know why that is.

Lord W. Well, it's because you were top of your profession. Were you like that before you played cricket? Was your father a Conservative?

F.S.T. I never asked my father how he voted. No, that's not right. There was a General Election, I think it was the first time I had a vote, and I asked my father what he was going to do. He said, 'You never ask anyone how they are going to vote. Never let me hear you say that again.'

Lord W. Ha! So you never knew?

F.S.T. I have an idea that he might have been Liberal.

Lord W. My father was Lib-Lab.

F.S.T. My background is not quite what people think it is. Lord Scales of Rawmarsh was my great-grandfather … Then, somewhere along the family tree, they do say that the title of the Earl of Northumberland was my family's rightful heritage. I've never tried to check it out but my great-uncle Tom fought the then Duke (successor to the Earls) of Northumberland in the High Court for the title.

But there were some papers missing and he lost the case.

Lord W. My father's family came from Rievaulx, in North Yorkshire, and he was actually born in a cottage next to the abbey. Around 1850 they started the social services by establishing workhouses, and my grandfather put in for the job. (I know this because the Helmsley Archaeological Society, when I became PM, started researching me and my family.) There was a tie between my grandfather and another candidate at twenty votes each. The wage was £1 a week and that was a lot of money in the middle of the nineteenth century. There was another meeting and the vote was still tied at twenty-twenty, so they then went to my grandfather and said, 'If you'll take eighteen bob instead of a pound you've got the job,' so he did. It was regarded as a very modern and forward-looking social service in those days. He did well and became workhouse master at York.

F.S.T. I was brought up right out in the country – there were only twelve houses where I lived – amongst horses. My father was a jockey and then he became a trainer. He turned to the mines only because the motorcar began to replace the horse as a mode of transport, children were coming along and he needed the money. So he became a miner at 37s a week and swore that the minute he reached the age of sixty-five he would retire and hoped never to see any of his sons go down a pit. My eldest brother did go into mining and he still is. I did a spell in the tally office of a pit after discussions between the Yorkshire County Cricket Club and my father because the county were anxious for me to develop as a fast-bowling prospect. Then, when I was awarded my cap in 1951, I was assured of a regular income and I was immediately called up for National Service. However, by playing football for Lincoln City . . .

Lord W. What position did you play?

F.S.T. I was a centre forward or outside right (I suppose I'd be called a striker today). But the football, plus professional cricket for League clubs on Saturday afternoon, plus five Test matches which I played in while serving in the RAF, plus games for Yorkshire when I got some leave, meant that I had £2800 in a deposit account in the old Yorkshire Penny Bank in Silver Street, Doncaster, by the time I came out of the RAF in 1953.

Lord W. I remember the Yorkshire Penny Bank. We used to take a penny to school and it could be banked there each week.

F.S.T. I drove a 1948 Rover motorcar.

Lord W. And I had an Austin Seven. I bought it just before the war for eleven quid and sold it for £3 15s.

Aircraftman Trueman (back row, second from left) in the RAF cricket team, 1952

When did you know you were going to become a *fast* bowler – as a kid?

F.S.T.   They say I was fast at school ... I don't know really. But where I was born, down in the very south of Yorkshire ...

Lord W.   My God, you might have been a Notts bowler or Derbyshire.

F.S.T.   When I started playing for Yorkshire, Notts checked to see just where I had been born and it was just in Yorkshire.

Lord W.   But you were within spitting distance of the boundary?

F.S.T.   Oh, yes. The nearest county ground to me was Worksop, where Notts play, and I was brought up on Larwood and Voce as household names.

Lord W.   Did you study them as bowlers?

F.S.T.   Never saw them bowl. But when I was at school we beat all the other schools in the area and the trophy was the Larwood Ball which is at Maltby Hall School now. But all round, my background is entirely different from yours.

Lord W.   Except for the accent, which I've never got rid of.

F.S.T.   Which I never would get rid of. I am a very proud Yorkshireman first and a very proud Englishman second.

Lord W.   But were you always a *fast* bowler – never tried spin ... never wanted to be a spin bowler?

1963:
Conrad Hunte
c Parks
b Trueman, 22

F.S.T. I did teach myself to bowl the cutter, which came in quite useful against the Australians at Leeds in '61. The first reference to me in *Wisden* does describe me as a spin bowler but I don't know where they got that from, especially as it was my first game for Yorkshire at Cambridge University in 1949. I'll never forget the buzz that went round the ground there because Ellis Robinson, the old off-spinner, asked me if I could bowl a bouncer. 'Oh, yes,' I said. So

Twenty years on. F.S.T., and his Courage Old England XI, in playful mood with
Basil d'Oliveira

Ellis told me, 'Let this fellow have one then. He can't play the short,
lifting ball at all.' So I bowled the bouncer, the batsman flung up
the bat to protect his face and Ellis caught him off the glove. And
that was my first wicket in first-class cricket. The buzz went right
round the ground because no one had seen an Englishman bowl a
bouncer since Larwood.

Lord W.   Did you ever play against Larwood?

F.S.T.   No, never, but I've seen a lot of him since he finished playing
and went to live in Australia. In 1958 I got George Duckworth to
introduce me to Lol and we took him into the dressing-room where
he was talking to the players when Bradman walked in. He spoke
to everyone else, took one look at Larwood and walked straight
past him without a word. Clearly, some bad feeling lingered on
from the bodyline era because in 1977, when Test players of all ages
and generations were gathered in Melbourne for the Centenary Test
celebrations, Bradman made the principal speech. It was a difficult
job, I know, to review a hundred years of Tests but it was very
noticeable that when he reached 1932 he said, 'We have now reached
the turbulent years, so we'll pass on.' And that was all he said about
the Larwood–Voce–Jardine tour. There must have been some *very*

bad feeling resulting from that tour, far worse than we have ever heard about publicly.

And talking of ill-feeling I don't know what it is, but I don't make friends of a lot of people – I keep myself to myself a lot of the time . . .

Lord W.   Your natural Yorkshire reticence!

F.S.T.   But it backfires on me sometimes. D'you know – there was a dinner at Lord's to mark fifty years of cricket between England and India, and I wasn't asked.

Lord W.   Is that right?

F.S.T.   Yes. Well . . . looking back to the 1952 series, you'd think I'd had a bit of something to do with Tests between England and India, wouldn't you? And that's what makes me wonder why I have never been honoured by my country. When I see some of the people walking around in cricket with CBEs and OBEs and MBEs and I think about the way some of them have behaved, well, I'd be ashamed if it was me. I don't know how I got my reputation, but I hear that I've been seen to drink twenty pints of beer of a night – I don't even drink beer. I'm told that I sleep with a different woman every night. (Wish to God I could manage it!) It is absolutely incredible. But people come up to me claiming to have been with me on such and such an occasion and saying, 'We got pissed together.' It's a sort of standard introduction and as soon as anyone says that I know it's somebody who's never met me in his life. So I don't know why it should be that I got that sort of reputation, but I'm damn sure that that's why I've never been recognized, even though I was the first man in history to get 300 Test wickets.

Lord W.   And against a better class of player, too, and when not so many Test matches were played. And they get a lot more money today, too.

F.S.T.   I got £50 for a Test when I played.

Lord W.   What do they get now?

F.S.T.   £1400. They can earn more in one season, now, than I earned in my entire career.

Lord W.   I think perhaps, Fred, that if you had had half the wickets and half the speed there would have been no problem! Did you ever see Wilfred Rhodes?

F.S.T.   I never saw him bowl, of course, but I met him on many occasions, especially after he went blind. It was marvellous, really, to sit with him while he recognized the quality of shots from the sound of bat on ball. He was a marvellous man.

Lord W.   There's one story about him which I remember. He was playing in South Africa in a Test and watched by a Yorkshireman

F.S.T. with Lord Wilson

who had emigrated. This chap was giving Wilfred all sorts of advice
– 'Watch it, Rhodes. Leave that one alone. Nah then, hit him out o'
t'bloody ground,' and all this was noted by a dear old lady sitting
close by. Eventually she asked, 'This Mr Rhodes ... is he any relation to the great Mr Rhodes?' The answer came promptly: 'The
great Mr Rhodes? He *is* the great Mr Rhodes!' But the old dear was
still puzzled. 'But I thought the great man was called *Cecil* Rhodes?'
The new South African pondered this for some minutes in silence
and then felt he had grasped what she was talking about. 'Cecil,' he
mused ... 'Cecil ... Ah, no, love. Tha's thinking of Cecil *Parkin*.'
The founder of Rhodesia clearly had no place in the thoughts of a
Yorkshire cricket fan.

F.S.T.   You've still a lot of Yorkshire connections, haven't you?

Lord W.   Well, I am Chancellor of Bradford University. I'm very keen
on Bradford and I've always had a high regard for their diplomacy
when I became Chancellor. I was speaking in Bradford on the Sunday before polling day when I first became PM (there were three
marginal seats there which we wanted to win) and over tea two or
three of the city fathers said they wanted me to take the job but
they had a bit of a problem in announcing it. If they did it immediately, it might look as though they were trying to help us win
those seats in Bradford, and if they left it until after the result of the
General Election, it might appear that they had asked me only
because I had become Prime Minister. So very cleverly they timed
the announcement for five past nine on the night of Polling Day

... after the stations had closed but before any result was known.

I went to live in Cheshire simply because my father lost his job in Huddersfield and his next one was on Merseyside. His employer in Huddersfield was a real tough nut. He'd say to my father: 'How many men have you sacked this week, Wilson?' and when my father said he hadn't sacked any he would be told, 'You've got to sack a quarter of your men every month – keep them on their toes.'

F.S.T.   Was it this sort of thing that turned you to politics and to Labour?

Lord W.   Not really. The family were Lib-Lab really and my father, being out of work at the time, acted as Winston Churchill's election agent in 1906 when the Liberals were swept to power. In those days there was a barbarous system whereby you had to stand for election again if you were appointed to office and Winston, after being appointed to the Board of Trade, had to stand again as a candidate and my father was his No. 2 agent.

F.S.T.   Did you admire Sir Winston Churchill?

Lord W.   Oh, enormously. He was all over the shop for long periods of time, but ... I was on his staff for a time during the war.

F.S.T.   Going back to your Huddersfield Town days ...

Lord W.   I used to go every Saturday morning, when they were at home. My mother would give me a shilling. It was a penny each way on the tram, and living in the Colne Valley we were on the route which went right through the town to Bradley and so past the ground. You had to be in the ground by eleven or you wouldn't get in. It was sixpence to go into the ground and then threepence, either for a pork pie – I usually had a pie – or a twopenny fish and a penn'orth of chips from a sort of canteen on the ground. So that left me with a penny which, by mutual consent, I trousered and that doubled my salary for the week. And once a fortnight I could watch them all – Alex Jackson, Charlie Wilson, Bob Kelly, McLean, little Billy Smith – that was a forward line! And Turner, Mercer, Taylor – Tom Wilson, centre half – an old-fashioned centre half.

F.S.T.   When you were made Prime Minister for the first time I sent you a telegram as one Yorkshireman to another, welcoming you to office, but I believe you got a different sort of telegram – from one or two people! – when you later described me as the greatest living Yorkshireman.

Lord W.   By Jove, I did. They came from all sorts of people, but especially one from J.B. Priestley – he didn't like the idea at all.

F.S.T.   Would you tell me what prompted the remark?

Lord W.   I can't really say ... I suppose I just felt it.

Food and Drink

Fish and chips × 1,500,000

SHOPPING LIST

Fish	697,000 pounds.
Dripping	230,000 pounds.
Potatoes	1,010,000 pounds.
Sauce	31,000 bottles.
Tea	10,000 pounds.
Butter	19,000 pounds.
Bread	39,400 loaves.
Milk	120,000 pints.
Sugar	19,000 pounds.
Salt	3,000 pounds.
Vinegar	13,000 pints

Harry Ramsden.

WELCOME TO

Harry Rams

Some of the ingredients needed to satisfy over a million and a half customers a year, which makes Harry Ramsden's the most famous fish and chip shop in the world

Fish and Chips

Five times almost every week for the past twenty-five years, Mrs Peggy Jones has eaten fish and chips for lunch. This information may cause a faint raising of the eyebrows amongst dieticians and heart specialists but it will occasion no great surprise to Yorkshiremen and women when I explain that Mrs Jones is the restaurant manageress at Harry Ramsden's, the world's greatest fish and chip shop. What else would they expect her to eat? No, if there is anything calculated to cause remark it is possibly the fact that the lady's weight is closer to seven stones than seventeen. There will, of course, be a minor outcry in certain quarters at the claim of 'the world's greatest', but it is difficult to see any rival claim which will stand close scrutiny.

Harry Ramsden's is no longer the largest in area or seating capacity but it was certainly the first of the large-scale establishments; its reputation had gone round the world before newer, and perhaps even more salubrious, emporia had even laid their foundation stones; and the sentimental attachment to it felt by Yorkshire people has never faltered over fifty years. If it is not absolutely the biggest, its operational figures, overall, must make more impressive reading than those of any rival firm: one and a half million fish and chip meals are served there every year involving 697,000 lb of fish – mostly haddock, but with a fair demand for the two alternatives, plaice and halibut; to go with the fish, 1,010,000 lb of potatoes are chopped up into chips; and to fry it all, 230,000 lb of beef dripping are melted in the frying ranges. In the chandeliered dining room, decorated in cream, orange and brown, 31,000 bottles of sauce are emptied onto the plates of fish and chips, and the sideplates of bread and butter take up 39,400 loaves a year and 19,000 lb of butter. Ten thousand pounds' weight of teabags go into the pots, to be served with 19,000 lb of sugar and 120,000 pints of milk. Over the meals are sprinkled and shaken 3000 lb of salt and 13,000 pints of vinegar.

Those are the bald, but impressive statistics. What makes Harry Ramsden's so different from a growing band of rivals is the sheer romance of its story. It was in the 1920s that old Harry set up his first shop in a wooden hut beside the junction of the A65 and the A6038 at White Cross (equally famous for its perambulators). There would not have been much trade from the motoring community in those days and the spot was not, at that time, particularly heavily populated. But if Harry had his eye on the future and could see the development of the car-owning family and the motorcoach outing, then it was an utterly inspired choice because travellers between Bradford and Otley or Ilkley, Leeds and Ilkley (and on to the Dales), or in reverse direction, were all going to pass his front door. Whatever the reason – and I can't for the life of me work out how it happened – after five years Harry's business had developed to such an extent that he moved, just thirty yards, to the other side of the road where new, stone-built premises, with a restaurant, were opened in 1931. It was called, quite simply, 'T'Biggest Chip 'Oile i' Yorkshire'. In 1972, with Harry now gone to the great frying range in the sky and a multicorporation running the business, it was extended again, given a complete facelift and redesignated 'T'Biggest Chip 'Oile i' t'World'. Now the terminology is interesting because it is usually only in Lancashire that the titular emphasis is placed on the sale of chips (how would the inhabitants of Coronation Street, for instance, ever eat if it were not for the 'chippie'?). In Yorkshire, it is almost invariably the 'fish shop' or 'fish 'oile' (a corruption of fish *hole*). But if the restaurant is today a glittering tabernacle to heavy-calorie ingestion, with acres of parking space, a children's playground, coin-operated slot machines (discreetly housed *outside* the restaurant), with a beautiful arrangement of potted plants *inside*, where customers can also buy seaside rock, lettered right through (and made in Blackpool!), it was Harry Ramsden whose foresight made it all possible. Rightly, it is his name which blazes over the entrance, his name by which the place will always be known.

It cost him £150 to start his first business, on the western side of the road; he arranged to sell it for £35,000 in July 1952, and a great gala occasion was arranged. Packages of fish and chips were sold at the price Harry originally charged in his first wooden hut: 1d (less than ½p) for a fish and a ½d for chips. And with the Yorkies' taste for a bargain, my countrymen queued for a mile down the Otley road to save a copper or two. There was a firework display and a cocktail party for the press of such formidable proportions that, thirty years later, hardened drinkers recall it with a delighted shudder.

And amidst all these festivities, old Harry found he just couldn't bear to part with his baby and the sale was called off! He died in 1963 and left £44,177, a notable triumph for private enterprise. The business was acquired by a man called Eddie Stokes, who in turn sold it to Associated Fisheries and, carrying on the tradition which had been established for so many years, the restaurant is open for twelve hours a day (11.30 a.m. to 11.30 p.m.) on 361¼ days a year. It closes on Christmas Eve for the second half of the day, all day on Christmas Day, Boxing Day and on the first Monday in February for the staff outing. This takes the form of a dinner dance in a local hotel – rarely more than ten miles away – and fish and chips is not one of the dishes on the menu. This is probably something of a disappointment to Peggy Jones, who explains her twenty-five years of advertising the product quite simply: 'I like them.'

Harry Ramsden's, then, is a Yorkshire institution and one which has sent away visitors from just about every part of the world with lingering memories of the quality of West Riding fish and chips – Americans, Canadians, Australians and New Zealanders, South Africans, Hawaiians, Yugoslavs, Poles, Germans. All-Black rugby tourists and Australian Test cricketers have dined there; I have seen a chauffeur-driven Rolls in the car park alongside a Women's Institute coach. Brian Close, until he was married, lived with his parents, brothers and sister in a house just a hundred yards away from the shop and he's probably lost track of the number of his guests, up for a drink after a day's play at Headingley or Park Avenue, who have enjoyed a fish and chip supper from Harry's.

It would be wrong, however, to regard Harry Ramsden's as the be-all and end-all of that particular trade in Yorkshire. For a hundred years, fish and chips have been a staple diet of the working class and it is a little difficult to explain just why the dish should become a special favourite in the north of England generally, in Yorkshire especially, and in the West Riding specifically. Friday lunchtime has long been established as the particular part of the week when housewives contemplate no cooking – every fish 'oile in the area will be busy frying from 11.30 onwards. But the trend started by old Harry was followed by a number of businessmen, setting out not only to cater for the day-long trade but to establish a dining-out tradition.

Mother Hubbard's started up on the Bradford ring road, not far from the city centre, and claimed for its stylish, 200-seat restaurant, a Civic Trust award for good design – and with some justification, too. I'd give the firm a special award of my own anyway, for branching out to open another place in Oldham, Lancashire. That is missionary work of the highest order because Lancastrians have long been starved of quality fish and chips. They sell hake, principally, rather than the haddock which is the staple fish in Yorkshire; they cook theirs in vegetable oil while we use beef dripping; their batter seems to have been thrown together while ours is carefully blended – in some cases to a recipe which is guarded as closely as the Crown Jewels. Aye, I reckon Mother Hubbard's, Oldham, deserves to prosper as much as any business I've ever heard of.

In 1982, there was a challenge to Harry Ramsden's claim to be the world's *biggest* fish and chip shop when work started on Fryer Tuck's in Bradford (I think that prize punster, Brian Johnston, must have thought up the names of so many Yorkshire shops – Stan's Plaice, The Merry Frier). Fryer Tuck's has operated since 1977; after opening an extension and putting on a more sophisticated menu, the managing director, John Trevor Saville, threw down the gauntlet: 'It is an indisputable fact that we are now the biggest fish and chip restaurant in the world. Our seating capacity is larger than Harry Ramsden's.'

Oh, aye, lad. Is that so? Well, there's more to being the world's *greatest* than sticking in a few extra seats. Contemptuously, Harry Ramsden's manager, Frank Begg, dismissed the claim: 'You've only got to look at their menu to see that Fryer Tuck's is not just a fish and chip restaurant. Harry Ramsden's started as a traditional shop and we still are. Fish and chips are all you can get here. Fryer Tuck's serves lobster, scampi and other seafoods.' And I take his point. They won't get many lads calling in at Fryer Tuck's on their way home from the pub at night for a lobster and a bag o' chips. That's not to say a lot of people won't enjoy sitting down to a *Thermidor* or *Newburg*, just the same.

But we have only looked at the big fish in this particular pond so far. Scattered around the county are thousands of little shops which rely simply upon out-sales – to people who religiously (sorry, Brian Johnston!) call every week for their Friday lunch, who like to eat them from the paper in their car or sitting on the wall outside the shop, or to pick up the evening meal on their way home from work (teatime opening is now very popular). It is quick, easy and relatively cheap and the quality is guaranteed.

Heretical though it sounds, it seems probable that the first shop selling fish *with* chips, was in London. In 1968, the National Federation of Fish Friers decided that distinction belonged to Malin's, at 560 Old Ford Road, and presented the shop with a plaque proclaiming that fact. In West Yorkshire, the claim to the greatest antiquity was made a few years ago by a shop in Yeadon which staged its centenary by using Harry Ramsden's gimmick of selling fish at one penny, chips at a ha'penny, with the free, added attraction of staff dressed in Victorian garb. And the Whitehead family, proprietors of the shop, used a batter recipe handed down from the lady, Hannah by name, who operated there in the 1870s.

Fish, in nineteenth-century England, was a cheap commodity and thus had a great appeal to the poor, who were numerous. It was cooked, with no great regard for hygiene, or the disposal of waste, in premises which would have caused the modern health inspector to faint on the spot. And such malodorous sites were not difficult to find! The marriage of fish with chips at the end of the nineteenth century became an established and popular meal, and all the events, discoveries, experiments, inventions and legislation leading up to that would fill a book in their own right. In fact, they have done so already. Gerald Priestland, formerly a distinguished foreign correspondent for the BBC and later its religious affairs correspondent, might at first sight seem an unlikely author of *Frying Tonight – the Saga of Fish and Chips*, but in 1972 he produced a brilliantly written and superbly humorous history, researched with great scholarship. It would probably come as something of a surprise to the average customer, standing in the queue at eleven o'clock on a Friday night, to learn that the Maoris, Eskimos, Incas, Jesus Christ and Dr Magnus Pyke all come into the story – but they do.

So perhaps it is not entirely inappropriate that the trade has become just a little more cosmopolitan in Yorkshire in the last couple of decades. There are Chinese takeaways selling fish and chips, and Indian and Pakistani immigrants have got in on the act. Shops have begun to sell a wider variety of food – curry sauce, pies, battered sausage, fritters of various kinds. But to the purist, haddock and chips remains the fish 'oile's *raison d'être*. Don Mosey has never recovered from the horrifying experience of taking Geoff Miller, the Derbyshire and England all-rounder, into a shop during a Test match at Headingley and hearing the philistine ask for 'haddock special with curry sauce on it'. That was in 1979. To this day, Don greets Dusty with a glance of withering scorn and a muttered 'Peasant!'

It's a pretty safe bet that you can stop at any fish 'oile in Yorkshire and rely on the quality of the food you buy. The gilded emporia are the showpieces, but it's the little shops you will find in every other street that feed the workers – and some of the pleasure seekers as well. Just five minutes' walk from the Test match ground at Headingley is Charlie Brett's, where there is usually a queue for the 'out-patients' end of the business and a full house in the café, both of which are accommodated in an ivy-covered cottage fronted by a rose garden. Of all the small fish shops in the county, this is a prime favourite with cricket lovers, and during a Yorkshire match or a Test, the hum of conversation is strongly cricket tinged.

It took quite a long time to persuade John Arlott to taste the delights of Charlie Brett's, despite its popularity with his friends amongst the London-based cricket writers. It was Peter Laker, the *Daily Mirror*'s cricket correspondent, who finally coaxed John to the ivy-covered-cottage-in-the-rose-garden early in the 1970s and, from then onwards, no Test match was played at Headingley without John dining there on one evening during the match with a whole string of England cricketers who have gone, over the years, as his guests. As John went through his last season as a BBC commentator, there was a farewell dinner to him at every Test venue (and a lot of places in between!), but for Headingley, John laid on his own party. He took over Charlie Brett's for the evening with a guest list which included almost the whole of the 'Test Match Special' commentary team and the English press corps. He managed to get 'Lord Edward' Dexter to the feast but could not quite persuade 'Pope' Jim Swanton. But it was something of an occasion, the memory of it treasured by Charlie and his family equally with the occasion of John's first call. Arlott was the wine correspondent of the *Guardian*, as well as its chief cricket writer, and he devoted that week's wine column to his visit to Charlie Brett's. The cutting, now yellowed with age, is framed and hangs on the wall of the restaurant. It was prepared with many a chuckle in the commentary box and a certain amount of evangelical assistance from a couple of John's colleagues there. When it finally appeared it read like this:

The recital of the costly splendours of the winelist of the White Horse at Chilworth [a previous article] calls for a balancing note from what no one in his right senses would call the other end of the social spectrum. Sausage and mash and bread and cheese are far too easy; almost any wine is proud to go with either. Fish and chips may seem less simple.

First, it is necessary to define fish and chips. According to the Mosey doctrine, fish and chips means fresh, preferably Grimsby-landed haddock, skinned, filleted and fried in the best Yorkshire beef dripping. The batter must be light, between firm and crisp; the chips should be solidly cut, fried in the same dripping and served dry and firm. He adds, 'This is real fish and chips and none authentic is produced more than ten miles from Bradford Town Hall.' Brett's falls within all of that. It is at North Lane, numbers 12 and 14, Headingley. Headingley is on the north side of Leeds and apart from cricket matches might be visited on the way to the superb small Norman church of Adel, Kirkstall Abbey, Roundhay Park, or the Romanesque St Aidan's with its Brangwyn mosaics and painted panels by Joseph Heu.

The ivy-covered-cottage-in-the-rose-garden

Brett's was founded in 1919 by Arthur Brett as a sideline to his carriage business. He stabled the wagons and horses on the other side of their semi-rural lane. It is now run by his son Charlie ('Charles on Sunday') whose wife and their daughter Jane run the dining room. Special haddock and chips, with tea and bread and butter, costs 60p – with a double portion of haddock, 82p. Soup as a first course is 15p; cheese salad and a sweet are available but these are not the serious matters; the fish and chips *are*, and the claim that Brett's is the *best* fish and chip shop in England, and therefore the world, must be taken seriously. The South does not know what this dish means. The haddock is full and fleshy with a splendid depth of flavour, utterly clean with no hint of over-cooked fat which so often taints the dish elsewhere. It is delivered straight from Grimsby into the cold cupboard at the back of the shop during the night and eaten within the day.

The chips are flowery, dry and biteable ('I never jib at paying over the odds to get right potatoes'). A sophisticated variant may be plaice (65p) but the haddock is the soul of the matter.

What to drink with this splendid plate? At Safeway, just over the main road, there is fine, rounded, Appelation Contrôlée, French-bottled Macon Blanc, at £1.20, which is good enough for any man. Mr Brett will allow you to bring in your bottle and will supply glasses free from corkage charges if you come, stay and leave in orderly fashion. He may even store your bottle in his ice box so that it is chilled for your meal.

For those who regard the Moseyan delimitation of the area of fine fish and chip production as heretical, the Co-op, in its 3400 nationwide off-licences, has a Graves at £1.75 a bottle, an Italian Soave for £1.05, drier and probably better with fish and chips. Chablis is £1.85 and the Yugoslav Lutomer Riesling £1.18, Liebfraumilch £1.22, Moseler Blümchen £1.20. A white Beaujolais, not easy to buy but Duchy Vintners of Helston have it at £25.90 a dozen inclusive of VAT, fits the plateful like a glove, and it will stay with bread and cheese afterwards if you've not got the crust to take red wine with you. Not all wine travels; good fish and chips does but it must be good, and dripping-fried. It should be taken, cooked, from the place of its birth, re-heated in a dry frying pan and though it is not *quite* the same, eaten with gratitude and plenty of pepper and salt. Vinegar? – mmm ... mmm ... to taste, but not the best of friends of wine. But part of fish-and-chips with hyphens.

Brett's is at the bottom of the last remaining front garden in North Lane and the dining-room, neat and tidy but not large, is through the shop. It is open 11.30 to 2 on weekdays, 4 p.m. to 7.30 on Mondays and Thursdays and well worth the journey.

Well, the prices quoted there – both fish and chips and wines – will date the article to the early seventies. Haddock and chips now cost £1.90, plaice and chips £1.98 and Brett's has now gone up-market to the extent of adding morning coffee-time to its opening hours. John Arlott, retired to his rock in the English Channel, can no longer be a regular patron but the affectionate contact between John and Charlie is maintained by birthday telephone calls from time to time. Charlie, who used to ride a motorbike in the Isle of Man TT Races and was a four-handicap member of Horsforth Golf Club, treasures the sporting links that have been built up and consolidated over the years and was delighted to receive a Christmas postcard in 1981 signed by the whole media party accompanying the England cricket tour in India, expressing a certain yearning for a few of his haddock specials as a variation of their curry diet. And as each new season comes round, there is a comforting air about the prospect of the lunchtime pilgrimage up to North Lane to taste once again the excellence of Charlie Brett's culinary art and the smiling welcome from Mrs Brett and Jane, plus the other helpers – Mrs Mary Gray, who, at seventy-four, has been serving in the restaurant for twenty years, and Mrs Muriel West, a mere beginner after only eighteen years. Charlie Brett's is not only a part of Yorkshire's fish and chip tradition – it's part of cricket's story as well.

And if the pedigree of the ivy-covered-cottage-in-the-rose-garden has not already been stamped, let's call upon one of Charlie's fondest memories to establish it beyond all question. Herbert Sutcliffe, one of the greatest of all Yorkshire batsmen, was – in retirement no less than his playing days – a patrician figure and almost regal in his style. 'He used to park his Rolls-Royce outside,' recalls Charlie, 'with his two damn great dogs in the back and come in for an order which never varied – haddock and chips with just a sprinkling of salt and vinegar and two fish, wrapped separately, with nothing on [i.e. no salt and vinegar]. One day I asked him what was the significance of this particular order and he told me: "I drive up the road and stop outside the Parkway Hotel [a large, residential place on the northeastern outskirts of Leeds]. I eat the fish and chips, the dogs have a fish each, and I sit looking at the hotel wishing they could serve food like this."'

Theakston's Brewery

They sailed their longships into the Humber and up the Ouse and from there fanned out into the smaller river valleys leading up to the high Pennines. And the Norsemen of a thousand years ago left their mark on twentieth-century maps with their topographical terms. Their *becks* run down their *gills* from their *fells*; they wander over *mosses*, through the *heath* and *ling*, skirting hamlets and villages which were Norse *setts*, *seats* and *sides*.

And with them, around 950 AD, came a man who settled near the North Yorkshire village which was to become Masham (Maasum) to the locals of today. His name, Anglicized over ten centuries, was Theakston. Through the aftermath of the Norman Conquest, through the Middle Ages, the Tudors, the Stuarts and the Hanoverians, the Theakstons led a quiet, unremarkable existence on their farms and smallholdings where Wensleydale gently subsides into the Vale of York. It was not until the reign of George IV that a Theakston broke with family tradition and left the land to ply a new trade and even then it was scarcely a spectacular plunge into the unknown. Young Robert Theakston moved just two miles across the fields from his father's farm at Wathermaske into the village of Masham to set up a brewery – or rather to take over the Black Bull and its brewhouse. His partner was John Wood, his friend and brother-in-law, and when they started in business together Sir Walter Scott was still writing the Waverley novels and their fellow Yorkshireman, William Wilberforce, still had six years to wait to see the fulfilment of *his* dream of the abolition of slavery.

This was scarcely an era when a small brewery in North Yorkshire was likely to make a dramatic impact upon the commerce of Britain, but quietly, steadily, the business of the Black Bull prospered until its brewhouse could no longer cope with the demand for its ale. A new brewhouse and maltings were built a few hundred yards away, and the founding Robert lived just long enough to see it go into production. By now John Wood was long since dead and old Robert saw the brewery they had created together pass into the hands of his two sons, Robert and Thomas. More than a hundred years later it is old Robert's great-great-grandson, Paul, who is chairman of the limited company which, in the last two decades, has seen a massive explosion of success in a world deep in the trough of economic depression. And it all came about because of two factors: first, the family business's concern with its own standards which have always been maintained with great care over so many years. The brewing formula evolved just under a century ago by Edwin, grandson of old Robert, is still basically that which gives us Theakston's excellent best bitter and the more renowned Old Peculier (note that 'e', by the way). The second factor, ironically, was the policy of the giant combines which, through the fifties and sixties, gobbled up so many of the small brewers of traditional English ale. The Big Six, as these huge conglomerates became, developed in the 1960s a policy of supplying their countless thousands of pubs with refined beer in metal kegs – 'pasteurized' beer, as it was contemptuously dismissed by the traditionalists. And the campaign was largely successful, backed as it was by the usual propaganda war. The dictum of the Big Six was, in effect, 'Thou shalt drink keg beer' and it enveloped us. We were brainwashed into believing that Double Diamond actually did work wonders, that Tetley Bittermen really did embody all the masculine appeal which the girls could not resist.

But as always in times of social revolution, there was a resistance movement lurking in the shadows, seeking the chance to counterattack. The Society for the Preservation of Beer from the Wood was too ponderous, too grandiose a title to induce many to rally to its colours. But CAMRA, a slick, streamlined abbreviation of Campaign for Real Ale ... ah, now that did rouse the faithful. The resistance movement was born; the beer-drinking Maquis combed the countryside, shunning pubs which served only the despised 'pasteurized' beer, and pointing the way to the Real Ale dispensaries. It became a cult form of drinking. And nearly 150 years after the brothers-in-law Robert and John had started up their business, Theakston hit the jackpot. Today their beer goes round the world – to the USA and the Middle East, to the Dutch, who have spent centuries learning how to recognize a good pint when they taste one. And it is still sold to pubs and clubs throughout the length of our own land.

In just over ten years the output of best bitter and Old Peculier (there's that 'e' again) has increased twenty-fold. From twenty-three employees in 1969, the brewery now has a payroll of more than 150

Before a German bomb dropped on the White Bear – Lightfoots staff *circa* 1905 ...

... and a Theakston's pub of the 1980s

and the 'new' brewhouse of 1875 cannot cope with the demand. It's still there and it's still working, homely and mellowed, looking rather like a film set for a Dickens novel, and to real ale-drinking purists it is very much a place of pilgrimage. But in 1974, the company bought up the old state brewery of Lloyd George, in Carlisle, where all Theakston's best bitter is now brewed.

But, like all success stories, this was not achieved without one or two problems on the way. Indeed, looking at the records of the old Peculier (ah! now we have it) Court of Masham, it seems that the Theakstons were lucky to stay in existence for old Robert to start his brewery in 1827 – brawling and failing to attend church got them into trouble from time to time. And what about 'Being rude to the Vicar – fined Six Pence'? Now that made me think; it would have cost me a bob or two, if that had been a twentieth-century offence, to play in the same Test side as the Reverend David Sheppard.

Generations of Theakstons served with distinction in two world

wars and in between found time to buy up the local opposition, Light-foot's Brewery. But as old Robert's mother had been a Lightfoot, perhaps it wasn't so much a takeover as a family merger. And the company records show that it brought Theakston not only the brewery but 'nine pubs and an excellent cricket team'. Nice to see they got their priorities right in 1919! The flagship of the Lightfoot fleet of nine pubs was the White Bear, but it went for a burton (to mix my metaphors a bit) in 1941 in a way that makes you want to weep. The year gives a clue, but even so it's just a bit difficult to think of a quiet village pub in rural North Yorkshire as a primary target for German bombers! But that's how Theakston lost the old White Bear. Maybe it was the fumes of the maturing Old Peculier, borne up into the night sky, that befuddled the Heinkel bomb aimer. Or perhaps he was just trying to get rid of his load after being driven away by the ack-ack defences of Tees-side. But the sad story is that a lone bomb demolished the White Bear. If it had been possible to trace the pilot he might well have lined up with the others in the dock at Nuremberg!

However, the new White Bear rose from the rubble after the war by the expediency of transferring the licence to a row of cottages near the former Lightfoot Brewery, knocking the houses inside out and creating a brand new pub with an old-world atmosphere – lots of dressed stone and polished wood. And it is here that pilgrims from a remarkable number of countries try their first pint of Old Peculier after visiting the shrine of old Robert, the founder – the 1875 brewery about a quarter of a mile away.

It was here that I met an old mate who, spot on in his timing, joined the sales staff of Theakston as the expansion was developing. Peter Squires is the firm's sales services manager but he will be better known to most people as a Yorkshire, England and British Lions wing three-quarter and, from 1972 to 1976, a Yorkshire cricketer.

So there you have a happy ending to the story – a story which reads something like one of those dynastic Victorian novels. I'm not a great beer man myself these days, but I do like a story with a happy ending. And I wonder what old Robert would make of it all if he could come back today. His Black Bull is now shops and offices. But his great-great-grandson sits in the chairman's seat just across the yard from the new White Bear.

Kit Calvert and Wensleydale Cheese

This, believe it or not, is an extract from the Gospel according to St Luke, Chapter 15:

A farmer 'ad tweea lads and yan on 'em, youngomer, sez teu t'aad feller, 'Fatther, give ez mi sharr ev t'farm 'ats ta cum ta mi.' An' seea he lets 'em sharr an' sharr alike.

Nut manny days efter, t'youngomer githered aw he'd gitten t'gither and teuk hiszel off into foreign parts, and thar weeasted his brass i' lowse leevin. An' when he'd warred aw, hard times cam ower t'land he was in an' he cu' ta hey nowt. Seea he went an' hired hizsel, an' his maister sent him inta t'fields ti sarra pigs an' he'd a fain itten t'pig meeat fer neeabody gev him owt. 'Twas then he com te his sensis an' he said, 'Hoo manny o' my fatther's sarvants hez eneugh an' ta spar' an' I'se fair hungered. Ah'll away heeame ta mi fatther an' Ah'll say, "Fatther, ah've sinned agen heaven aṅ' ye an' Ah's nut fit ta bi co'ad yan o' yours. Tak' mi on as a sarvant lad." '

Wi' that he gat up an' set off an' his fatther spied him cummen when he war a long way off an' he was wheea fer him an' ran oot ta meeat him an' threw his arms roond his neck an' kissed him fer he war fain ta see him. An' t'lad said, 'Fatther, Ah've sinned agen heaven an' dun a gert wrang t'ye an' Ah's nut fit t'bi coa'd a lad ev yours.'

But t'fatther coa'd sarvants, tellen 'em ta hurry up and t'fetch best suit o'cleeas th' cud finnd an' help him t'don, and git a ring fer his finger and shoon fer his feet an' fetch fattest cawf in an' kill't: 'Sooa ez we may aw itt an' bi joyful, fer mi lad 'at Ah thowt was deead's alive. He had him lost but noo he's fun ageean.' An' th' started ta enjoy th'sels.

Noo t'owder lad was oot i' t'fields an' as he co' neear t'hoose he heeard music an' dancin'. An' coa'en yan ev t'sarvants aside he ast what wez on, an' t'sarvant teld him, 'Thi bruther's cum'd heeame and becos he's back seeafe an' soond, thi fatther's kill't t'fat cauf.'

He than went crazy an' wadn't gang in, seea his fatther cam' oot t'tice him but he pleeaned te his fatther: 'Aw t'yeears o' mi life ev Ah bin like a sarvant, dun aw thoo ast er teld mi an' yet nivver ez mich ez a lile gooat hez t'gin mi, seea's Ah cud hev a merry neet wi' mi mates. But ez seun ez this weeastrel co's back, efter squanderin' aw thoo gev him i' lowse leevin' an' fancy wimmin, thoo kills t'best stalled cauf fer him.'

But t'fatther sez tew him: 'Mi lad! Thoos awlis wi' mi an' aw Ah hev is thine. It's nabbut reet yan sud mak' merry an' bi joyful fer thi' bruther 'at we thowt was deead's alive. He was lost an' noo he's fun.'

The Parable of the Prodigal Son, as it was once told by the local preachers of Wensleydale. The difficult work of translating the spoken word into written form was undertaken by Kit Calvert, probably the best-known and best-loved man in the two northern dales and universally known as the Complete Dalesman. It is difficult to quarrel with the title. I don't think anyone would want to, anyway. And let's give a credit, too, to the typesetters of Butler & Tanner Ltd, who must have had one hell of a job getting all the apostrophes in the right place!

Not content with that little masterpiece, Kit threw in for good measure two other parables from the same chapter of St Luke – The Lost Piece of Silver ('Er what wumman wi' ten bits o'silver, if she was ta loss yan on 'em, wadn't leet a cannel an' ratch ivery neuk an' coorner till she finnds it?') and the Lost Sheep ('Whars t'man amang ye, if he hed a hunderd sheep an' lost yan on 'em, wadn't leeave aw t'others on t'fell an' gang an' laate t'straggler till he finnds it?'). He then turned his attention to St Luke 2 – the Christmas story – at the request of the vicar of Kendal, in neighbouring Cumbria, and went to the parish church there to read it. St John 19 (Trial and Crucifixion) and 21 (Filling the Nets of the Fishermen) followed, and then the Twenty-Third Psalm ('He lets m'bassock i' t'best pastur an' taks mi bi t'watter side whar o's wyet on peeaceful'). It's marvellous stuff. But then Kit Calvert was as much at home with words as he was through his eighty years, with Wensleydale cheesemaking, farming, livestock and heading the Hawes Gala procession in his pony and trap. What could be more beautiful in its simplicity than the way he once described the death of his wife: 'She was called home on July 11th, 1975, after forty-four years of our happiness together'?

The blue eyes twinkled under the sparse white brows, the brown trilby hat set firmly on his head, even indoors, as Kit Calvert talked with sturdy pride of his life in the dale he loves. At first it is difficult to remember that this man fought bureaucracy as few individuals have fought it, that he took over as secretary of a bankrupt business where he waged a series of boardroom battles worthy of one of those dynastic serials on television, that the business Kit Calvert revived in 1935 with a working capital of £1085 was sold thirty-one years later for £487,000.

A more unlikely tycoon is difficult to envisage, but then who would think of tycoonery in terms of Wensleydale cheese? Far more important to Kit Calvert than making money was the work of saving a foundering business which was a lifeline for the valley farmers. And after retiring from business he became an even more unlikely tycoon, buying not a string of racehorses, but a three-year-old black and white pony, Dolly, and then a donkey, Jack. He died, mourned by a whole valley, in 1983.

Dolly, a sprightly if venerable old lady of eighteen, is almost as well known around Hawes, harnessed to either a gig, governess cart or an Irish jaunting cart, as Kit himself. She's something of a star, leading the annual gala procession, and has appeared on television in episodes of James Herriot's 'All Creatures Great and Small'. Jack, the third member of this trio of firm friends, was also for many years a prime attraction on gala day until he disgraced himself (in that perverse way that is the speciality of donkeys) by refusing at the water splash in the Gala Day race and depositing his rider in the drink. Dolly and Jack share a paddock behind Kit's bungalow and until his death no day passed without an affectionate exchange of views by the three of them.

Kit Calvert was born on 26 April 1903, at Burtersett, a mile and a half up the fellside above Hawes, the son and grandson of quarrymen. For just under eight years – starting when he was five! – he walked the round trip of three miles to school in Hawes five days a week winter and summer, carrying lunch in a waterproof satchel strapped to his back. The menu never varied – with his father, even on the top rate, earning 18s a week (90p), there was little scope for a varied diet. It was two slices of buttered bread with either treacle, marmalade or jam between them, and half a round bannock with currants in it. Wet clogs and stockings in the winter rain were discarded on arrival and left to dry in the classroom while lessons proceeded. Spending money was ½d a week, ritually handed out on Tuesday (market day), which bought a handful of sweets at Mrs Metcalfe's general grocery store. Kit left school shortly before his thirteenth birthday, but he had already earned his first wage – 4d (about 1½p) – from the proprietress of a boarding house, plus a lunch, for one working day – Saturday. He was then ten years old and his duties were: wash the flagged footpath and sweep the cobbled yard; polish the brass and steel fire-irons; clean the brass taps in the bathroom and then any other jobs about the house which could be found for him. His employer was imaginative in this respect. Somehow it is not difficult to recall that just over the hill in Wharfe-dale, Charles Kingsley had written the story of an exploited apprentice!

At thirteen, Kit was earning 5s (25p) a week plus full board, working for a lead-miner-turned-farmer who was crippled by a cough from his mining days, but when Kit asked for 1s a week rise, the farmer could not afford to pay it. So off went young Calvert to exercise the farm-hand's time-honoured right to stand in the market place and hire himself to anyone who would pay the best wages. Kit was staggered to learn that a cattle dealer in Bainbridge, three miles from home, valued his services at £1 a week plus full board. He soon discovered the reason for this: his new boss was fond of a drink and Kit earned his £1 the hard way. Five years passed and then an accident ended his working days on the land. A spell of part-time work at the auction mart taught him the value of livestock and he began to invest his few shillings of savings in calves and lambs until he had his first £100 – an enormous sum for a working man, especially in the acutely depressed agricultural industry. Then a farmer he had helped in his spare time died and left Kit around £300. He rented a piece of land at £70 a year and sold milk over the kitchen table to neighbours, taking what was left over to the local cheese factory, only 200 yards away.

Now the story of Wensleydale cheesemaking is a long one, going back to the great Norman Earl Alan, who was concerned about the spiritual welfare of his troops garrisoned at Richmond and so asked for monks to be sent from Normandy. The Cistercians were practical men and the shrewd old abbot agreed only on condition that land was granted to his monks so that they could be self-sufficient. The land they were given was on the northern side of the Ure valley, between Askrigg and the break in the Pennines beyond Hawes, and today it is still known as Abbotside. And that is where Wensleydale cheese was first made – from the milk of the monks' ewes grazing on the land where the forest and scrub had been painstakingly cleared. But the monks couldn't grow corn there, so they asked for more fertile land and were given the area farther down the valley where they built their abbey of Jervaulx. However, they were thrifty souls and retained the land at Abbotside, so it was their tenants who now produced the cheese to be taken to the abbey either for the monks to eat or to be sold. The business had been established before the end of the twelfth century and it continued in just the same way until the Dissolution, after which it was discovered that the cheese could be made just as well, and with less trouble, from cows' milk. For the next three and a half centuries Wensleydale cheese continued to be made, still to the monks' recipe, using a process known as 'pickling'. This involved running the cheese into tins coated with brine, leaving it there for three days but turning it every day. It was not until 1874 that a visitor to the area – the head of an agricultural college in Bucks – pointed out that this was a laborious way of making cheese. He experimented, and discovered that entirely satisfactory results could be achieved by introducing dry salt directly into the cheese at an earlier stage and, overnight, the stage was set for mass production.

But by 1930 every branch of agriculture, including cheesemaking, was in a desperate state. Kit Calvert, now married, could get only £2 each for his lambs in 1931; the following year the price was 31s, and in 1933 it was down to 17s 3d – 86p for a lamb! His wife sold milk at 1½d a pint and whatever was unsold was sent to the dairy, to be made into cheese or butter, at 5d a gallon in summer, 8d in winter. But Kit's business sense was developing. He arranged for a farmer neighbour to slaughter a couple of lambs each week and to hawk the meat from door to door at what would be bargain prices for housewives. I don't suppose the local butcher was particularly happy about the competition but a farmer in the 1930s could not afford the luxury of worrying about such matters. From the meat sales, Kit was to get a basic 17s 3d – as he would if he had sold the lambs whole – and any amount above that, split with the slaughterer. It worked out that Kit received just over £1 for each lamb. Then, in 1933, the owner of the dairy became insolvent and, although the business was revived briefly, it collapsed again in little more than a year. Gone was the cheesemaking industry in Hawes.

The old blue eyes saddened for a moment as Kit Calvert reflected on the next part of the story. He puffed in sad, silent recollection on the clay pipe (or the same type of clay pipe – he regularly received them as Christmas presents) that he had smoked for years. 'For years we had all been selling milk at uneconomic prices. Many farmers had gone bankrupt; some had been driven to suicide. It was a dark, forbidding world for the farmer in the 1930s and no one could see how it was ever going to get any better.'

After the collapse of the Hawes creamery, most local farmers had started to send their milk by train through the Pennines to Appleby, to the depot of a large dairy company but this couldn't take *all* the milk yield of the district. It rankled with Kit Calvert that a small but (to him) vital local industry had been allowed to die. He was sure it could be made viable and take its place (which he saw as extremely important) as a local industry. He thought and thought – puffing a good deal of smoke through one of those clay pipes, I'm sure. Then he called a meeting of local milk producers and tried to persuade them to reopen the local dairy and to buy shares in the new company. No one offered to risk a single penny. He tried again: 'I'll show my own faith in the idea by investing £100 myself.'

His bank had just told him he was £234 overdrawn and unless this was reduced to £200 in *one week* it would foreclose on his stock of sheep and cattle. The bank also demanded the deeds of the Calvert house as security for the overdraft. Kit refused to hand them over and, instead, used the house to secure a loan with which he reduced the overdraft by £35 leaving him £100 to buy twenty £5 shares in the new dairy business he was trying to promote! Still the local farmers were unwilling to support the venture. So Kit now turned to local tradesmen and persuaded a few to buy small blocks of shares. Then he turned again to the farmers – with just the faintest hint of blackmail.

The dairy depot in Appleby and the recently formed Milk Marketing Board took about 500 gallons of milk a day from the Hawes area. That was less than half the local production and the only other outlet for the producers (apart from over-the-table sales) would be the Wensleydale creamery – if it was reopened. Kit told the farmers they couldn't expect help from a business they were unwilling to support themselves – at least to the extent of two £5 shares. So a little more money trickled in. Arrangements were made to form a company with the board of directors made up of shareholders with an investment of not less than £25 (five shares) and this persuaded a few reluctant farmers to shell out another £15 apiece. If they were going to have any brass at all in this new company, they wanted to know what was happening to it! And so Kit Calvert set out on his great financial adventure with a company capital of £1085.

He ran into his first snag straightaway. The man who held the creamery building on a £950 mortgage refused either to lease or rent the building to the new company. So Kit's board bought it for £800 and promptly remortgaged it for £600. The first £200 of capital had gone but at least they had somewhere to make cheese, even if they hadn't yet the apparatus. Next came the discovery that they had to provide £500 security to the Milk Marketing Board to cover one month's milk prices and they got round this by buying £500 worth of government stock which the Milk Board held as their security. That left £385 to buy vats and shelves to store the cheese, a wagon to collect the milk (few farmers had their own motorized transport and still fewer had anything big enough to carry a cargo of milk churns) and then 200–300 pigs to drink the whey – the byproduct of cheesemaking. There were one or two other problems, too, at least one of them of a major financial nature, but Kit Calvert optimistically pressed on. A licence was obtained to make cheese and butter and arrangements were made for 500 gallons of milk a day to be processed.

On 20 May 1935, Wensleydale Dairy Products Ltd went into production with a board of nine directors, a cheesemaker at 35s a week

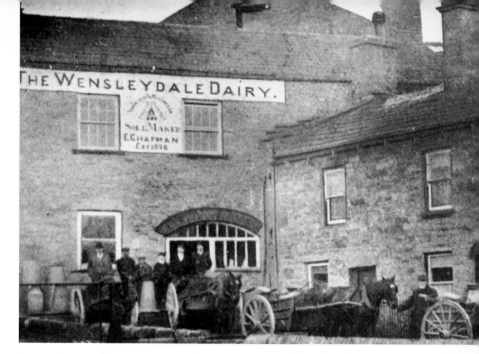

Where it
all began

(to go up to £2 as soon as the company could afford it), an assistant
cheesemaker at 25s and a fourteen-year-old general help at 7s 6d. The
company secretary was Kit Calvert. He agreed to work for one year
without salary and the board was to decide what to pay him after he
had produced his first balance sheet. A buttermaker joined the staff a
few months later at 45s a week and the staff was completed by a lorry
driver who doubled up as milk collector and as the-man-who-looked-
after-the-pigs (35s a week).

A one-ton Ford truck was bought to collect the milk and, working
out that the cost of buying it on hire purchase was £290 against a cash
sale of £240, the company secretary somehow persuaded five of his
directors to guarantee a bank loan which was paid off in seven months
and cost the company less than £9 in charges. In terms of high finance,
that meant a saving of more than £40 and every penny was something
more than precious in this precarious launching of Upper Wensleydale's new industrial venture.

Again, problems. A month's supply of milk had to be paid for not
later than the 10th of the following month, so cash flow was vital. Yet
such is the nature of cheesemaking that, once the milk is bought, the
cheese is not ready for sale for some time. Reserve capital is necessary
and the company had none. Cheeses from the factory were normally
great big 16-lb whoppers which had to be carved up and weighed by
shopkeepers into saleable portions. Kit hit upon the idea of producing
1-lb cheeses (which were ready for sale in four days) and talked farmers' wives, and their children, into selling them at farm gates or local
beauty spots like Aysgarth Falls, to the day trippers. Even at 6s a
dozen, the price at which these miniature cheeses left the creamery,

they solved the cash-flow problem and nearly fifty years later Kit was still speaking of them with affection. They probably saved the life of the company.

But then he encountered difficulties much closer to home. His board was composed of men he had known all his life and – perhaps more to the point – twelve who had known him. They were hard-headed Yorkshiremen, essentially conservative and ultra-careful in all business matters, concerned about the spending of every penny, with a horror of 'speculation'. And the most conservative and ultra-careful of them all was the chairman, Jimmy Dinsdale.

Mr Dinsdale was a retired farmer and therefore had time on his hands to watch young Calvert, his thirty-two-year-old company secretary. He didn't like, and was highly suspicious of, anything which broke traditional patterns – like making miniature Wensleydales and flogging them at farm gates. Kit was battling with competition from eight other manufacturers who had been in business for years, most of them with larger outputs than himself. He knew he had a fight on his hands to find, and hold, his markets and the last thing he wanted was a chairman who feared new initiatives breathing down his neck.

Nonetheless, by the end of the first year's trading, Wensleydale Dairy Products Ltd showed a profit of just over £1500 – nearly half as much again as the capital sum which had seen them start up the business. Now came the time for the board to decide on Kit's salary and, although he was a director and, indeed, the principal shareholder, he was asked to step outside while the matter was discussed. When he was recalled, he was told that his wage was to be £1, payable from the time the company had started trading. So his reward for turning a bankrupt company into one making a £1500 profit in his first year was £50.

'I was deeply upset and offended,' he recalled, 'but I didn't complain.'

After thinking it over, however, he told the chairman that while he accepted the first year's wages, he was not prepared to carry on at those rates, and when Mr Dinsdale called another meeting of the directors, they increased the offer to 25s a week! Kit refused and was asked what he thought he ought to be paid. He replied, 'At least £3 a week.' I can just see the expression on the faces of those tight old blighters. One of them choked on his words. 'No workman in Hawes is worth £3 a week,' he spluttered. It must have been a boardroom battle to beat anything ever seen in the City of London because these were fellows who wouldn't dress anything up in smooth phrases. They were used to conducting *their* business deals over sheep-pen rails, down at the auction mart. I'd give a lot to have been a fly on that boardroom wall. Kit sailed into them. 'And what about t'cheesemaker? He's due for a rise. He agreed to take 35s a week until we could afford to pay him £2. We can afford to do it now.' And then came a bit of real Yorkshire – a classic case of looking after t'brass. 'He's not asked for a rise,' said the chairman. 'We don't give money to anyone until he's asked for it.' Kit was told to say 'nowt' to the cheesemaker, but he went off and put the point that a five-bob a week rise was due to him. And what did he reply? Need you ask? 'It's mine by right and I'm damned if I'll *ask* for it.'

Kit decided it was now all becoming too daft for words, so back he went to the board and said, 'If he doesn't get his five shillings, I'm resigning here and now.' The cheesemaker got his rise, but the old chairman hadn't finished with Kit. No young upstart was going to get the better of Jimmy Dinsdale. Ten days after that board meeting, Kit read an advertisement in the local paper: 'Secretary wanted for Wensleydale Dairy Products Ltd. Applications to the Chairman. Salary to be negotiated.'

The power struggle was now in full cry in that unlikely setting beside the slow, lazy waters of the Ure. Kit Calvert took stock of the situation. He went to see the owner of an old mill at Bainbridge, five miles down the valley and asked, if he got a licence, could he lease the property to start his own creamery. The landlord said yes and within an hour the story was back in Hawes where it circulated through the town like a forest fire. With this little plot simmering nicely, Kit went along to the Wensleydale Products meeting called to sift the applications for a new secretary.

The chairman's welcome was not exactly cordial. 'You can't sit in this meeting,' he said. 'The only business is to find your successor as secretary.' 'That's right,' agreed Kit amiably. 'I'm a director so I just thought I'd drop in and help you.' A short list of three was drawn up from seventeen applicants and the meeting was adjourned to a later date.

The following morning, chairman Dinsdale steamed into Kit's office to announce with heavy satisfaction that he had it 'on good authority' that Kit wouldn't get a licence to run his own business in Bainbridge so he was wasting his time. The plot was thickening quickly. Next, Kit rang up a senior Milk Marketing Board official in Newcastle and asked if he would come over to see him in Hawes. The following Thursday, Mr Pepperall from the MMB arrived in town. He had a cup of tea at the Calvert residence and his arrival did not pass unnoticed. Word drifted around town: 'Kit Calvert's got a bigwig with him from t'Milk Board.' The pair of them walked down the main street where Kit casually introduced Mr Pepperall to Mr Chapman the grocer – who just happened to be a director of Wensleydale Products. No business was discussed; it was just a friendly social call on a fellow director, but the mere fact of who Mr Pepperall was had now begun to take on a sinister significance to the other directors. After all, it had been Kit's idea ro revive the cheesemaking industry; he was the one who had done all the talking to the Milk Board; he was the one who knew the men in high places; and he did seem pretty friendly with this chap Pepperall who had come a long way just to see him. Jimmy Dinsdale had only got *his* tale – that Kit wouldn't get a licence for his own business – from the local secretary of the National Farmers' Union. It could be wrong. In fact it was beginning to look as though it *was* wrong.

Kit drifted into the Board Hotel with the big man from Newcastle and they 'just happened' to run into Mr Blenkinsop, another director of Wensleydale Products. Again it was a friendly, social chat – but the seeds of doubt were now growing to full bloom. Next, the Calvert-Pepperall duo strolled across the river to the local beauty spot, Hardraw Scaur Falls, passed a pleasant hour there and then walked back into Hawes for a meal before Mr Pepperall set off home to Newcastle. Not a word of business had been discussed, and Mr P. must have been mightily intrigued about what was going on. He told Kit, 'I've had a very pleasant afternoon, but I'm sorry I haven't been able to help you at all.' 'Don't worry, sir,' said the arch-plotter, 'I'm sure it has been a useful afternoon.'

And indeed it had. While they had been savouring the rural delights of Hardraw Scaur, a hurriedly convened meeting of six of the nine directors had been taking place in the Board Hotel. Lounging outside the pub was one Joss Hutchinson, ostensibly carrying out his duties as the market tolls collector, but also half a crown better off for reporting to Kit the comings and goings of his fellow directors. Kit went home well satisfied with his day's work.

We shall never know what was said in that unofficial board meeting but the atmosphere at the next official meeting was distinctly more cordial towards the company secretary. They were sorry, said the other directors, that he had not applied for his own job because he would certainly have been on the short list – or maybe a short list would not even have been necessary. Would he not now reconsider his position and apply for the post? 'No,' replied Kit, 'but if this meeting is in order I'll do my best to help pick a new secretary.'

Well, some of the directors might have changed their views but not the chairman, not old Jimmy Dinsdale. He still wasn't going to have a thirty-two-year-old upstart getting his own way. He leaped to his feet now and thundered, 'Of course the meeting is in order. *I* convened it.'

It was obviously a situation that impressed itself on Kit Calvert to a marked degree because more than forty years later his memory of the dialogue which followed was very clear:

Calvert: I know you convened the meeting but what is the business?

Chairman: To select a secretary from the three candidates we are about to interview.

Calvert: How did these men know we needed a secretary?

Chairman: From an advert in the *Stockton and Darlington Times*.

Calvert: Who sent the advert to the paper?

Chairman: I did – because you resigned.

Calvert (turning to the other directors): Did I? And did *you* authorize the advert being published?

Confusion. Muttered debate. A request (again) for Kit to apply for the job himself.

Calvert: No. Not with those three chaps out there. Not until the chairman goes out to tell them they are not required.

Chairman: Never.

Calvert: Then I'll not have my name considered.

They seemed to have reached deadlock until one of the other directors offered to go out and tell the waiting candidates that they were no longer required. Kit wouldn't allow this. The chairman had to do it himself. And after a lot of snarling and teeth-grinding, Jim Dinsdale went out to see the three applicants. What it must have cost him in lost pride, only the good Lord knows.

But Kit Calvert still hadn't finished with him. When the chairman came back into the room, Mr Blenkinsop (whose 'chance' meeting with Kit and the man from the Milk Board must have contributed mightily to giving the directors cold feet) moved that the company engage Mr Calvert as secretary at a wage of £3 a week. Before the motion could be put, Kit intervened: 'Wait a bit. I'm not taking £3 a week.'

What?

'Yes. I would have taken £3 and given you of my best, but now it's all different. I want £4 a week, to be recognized as manager and not be harried by the chairman in things I believe to be in the best interests of the company.'

There was a long, long debate. It must have been just one pill too many for Jimmy Dinsdale to swallow and some of the directors must have felt that Kit had gone a bit too far. But the threat, spread with

Kit Calvert's
(centre back)
on his
'retirement',
1968

a simple ingeniousness which guaranteed its potency, of the man who had worked a few miracles in the past year now starting up a rival business only five miles away was enough to sway the waverers. One by one the directors ranged themselves against the chairman and Kit Calvert was appointed secretary and manager at £4 a week. Trying to salvage something from the total wreckage of his pride, the chairman obtained from every director a solemn pledge that nothing of the boardroom business would ever be disclosed outside that room.

Kit Calvert went home to supper, well pleased with his day's work but with no thought of communicating the cause of his satisfaction to anyone else. A promise is a promise. Before he had finished eating, the local joiner called at his house. 'Isn't thy ears burning?' he asked. 'No. What for?' replied Kit. 'For what thoo's done t'owd Jim Dinsdale ... and torn a wage o' fower pund a week out o' t'company.' There are *no* secrets in a community like that.

Wensleydale Dairy Products Ltd got on with its business pretty well after that. By 1937 the company was ready to buy its first delivery van – for £25, second-hand, 12 cwt – with big advertisements on each side (Wilkinson's Pomfret Cakes – I hope they appreciated the 'plugs') in which Kit drove around the market towns of Yorkshire, Lancashire and Cumbria. In the same year they branched out with a new dairy in Richmond which supplied milk to the Army at Catterick Camp and turned surplus gallonage into cheese.

I suppose Kit Calvert can be thought of as just another awkward old so-and-so of a Yorkshireman, as so many of us have been termed over the years, whatever our calling, but to me he is a bit of a hero. I wish we produced a lot more like Kit Calvert, the Complete Dalesman.

Brian Rix

From playing farce to helping the mentally handicapped, Brian Rix's career might be said to have spanned the whole field of human emotions. He has been actor, aircrew cadet, Bevin boy, actor-manager and is now secretary general of the National Society for Mentally Handicapped Children and Adults. Throughout it all he has remained a characteristically blunt Yorkshireman with an intense love of the county – and its cricket. The conversation took place at Lord's in August 1983.

F.S.T.   I am always fascinated by the very strong theatrical connection that Hull has – yourself, Ian Carmichael, Tom Courtenay, Dickie Henderson's parents came from Hull, John Alderton – he's not quite a Yorkshireman but he dearly wishes he was – they all have Hull connections. Why is this, do you think?

B.R.   I think one of the principal reasons is there has always been a deep feeling of resentment in Hull at being sort of cut off from the rest of the county. As far as links with everywhere else were concerned, you always had to change at Doncaster and it created a distinct impression of isolation. This feeling of resentment was emphasized during the war because when the Germans raided Hull it was always referred to as 'the northeast coast', never 'Hull'. Hull got the shit knocked out of it by the Luftwaffe. The very shit knocked out of it. Did you know that 97 per cent of all the houses in Hull were damaged in air raids? No, I'll bet you didn't. But 97 *per cent* ... Yet London got the billing, Coventry got the billing, Liverpool got the billing. Never Hull. We got blitzes galore yet very rarely did anyone know what was going on there. And there has always been a feeling in Hull that it was the end of the line – literally, and in every other way. Direct trains never went there, bombers never went there (according to the news bulletins), York-shire cricketers were never chosen from there. And that's why there was always this strong feeling of independence there. Right – you don't acknowledge us, we'll bloody well get on with living our lives just the same.

It may well be that that is the reason for the very strong amateur theatrical tradition in the area. It's a great deal to do with a tradition of making your own entertainment – the Hull Savoyards, the Hull Operatic, the Hornsea Operatic – there were lots and lots of these societies, good amateur companies. Hull, too, don't forget, had its own telephone exchange and that is how Rediffusion started. The Hull trawler owners at the time had a lot of money and some of them got together and said, 'Look, we're digging up the roads to put the telephone equipment in. Why don't we lay some lines and we'll put in the first cable radio?' And that's how Rediffusion started. You paid sixpence a week and you got one of those old-fashioned curved loudspeakers – my grandparents had one – and you tuned in to Rediffusion. And it was done with Hull trawlermen's money. So this great company which spread right across the country started in Hull.

F.S.T.   And then there were the old East Yorkshire buses with that funny rounded top. They do say that top was specially designed to fit through the curved archways of places like Beverley. Is that true?

B.R.   That's absolutely true, yes. You see, that's interesting ... all those monks, not only in Beverley, but in Hull as well – there's Whitefriargate in Hull, Blackfriargate ... and Hornsea Mere, that wonderful fishing area, once the monks used to fight battles over it for the fishing rights. You go into Hull itself, think of the historical background ... My father's first office was in the Land of Green Ginger, where Daniel Defoe starts *Robinson Crusoe*. Sadly, all that's been discarded. People don't think so much about that sort of thing today. They look at the historical landmarks of other cities but they don't think about Hull in the same way. They think, Oh, Hull – smelly old fish, and that's all. It's tragic; it's infuriating.

F.S.T.   Oh, yes. I've always found Hull people tremendously proud of their heritage and I've a lot of connections with the area mainly because of Rugby League. I've always been a fanatical supporter of the game – nothing better than watching Hull FC or Hull KR.

B.R.   Sorry about that, Fred. My father, who was a supporter, with my uncle, of Hull City, became a director of the club.

F.S.T.   It used to be a city of level crossings, as well.

B.R.   Indeed. In the pre-Beeching days, from Hornsea you would stop twelve times on the way to Hull for level crossings.

F.S.T.   And not many people know it, but there was once, at Hull Kingston Rovers ground, a very thriving baseball club.

B.R.   Yes, there was. I didn't see it but I remember seeing it reported in the *Hull Daily Mail*. And speedway, too. My father, under a nom de plume, 'Shellback', used to write in the Saturday sports edition. A 'shellback' is a man who has come home from the sea. He was a bloody good writer, too, my old man.

F.S.T.   It's always been a bit of a windy corner of the country, too, around there.

B.R.   Oh, indeed. The ball would always move on a breezy morning at the Circle ground. At Scarborough, up the coast, they used to have sea frets. In my day, when I was a boy, they were called sea rooks. I don't know why.

F.S.T.   The coldest day I have ever known in cricket, anywhere in the world, was at Hull when we were playing Somerset once. It was so cold that Paul Gibb, one of the umpires, had to leave the field to use the toilet and after what seemed an eternity the other umpire (it might have been Bert Rhodes – I can't remember) had to go to see what was the matter. It was so cold that Paul hadn't been able to fasten his trouser buttons! And I know that most of our players fielded in long-johns. When it's cold at Hull, it's really cold.

B.R.   I actually saw Sutcliffe and Hutton get their 315 by tea against Leicestershire at Hull in 1937 and Sutcliffe said to Hutton – Sir Leonard will tell you if you ask him – 'Shall we go on for the first-wicket record?' (555 – Holmes and Sutcliffe). Hutton said, 'Yes, OK,' and was out first ball after tea! I was there. I actually saw that. I think they'd both got something like 152 each by tea. Can you imagine it now?

F.S.T.   There was a famous match against Sussex in 1922 when Yorkshire bowled them out for about 26. Abe Waddington used to tell me about that – he took 7 for 6.

B.R.   I saw Macaulay ... I saw Hammond (he never made any runs when I saw him bat) ... I saw Bradman (*he* never made any runs when I watched him, either) – all either at Scarborough or Hull, but I never saw any of the greats make runs. I saw the Yorkshire greats make runs, but none of the others. I remember Hedley Verity, with a fast ball, which he disguised so incredibly. He would use it about every third over but it was beautifully disguised.

F.S.T.   Great names ... great memories. But what about your own personal memories. What do you recall of your own childhood?

B.R.   I was born in Cottingham, five or six miles from the city, left when I was four and never went back there until my mother's funeral fifty-odd years later. My brother pointed to the outside wall of the room in which I had been born and I asked him if there was a big brick wall, and a gate with metal supports and a railway station round the corner. He said, 'Let's go and have a look,' and there it was, round the corner, just as I had described. I had remembered it from more than fifty years back because I had fallen out of my pram on the level crossing there!

F.S.T.   I can see there's nothing wrong with your memory, Brian. Carry on, please.

B.R.   We moved to Hornsea where I went, first, to nursery school and then to St Bede's at Hornsea, where I started to learn to play cricket properly. I first had a trial for Yorkshire schoolboys when I was twelve and a bit; I was the youngest in the trial and made 54 not out and took 8 wickets for 17. The 'not out' should read 'retired' because I was made to retire by the selectors who wanted to see somebody else. I did well at prep-school cricket and went on to Bootham School, in York, which I hated. Why? Because I was bullied unmercifully. It happened because I was moved there during the summer term of 1937 and was pushed straight into the Second XI at the age of thirteen and played in the First XI before the end of the season. My peers in school cricket were very jealous and angry and I didn't know how to cope with the situation. I started to play for Hull at cricket when I was sixteen, opening the batting and the bowling. I didn't realize until I went into the Air Force at twenty that I had been doing all this while short-sighted and I have worn glasses ever since. It was the Air Force who said to me, 'You've been driving illegally for three years, or whatever, because you can't read a numberplate at the regulation distance.' Strangely enough, this did not interrupt my PNB (pilot–navigator–bomb-aimer) training and I carried on with some new lenses they gave me. What did finish it was sinus problems which affected my hearing, all stemming from having had measles when I was a kid. They had to hoof me out then and I went down the mines, at Askham Main colliery.

F.S.T.   So didn't you have breathing problems in the mines?

B.R.   Exactly. They found I had terrible breathing problems so they hoofed me back into the Air Force again where I became a medical nursing orderly instructor.

F.S.T.   So how did you start in the theatre?

B.R.   Well, this was before I had joined the Air Force. I had my audition in Hull and got my first job in Hull at the New Theatre. My sister worked with Donald Wolfit and I knew him, consequently.

I knocked on his dressing-room door and did my first interview there and my first audition there. I got the job by reciting a Robert Service poem called 'Bessie's Boil'.

F.S.T.   Bessie's *what?*

B.R.   Boil. It's about a woman who has a boil on her bottom. It ends with, 'Aye, missis. It wants to be cut, anyone can see that. You want to be at the 'ospital where all the doctors are at. You see, missis, this part o' the 'ospital is cloased on account o' repairs. Us fellers is only painters, we're painting the 'alls and the stairs.' And that was my party piece for the audition because I knew nothing else.

F.S.T.   And that got you into a company playing Shakespeare?

B.R.   Yes – I played then in *Hamlet, Twelfth Night, King Lear*. Years later Wolfit said to me he'd always thought I was going to be a comic actor but at that time his company was made up of actors who were too young for military service, too old for military service or what was known as temperamentally unsuited to military service, of which there were quite a few. You kept your back to the wall on certain occasions! But he was a good first boss as far as I was concerned. I was paid £3 a week and I celebrated my appointment in Fields Café which was near the New Theatre in Hull, in King Edward Street. I had egg and baked beans on toast. To have an egg was a great thing in 1942. Then I was attested for the RAF and put on ten months' deferred service which turned out to be two years' deferred service, so I left Wolfit and went on to Harrogate, to the White Rose Players and ultimately joined the Air Force on D-Day, which was a bit remarkable.

F.S.T.   So the RAF and then the pits and the RAF again and you came out in 1947?

B.R.   Yes. I had a bit of money saved and I went to my father and uncle and borrowed £450 from each of them and put in £100 of my own. My father and my uncle were shipowners and they were also in petrol. (You can still get Rix petrol in Hull, did you know that?) And with £1000 I started my own company in Ilkley, at the King's Hall.

F.S.T.   I've passed it dozens of times.

B.R.   I called it the King's Hall *Theatre*, of course. That was the scene of the famous first night, Easter Monday, 1948, when the curtain came down only on the right-hand side of the stage and the actors had pushed a desk to the left-hand side so they could be seen. And I couldn't get on to make my entrance because the door through which I had to enter kept hitting the desk. So I walked round and made my first entrance on my first night as an actor-manager by climbing in through the window at the back of the set. So, apart from the polite ripple of applause for the new actor-manager in Ilkley, there was hilarious laughter because the play was *Nothing but the Truth* and the first scene is in a New York skyscraper about thirty-six floors up!

F.S.T.   And you made an entrance through a window! Great story.

B.R.   Perfectly true, I assure you. And it goes on. We had hired some tails from a local firm for Colin Collins, our stage director, and he climbed up onto a grid to lower a rope – in full view of the audience. Colin was up there and we stood solemnly in the centre of the stage and pushed the desk back when both sides of the curtain were in place, and we thought we could get on with the show. Colin came down and he was destroyed. There was a hundred years of filth up there and his suit of tails was utterly destroyed. I took it back to the hire firm and they refused to accept it and I had to pay an awful lot of money to replace it. So I hung on to the tails, putting them in one of the wardrobe baskets, and ten years later Leo Franklyn wore that suit for four years during the run of *Simple Spymen*. A good example of Yorkshire thrift, don't you think?

F.S.T.   Exactly. I like that.

B.R.   Yes. It cost me a bomb in Ilkley but I got four years' work out of it in a play ten years afterwards. I'm rather proud of that as a Yorkshireman, never mind as an actor-manager. So that's the whole Yorkshire background – cricket, childhood, school, theatre. Oh, and I mustn't forget that at Bootham School we were evacuated to Ampleforth College and the very last time I played for MCC was against Ampleforth when you and I did the bowling, Fred. You got 6 and I think I got the other 4.

F.S.T.   Aye, and I remember you dropped a catch off me in the slips as well.

B.R.   I would have had a bet that you'd remember that. We've known each other a long time, haven't we? I suppose it was at the time I was at the Whitehall that we met. A lot of cricketers used to come to see the shows because it was always bloody well raining up at Lord's. And you were very friendly with Dickie Henderson then, weren't you?

F.S.T.   Yes. A great old mate, Dickie. But let's get back to you . . .

B.R.   Right. After I had lost every penny of my £1000 in Ilkley, I tried Bridlington, which once again was absolute bloody nonsense because, as you know, Bridlington is a summer holiday resort and I opened there in November. There I was, playing in the Grand Pavilion, Bridlington, a huge barn of a place, and trying to persuade a few locals to come and see us. Well, it wasn't all that successful but it was a bit better than Ilkley, and in the following year, 1949, two things happened: first of all I met Elspeth [Gray] and married her and I also ran into a play called *Reluctant Heroes* which I put on for the first time in Bridlington. I realized I had got a great success so I went on tour with it in 1950 and it was during that year that I fought my way into the Whitehall Theatre.

F.S.T.   Just how did you happen to meet Elspeth?

B.R.   I had started another company in Margate, in addition to the one in Bridlington – I was very ambitious! – and when I was auditioning for the Margate company I was sitting with a hangover, crouched over a gasfire in the Interval Club in Dean Street, and thinking, I wish I was anywhere but here, you know? And in walked Elspeth. I remember like now exactly how she was looking and how she was dressed. She had on a beautiful green tweed costume, and the eyes and the red hair. It was the most amazing vision and I gulped and I spluttered and I chased after her for the rest of that night. There was a job for her in Margate but as soon as I caught up with her I said, 'I have a vacancy for an assistant stage manager in Bridlington' and pushed her into the job. I offered her the vast sum of £4 10s a week. She'd been a Rank Charm Girl and had just done a film, *Tottie True*, and been paid real money. So eventually she came for £8, and as I was only paying myself £12, we got married on a joint income of £20 a week.

We were married with me looking like someone out of Belsen because I had not eaten for about three weeks. I had contracted a condition that is usually found in sheep – God knows how I'd picked it up – which attacks the throat. The more penicillin they gave me the worse it got, so my wedding pictures show me as painfully thin and gaunt ... alongside this vision which had completely knocked me over at first sight.

As the kids grew up we continued to go back to Yorkshire to visit my parents and to have holidays. I know one's view of things, long afterwards, is seen through rose-coloured spectacles but – think of Fraisthorpe with the sun shining on those amazing sands, maybe two miles of silver glinting in the sun. Our kids used to go up there and have a lovely time. I like going to the Dales. I have been back to the York Arms at Ramsgill. I had been there as a kid and I was fascinated to find it hadn't changed at all. I was up at Pickering earlier this year – think of all the walks and drives there are around there. Suddenly you remember just how beautiful Yorkshire is. Even Fylingdales with its early-warning system – those globes look romantic and different because of their setting. They don't look like some dreadful thing of war; they look like something out of science fiction.

F.S.T.   So Yorkshire still exercises a pull on you?

B.R.   If the climate were kinder I could think of no nicer or more beautiful place to live.

F.S.T.   So, just to complete your life in the theatre . . .

B.R.   Altogether I spent seventeen years at the Whitehall and seven years at the Garrick so I bestraddled Trafalgar Square for twenty-four years. I only did eleven plays in those twenty-four years.

F.S.T.   So why did you leave the theatre in the end?

B.R.   Because I was in danger of becoming boring to myself as well as to the public, and I could only see myself, in the end, as one of those rather sad actors who are going downhill. I felt I had to try to break away so I went into theatre management for a time and it was a disaster. I was working for someone else and, having been my own boss for so long, I couldn't do it.

So I was wondering what I was going to do with my life when I saw in the *Guardian* an advertisement for a secretary general of Mencap (the National Society for Mentally Handicapped Children and Adults). I was with Elspeth, driving in Devon, and I just knew that this was the job I was looking for. It was the right decision. It has been just the same as the early days at the Whitehall or being an actor-manager – it has been exciting, forming new relationships, formulating new ideas, and I think how lucky I am to get a completely new lease of life because, after all, I am nearly sixty. Another interesting factor is that although I loathed school because I was bullied and for all sorts of other reasons, Bootham was a very good, sound Quaker background. At Mencap I found that my predecessor was a Quaker, my deputy is a Quaker, *his* predecessor was a Quaker, our director of education is a Quaker . . . There, I've returned to a field which I thought I had forgotten and left behind all those years ago.

F.S.T.   Do you feel a great personal motivation in helping the mentally handicapped?

B.R.   Well, I think once you have a child who is mentally handicapped you are so shattered and so changed . . . You will never get over the resentment – for the child, not for yourself. You are very angry, and determined to do something. I regard it as a great honour and a great privilege and great sheer slice of luck that I was in that position. The mentally handicapped represent the greatest single problem in the country, apart from old age. We know there are half a million mentally handicapped people who fall into our category, but the Professor of Child Studies at Bristol University maintains that about 13 per cent of the entire British population have an IQ of under 100 and that means that about six and a half million people have difficulties – learning difficulties. That's a lot of people. But I don't think that had anything to do with it originally. What had to do with it was that I had a daughter. Once you are involved – if you are the sort of person who gets involved, and I am – you get wound up and you get into it and from then on you can think of nothing else except what you can do to help.

F.S.T. with Brian Rix

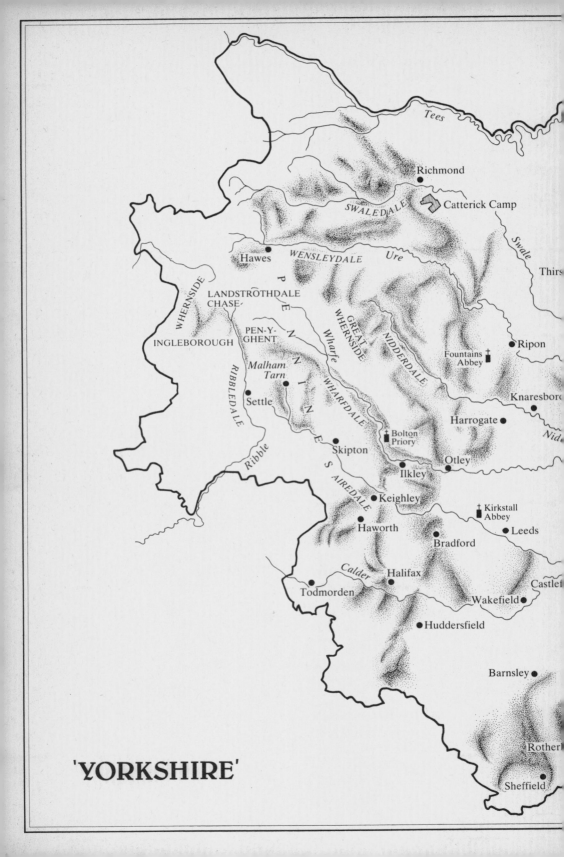